Sunset Breads

STEP-BY-STEP TECHNIQUES

By the Editors of Sunset Books and Sunset Magazine

Lane Publishing Co. Menlo Park, California

Fresh from the Oven . . .

Even in today's sophisticated world, few foods are as appealing as a simple loaf of freshly baked bread—and few are as satisfying to prepare. In this book, we offer a thorough guide to the art of baking bread at home. Whether you're a beginner who needs basic recipes and solid information on ingredients and techniques, or an experienced baker seeking unusual ethnic recipes, new shaping tricks, and ideas for entertaining, you'll find in the following pages a breadbasketful of ideas.

For their generosity in sharing props for use in our photographs, we extend special thanks to House of Today, William Ober Co., Agapanthus, and Williams-Sonoma Kitchenware. And for her culinary assistance with our photography, we thank Linda McCrary.

Cover: From simple, down-to-earth ingredients, wonderful things are possible—for example, challah (page 44), a rich and golden braided bread created from a straightforward yeast dough. Our recipe includes easy-to-follow diagrams to help in shaping. Traditionally served for the Jewish sabbath, challah is delicious for any occasion; its festive appearance and home-baked flavor are sure to evoke many a compliment for the baker. Photograph by Tom Wyatt. Cover design by Naganuma Design & Direction and Lynne B. Morrall.

Editor, Sunset Books: David E. Clark

First printing May 1984

 Library of Congress Catalog Card Number: 83-82505. ISBN 0-376-02748-7. Lithographed in the United States.

Coordinating Editor
Maureen Williams Zimmerman

Research & Text
Claire Coleman

Contributing Editor
Susan Warton

Special Consultant
Kandace Esplund Reeves
Associate Editor, Sunset Magazine

Design
Joe di Chiarro

Illustrations
Jacqueline Osborn

Photo Stylist
JoAnn Masaoka

Photography by Tom Wyatt

Additional photography: Glenn Christiansen: 30 (#6); Darrow M. Watt: 3, 14 (#1–5), 22, 103 (#6), 111; Nikolay Zurek: 14 (#6).

Contents

4 All About Bread
Everything you need to know about ingredients and techniques

10 Yeast Bread Techniques
A sampler of simple recipes, each using a different method for baking yeast bread

22 Savory Yeast Breads
Classic loaves and rolls, as well as an abundance of new recipe ideas

58 Sweet & Festive Yeast Breads
Sumptuous sweet rolls, grand coffee cakes, and special holiday breads galore

82 Sourdough Breads
From crusty sourdough French loaves to sweet and tangy breakfast breads

98 Griddle & Fried Breads
Change-of-pace breads: goodies from the griddle, and sizzling deep-fried treats

110 Quick Breads
An assortment of muffins, biscuits, and breads to bake when time is short

126 Index

Whole-grain goodness is what comes from the oven when you bake (clockwise from top) Pebble-top Oatmeal Bread (page 32), Dark Rye Bread (page 26), and Three Wheat Batter Bread (page 24).

Special Features

13 Troubleshooting Guide
21 Flours & Grains
33 Custom-made Crusts
36 Short-cut Bread Mix
53 Baking in Quantity
74 Golden Basket Bread
79 Fanciful Bread Sculpture
86 Old-fashioned Sourdough Starter
119 Butters for Your Bread
128 Metric Conversion Chart

All About Bread

Nourishing, comforting, and reassuringly down-to-earth, bread is perhaps the most fundamental of foods. From its earliest incarnation as a rough loaf baked on stones over a primitive fire, to its greatest glories as a delicate French croissant or a buttery brioche, bread has always been a symbol of sustenance, of strength, of life itself.

Bread appears in so many guises that one kind may seem to bear little relation to another. It is baked, boiled, steamed, fried; shaped in long, crisp sticks and in soft, flat cakes; leavened by yeast, by baking powder, and by sourdough starter (and sometimes not leavened at all); flavored with fruits and sugar, and with onions, herbs, and seeds.

While each loaf may have its own personality, all bread has in common several basic components. For the home baker, it's useful to have a working knowledge of these ingredients and their function in baking. Also important is an understanding of the procedures involved—whether you choose to bake a simple batch of muffins to serve the family, or an elaborate yeasted creation for company.

What's in a Loaf—and Why

The staff of life is a supremely satisfying food. Following is a list of the basic ingredients which—through handiwork and something like magic—interplay to build a wholesome loaf.

Leavenings

Leavenings produce the carbon dioxide gas that lightens doughs and batters. Baking powder and baking soda are chemical leavenings; yeast is a biological leavening.

Baking powder is sold in three forms. *Tartrate* acts instantly when combined with liquid. *Phosphate* is activated partially by liquid, partially by heat. *Double-acting* baking powder is activated mainly by heat, releasing most of its carbon dioxide in the baking process. (*Recipes in this book were tested with double-acting baking powder.*)

Baking soda releases gas only when mixed with an acid agent, such as buttermilk, sour milk, or lemon juice.

Yeast is a microscopic plant; when activated by warm water it gives off the bubbles of carbon dioxide that make dough rise. Yeast is most commonly available in a granular form—called "active dry yeast"—sold in envelopes that contain about 1 tablespoon each, or in small jars. It can be stored in a cool, dry place for about a year—be sure to notice the expiration date printed on the package. Yeast is also sold in a compressed cake; the quantity is the same, but yeast in this form is much more perishable and must be refrigerated. It usually lasts up to 2 weeks. Test by crumbling it—if it crumbles readily, it's still good.

The recipes in this book call for the dry form of yeast. The reason is that we've found it more widely available and more convenient for most bakers. Should you want to substitute compressed yeast, just be sure you dissolve it in lukewarm water (about 95°) rather than the warm water (about 110°) that's specified in the recipes.

Flour

Flour provides the structure of bread. Many kinds of flour—even ground acorns—have been kneaded into loaves over the long history of bread making. A few interesting varieties are described under Flours & Grains on page 21.

For yeast breads, at least part of the flour must be wheat, which contains a curious protein called "gluten." When wheat flour is moistened and beaten, the gluten becomes very elastic, allowing the dough to stretch as the yeast leavens it, and giving the loaf enough strength to keep its shape when baked. Rye flour is also glutenous, though less so than wheat, which is why it's usually combined with whole wheat or all-purpose flour to make bread.

Liquids

Liquids in yeast breads always include at least ¼ cup warm water for dissolving the yeast.

In addition, various other liquids are often mixed into bread, each imparting a distinctive flavor and texture. Milk creates a velvety grain; eggs, beaten and used as part of the liquid, lend the loaf a richness, tenderness, and slightly golden tone. Both milk and eggs, of course, also enrich the bread with added nutrients. Occasionally, fruit juice is used in bread to give it a special flavor. Bread made entirely with water (French bread is an example) is distinctively coarse-textured, chewy, and crusty.

Sugar and Salt

Sugar provides food for the yeast so it can grow; salt slows down the action of the yeast, keeping the dough on just the right leavening schedule for good texture and flavor. Besides their purely chemical roles, both salt and sugar (or the brown sugar, honey, or molasses often used in dark breads to bring out their more robust flavor) are essential for good taste. Also, the sugar in bread helps to brown the crust.

Fats

Fats make breads tender, moist, and palatable. Salad oil is convenient to use, because in most recipes the fat is added in liquid form. But many bakers prefer to use melted butter or margarine because they contribute such rich flavor.

Flavorings

Special ingredients such as herbs, spices, cheese, dried fruits, and nuts, offer the bread baker a wide field for experimentation. They aren't essential to the basic creation, but they can be exciting additions for special flavor.

BLEND ACTIVE
y Yeast
WT. 1/4 OZ.

Understanding Yeast Baking

Yeast breads have the reputation of being chancy and difficult. But once you've given it a try, you'll find that yeast baking is really quite easy, and very rewarding.

Mixing

The secret to a shapely, springy loaf of bread is the care and thoroughness given to the mixing and kneading of the dough. These are the steps that develop the gluten in the flour.

In most recipes, the yeast is dissolved first, then other ingredients are mixed in, the flour last of all. In the dissolving of the yeast, temperature is crucial: if the water is too cool, the yeast action will be sluggish; if it's too hot, it will destroy the yeast and the dough will fail to rise. For active dry yeast, the water should be about 110°—noticeably warm, but not hot. For compressed yeast, it should be about 95°—close to skin temperature. Test with a thermometer (see page 9) until you can recognize the right warmth by feel.

To measure flour accurately, stir it a bit in the container, lightly spoon it into a cup designed for measuring dry ingredients, and then level it off with a straight-edged knife. In bread making, there's no need to sift flour. On the other hand, you should never pack it in the cup or shake it down.

The amount of flour needed in any recipe or on any given day will vary according to minute amounts of moisture in the flour, as well as temperature and humidity of the air. So measure a little more than you'll probably need—and learn to recognize when the dough looks and feels right at each stage.

When you add the flour, sprinkle it over the yeast mixture 1 cup at a time, stirring until evenly moistened. When enough flour has been stirred in to form a thick batter (about ⅔ the amount of flour given in a recipe), beat the batter very well with a wooden spoon or with a heavy-duty electric mixer on medium speed. After you've beaten for about 5 minutes, you can see the gluten developing—the batter becomes glossy and elastic, stretching with the motion of the spoon. From this point on, it readily absorbs more flour and tends to stick to itself rather than to you, gradually forming a ball.

By hand, stir in enough of the remaining flour to make a dough stiff enough to pull away from the sides of the bowl.

Good bread starts with good ingredients, so fill your mixing bowl with fresh and wholesome foods. Milk, butter, eggs, yeast, spices, honey and brown sugar, flours and grains—these are the components of a luscious and nourishing loaf.

Kneading

Spread about ½ cup flour on a board, heavily coating the center area. Turn the dough out onto this area and sprinkle it lightly with flour. Now the dough is ready for kneading, which will complete the gluten formation.

As you knead, make sure the dough is never without a light coating of flour. Your objective is to shape it into a ball, keeping the underside smooth and unbroken.

Contrary to popular belief, kneading is not a very good way to work off frustrations—frequency, rhythm, and a gentle touch, rather than brute force, do the job best.

To knead, reach under the edge of dough farthest from you. Pull it toward you in a rolling motion (don't pull enough to tear the surface) and fold the dough almost in half. Then, with your finger tips or the heel of your palm, gently roll the ball away from you to lightly seal the fold. When the fold line is returned to the top center of the dough, rotate the dough a quarter turn and continue this folding-rolling motion, making a turn each time. Work quickly, for dough grows sticky if allowed to stand; you should be able to fold/roll at least 20 to 25 times in 30 seconds. Spread more flour onto the board gradually as needed for easy handling. If tears occur on the surface, try to fold them in rather than add more flour to cover them; if the dough sticks to the board, lift it up, scrape the board clean, reflour, and continue.

If you work quickly, 5 minutes of kneading may be enough. But it's virtually impossible to overknead by hand, and the longer you spend at it (perhaps 20 or 30 minutes), the higher and fluffier your finished loaf is likely to be. Again, it's best to judge by feel. When the dough becomes smooth and no longer sticky, its surface faintly pebbled with air bubbles, hold it to your cheek. If it has the firm bounce and velvety touch of a baby's bottom, you've kneaded it long enough.

If you've mixed your dough in a heavy-duty mixer with a dough hook, all this will go much more quickly. Use the criteria of appearance and feel mentioned above to judge when the dough has been kneaded long enough.

Letting It Rise

After the dough has been thoroughly kneaded, it almost takes care of itself. Your job is to give it a warm (70° to 80°, unless otherwise stated in recipe), draft-free place for rising—sometimes called "proofing." (Dough will rise at cooler temperatures, but will take a bit longer.) Most yeast breads rise twice: the first time until doubled in bulk, and the second time until almost doubled.

For the first rising, turn the dough over in a greased bowl (the wiped-out mixing bowl will do nicely) to grease it all over. Cover it with a damp cloth or clear plastic wrap (the latter will keep it a bit warmer). In most households, the most convenient warm place to leave the dough is inside a switched-off oven. If your oven feels cool, turn it to the lowest setting for a minute or two, then switch it off before putting the bread inside.

Like so many aspects of bread making, rising times are variable, depending mainly on temperature but also on the heaviness of the dough (whole grain doughs take longer than white; richer doughs take longer than those lower in fat). To test whether dough has risen adequately, check it by poking two fingers into it (see illustration on page 15). If the indentations remain, the dough has risen enough.

Turn it out onto a lightly floured board and knead briefly to release air bubbles. At this point, you divide and shape the dough as the recipe specifies.

The dough's second rising, after it's shaped, usually takes about half as long as the first rising. Use the same test for readiness as you did after the first rising: make a slight dent in the dough where it's least likely to show. If the indentation remains, the bread is ready for the oven.

Shaping

To shape a conventional loaf, see Step 5 of the Basic White Bread photo sequence on page 14. For an occasional change of pace from the standard oblong loaf, try these alternatives.

> ***The expression "to proof" bread dough originally meant literally to prove that the yeast was alive and active—not always a sure thing until modern times.***

Freeform loaves. Rounds and ovals are easy to shape because the dough tends to be round anyway. Keep in mind that stiffer doughs will hold their shape during rising and baking better than softer doughs; you wouldn't bake a batter bread as a freeform loaf, for example. After dividing the dough, lightly knead and pat it into a ball. Gently pull around the rim to flatten the ball slightly and smooth its top; pinch underneath to seal any crevices. To form an oval, just roll with your hands and gently pull both ends to elongate ball slightly.

Let freeform loaves rise, covered, on greased baking sheets. When ready to bake, you can slash their surfaces (see page 33).

Long loaves. Shape these by rolling the dough back and forth with your hands, gently pulling it to form a smooth rope. Don't make the loaves too long, though, or they may outgrow the baking sheet as they rise. Cover and let rise.

Rolled-up shapes. These are particularly attractive when wrapped around a filling, jelly-roll fashion. (And some people like this method for shaping a standard loaf without a filling.) Roll out the dough into a smooth rectangle of the size specified in the recipe (or roll out until the two short sides of the rectangle almost equal the length of your loaf pan). Spread the filling over the dough; then, starting at one short edge, roll the dough up tightly into a log, pinching the edges to seal. Pull the ends underneath, place seam side down in a greased loaf pan, cover, and let rise.

Braids. Divide the dough for one loaf into three or four equal portions. Shape each into a smooth rope as directed for long loaves. Lay the ropes side by side on a greased baking sheet; pinch them together at one end. Working from right to left, lay the first rope over the next one and under the third (and over the fourth, if using four strands). See pages 42 and 44. Repeat, always starting at the right, until the braid is complete. Pinch the ends to seal, and tuck underneath. Cover and let rise.

Unusual pans. Virtually any baking pan (and even clay flower pots or recycled cans) will take the place of a standard loaf pan. Just be sure that the volume of the alternative container is about equal to that of the pan suggested in the recipe—compare by measuring how much water it takes to fill them. For a loaf with an attractively rounded top, the dough should generally fill about two-thirds of whatever container you bake it in.

Baking

Baking the bread is easy—just follow the recipe directions, and always preheat the oven. Do keep in mind that glass pans bake hotter than metal ones, so it's best to reduce the oven temperature by 25° if you're using a glass pan. And if you're baking two loaves in the same oven on large baking sheets, you should position them for maximum heat circulation: first adjust oven racks so they are in the middle third of the oven; then, keeping pan edges at least an inch from the sides of the oven, stagger pan positions. About halfway through baking, switch pans.

As soon as you take the bread from the oven, turn it out of its pan to cool on a rack, unless otherwise directed in the recipe. If you plan to serve it soon, let it cool for 10 to 15 minutes before slicing.

Storing

To store bread for a few days, let it cool completely, wrap it airtight, and store it either in the refrigerator or in the bread box. Bread also freezes beautifully for as long as 3 months. To freeze, wrap each loaf of cooled bread airtight in foil, then package in a plastic bag, label it, and place it in the freezer. When freezing sweet breads that call for glazing, you should add the glaze after the bread is reheated—not before freezing.

To reheat frozen bread, place on a baking sheet in a 350° oven for about 15 minutes for rolls and small loaves, 30 minutes for large loaves. There's no need to thaw the rolls and small loaves first, but large loaves should be unwrapped and allowed to thaw partially before reheating. If the bread has a soft crust, protect it during reheating with a loose wrapping of foil; if the bread is crusty, reheat it uncovered.

Baking Bread in High Country

Baking high in the mountains—above 3000 feet—requires some adjustment of recipes.

When you make quick breads at high elevations, the baking powder and baking soda produce gases at a greatly accelerated rate. In the early stages of baking this can create too great a volume; then the gas cells burst, causing your bread to collapse. Specialists in high elevation cooking sometimes suggest that the baking powder and baking soda in recipes for biscuits, muffins, and quick breads be decreased by one-fourth.

Yeast breads are affected even more by high elevations. Yeast bread dough rises more rapidly in high country, so you must punch it down after the first rising and let it rise again until fully doubled in bulk before continuing with the recipe. Unless you're in a hurry, use slightly less yeast, too. But you may need to use a little more liquid in the dough, because liquid evaporates faster at high elevations, and ingredients dry out more quickly.

The Baker's Tools

The only tools that are really necessary for baking bread are a mixing bowl, measuring cups and spoons, and a baking pan—and even there, you could improvise if you had to. But a number of other items can help ensure beautiful results.

To be sure you dissolve your yeast in water that is the correct temperature, it's a good idea to use a **thermometer** that reads accurately at 90° to 120°. These may be sold as "yeast" or "dough" thermometers; some meat thermometers are appropriate for yeast baking, too.

For mixing the dough, a large, heavy **pottery bowl** is ideal; it retains warmth and remains steady during beating (especially if you set it on a damp cloth). But any bowl of about 4-quart size will do. Use a sturdy **wooden spoon** to beat in the flour.

A **heavy-duty mixer** with a dough hook can mix *and* knead the dough for you if you want to save time and effort. A **food processor** fitted with a plastic dough blade can also do the job, but check the manufacturer's directions first.

For shaping the dough, a **rolling pin** and a **sharp knife** are often used. A **pastry brush** for glazing is also a helpful item. For following the recipes in this book, your baking equipment should include two standard 9 by 5-inch and two 4½ by 8½-inch **loaf pans** and at least two **baking sheets** (the 12 by 15-inch size is fine for many of our recipes, but you may also want to invest in some 14 by 17-inch sheets for long loaves and large batches of rolls). Some breads are baked in **casserole dishes, cake or pie pans,** or **muffin tins;** and a few recipes in this book call for special equipment such as a **waffle iron, pastry bag, deep-frying thermometer,** or **doughnut cutter.**

After the bread comes out of the oven, you'll want to set it on a **cooling rack,** so that the steam can escape and the bread doesn't become soggy. And, last but certainly not least, you should have a large **serrated bread knife** so you can cut your bread into smooth, even slices.

Yeast Bread Techniques

For wholesome, honest goodness, there's nothing like a loaf of freshly baked bread. And anyone—even the most inexperienced cook—can achieve this old-fashioned treat.

This chapter presents a lesson in the art of yeast baking for beginners. Each recipe uses a different technique for making yeast bread. Each has its advantages: Some have time-saving features for convenient breadmaking; other simplify steps so breadmaking is easier than you might have thought possible.

Of course, we include the conventional method, typified by Basic White Bread (page 15). But we also introduce you to the sponge method, to refrigerator and freezer bread, to batter bread, and others, all designed to give you a taste of the best in easy yeast baking.

Each tender and toothsome loaf at right was made by a different technique. Clockwise from lower left: Cinnamon Swirl Loaf (page 16), Rich White Batter Bread (page 18), Sponge-method Peasant Rye Bread (page 17), and One-rise Whole Wheat Bread (page 12).

One-rise Whole Wheat Bread

Pictured on page 11

A standard yeast bread needs two risings. But by warming the flour and using extra yeast, you can bake this light-textured loaf with only one rising. All you need to do is mix, shape, wait an hour, and bake. You'll come out with a 100 percent whole wheat loaf that's delicious plain, in sandwiches, or for buttered toast.

About 4⅓ cups whole wheat flour
2 packages active dry yeast
2 tablespoons molasses or honey
1¾ cups warm water (about 110°)
¼ cup salad oil
1½ teaspoons salt
⅓ cup wheat germ

Measure 4⅓ cups flour into a bowl; place in a warm oven (about 150°) until warmed through (about 10 minutes).

Meanwhile, in large bowl of a heavy-duty electric mixer or another large bowl, dissolve yeast and molasses in ¾ cup of the water; let stand until bubbly (about 15 minutes). Stir in remaining 1 cup water, the oil, salt, and wheat germ. Add flour about 1 cup at a time, beating well with a heavy-duty mixer or vigorously by hand after each addition.

When dough begins to clean sides of bowl, turn out onto a board sprinkled with about 1 tablespoon flour. Knead just enough to shape into a smooth loaf. Place in a greased 9 by 5-inch loaf pan and cover lightly with plastic wrap. Let rise in a warm place until dough is about 1 inch above rim of pan (30 to 40 minutes).

Bake in a preheated 400° oven (375° for a glass pan) for 35 minutes or until loaf is well browned and sounds hollow when tapped. Turn out onto a rack to cool. Makes 1 loaf.

In Old English, a landholder was called **hlaford,** *meaning "loaf keeper," or the one who handed out bread. His wife was called* **hlafdigge,** *or "kneader of loaves." In time, a few letters were dropped and these words became "lord" and "lady."*

Super-simple Refrigerator Bread

This light and tender white bread takes a short cut from the standard baking technique—there's no kneading.

Leaving out kneading sounds much easier—but remember that this puts added emphasis on the mixing step, since mixing is your only opportunity to develop the gluten for a high-rising loaf. So be sure to beat the dough thoroughly after each addition of flour.

The first rising takes place in the refrigerator, and you can leave the dough there for as long as 24 hours. Then you just shape it into loaves, let it rise again, and bake.

There is a sourdough version of this bread on page 84. Other recipes that involve the refrigerator method include Armenian Peda Bread (page 40), Quantity Refrigerator Bread (page 53), Sweet Cinnamon Pretzels (page 68), Buttery Almond Bear Claws (page 69), and Golden Basket Bread (page 74).

⅓ cup *each* sugar and solid vegetable shortening
1 tablespoon salt
2 cups boiling water
2 packages active dry yeast
1 teaspoon sugar
¼ cup warm water (about 110°)
2 eggs, well beaten
7½ to 8 cups all-purpose flour

In a large bowl, combine the ⅓ cup sugar, the shortening, salt, and boiling water; cool to lukewarm. Dissolve yeast and the 1 teaspoon sugar in the ¼ cup water; let stand until bubbly (about 15 minutes).

Combine yeast mixture with lukewarm mixture; stir in eggs. Beat in 4 cups of the flour; then gradually stir in as much of the remaining flour as dough will absorb (at least 3½ cups), mixing well. Place in a greased bowl; cover and chill for at least 6 hours or up to 24 hours.

To bake, divide dough in half. With greased hands, shape each half into a smooth loaf. Place each in a greased 9 by 5-inch loaf pan; cover and let rise in a warm place until almost doubled (about 2 hours).

Bake in a preheated 350° oven (325° for glass pans) for 30 to 35 minutes or until well browned. Turn out onto a rack to cool. Makes 2 loaves.

Troubleshooting Guide

If you're a novice baker, you may feel just a bit daunted by all the variables in making yeast bread, and wonder what to do if things don't go just as the recipe says. It's true that yeast baking is not an exact science—but it's also true that it's a forgiving one. Here are answers to some questions you may have.

How do you know if the water temperature is right? It's always best to use a thermometer, at least until you learn to recognize the feel of water at about 110°. That way, you'll be sure the water is warm enough to get the yeast going, but not so hot as to kill it. If you must err, err on the side of coolness. As long as the yeast dissolves, it will eventually begin its rising action, though it may take some extra time. But if you kill your yeast with hot water, you'll have to start over.

How can you tell if the yeast is active? Envelopes of active dry yeast are dated to tell you how long the yeast will be active. But if you buy bulk yeast, it's not always easy to tell. You can test your yeast, though, by taking a simple step—one that's built into many bread recipes. When dissolving the yeast in the warm water, add 1 to 3 teaspoons of the sugar or honey called for in the recipe. (If none is called for, you can just add a teaspoon or so without affecting the flavor of the bread.) Let stand for 5 to 15 minutes or until bubbly; the bubbling tells you that the yeast is still fresh and active.

What if the phone rings? Don't worry about short interruptions—up to half an hour. If you've just dissolved the yeast, cover it and leave it at room temperature—it won't hurt it to ferment for awhile. If you're mixing or kneading the dough, cover it to keep it from drying out.

Should it be inconvenient to shape the loaves when the dough has doubled, just punch it down and let it rise again—this time at room temperature. You can punch it down two or three times and still bake excellent bread. Watch closely, though—each successive rising will happen a little faster.

You can postpone the last steps—shaping, second rising, and baking—by placing the dough, covered with plastic wrap, in the refrigerator during the first rising. You can leave it there for several hours; the rising action will continue, but at a much slower pace. When you're ready, let the dough finish rising, covered, in a warm place.

How can you tell if you've kneaded in enough flour? If you've kneaded for 10 or 15 minutes and are still not sure you've worked in enough flour, invert a bowl over your dough and let it rest for about 15 minutes. When you return, if the dough is sticky and has spread out sideways rather than starting to rise, knead in more flour.

What if the dough rises too long? If you happen to leave the dough too long so that it rises too high (becomes "overproofed"), the solution is to punch it down, knead it a bit to release air, and let it rise again. Overproofed dough looks as though it has ballooned beyond double its original size. Its "skin" is thin and transparent, with bubbles just beneath the surface. If left long enough, it may deflate itself, in which case you just punch it down and let it rise again. You can do the same thing if you've let your shaped loaves rise too long. Knead the dough lightly to release air, then reshape and let rise again (watch carefully—the loaves will rise faster).

What if the bottoms of your loaves aren't browned enough when you turn them out of the pans? If you prefer a browner crust, you can return your loaves to the oven—either in their baking pans or directly on the oven rack. A few extra minutes will give you a darker, crisper crust.

Basic White Bread *(Recipe on facing page)*

1 *Dissolve yeast and sugar in warm water. After about 15 minutes, mixture will have a distinct light, bubbly layer on top—this means that yeast is active.*

2 *Dough is ready to knead when it is stiff enough to pull away from sides of bowl with a wooden spoon.*

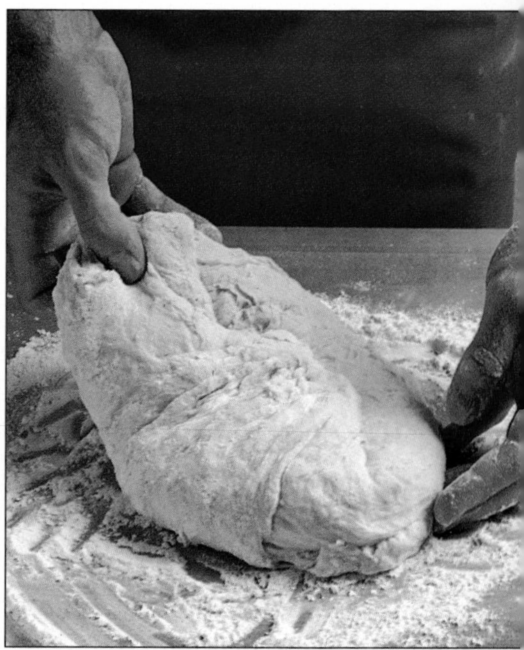

3 *Turn dough out onto floured board and sprinkle with flour. Begin to knead, adding flour as necessary to prevent sticking.*

4 *Use a folding-pushing motion, rotating dough a quarter turn each time and adding flour as necessary. Kneading is finished when dough is nonsticky, smooth, satiny.*

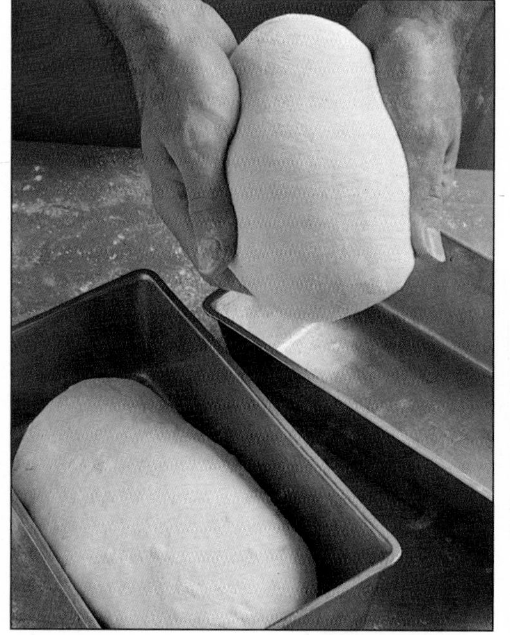

5 *Form each dough half into a loaf by gently pulling top surface toward underside to make top smooth; pinch seam and turn ends under. Put loaves, seam side down, in greased pans for second rising.*

6 *Freshly baked white bread is a treat that needs little adornment—just butter and jam can turn it into a feast. It's excellent toasted, too, or used for sandwiches.*

Basic White Bread

Pictured on facing page

Here's a step-by-step illustrated lesson in the art of bread making, using the standard method. Most yeast bread recipes follow this technique, which involves thorough kneading and two risings to produce an even, fine-textured product.

On these pages you'll learn what to expect and what to do at each stage to make two beautiful loaves of white bread.

- **¼ cup warm water (about 110°)**
- **1 package active dry yeast**
- **2 tablespoons sugar**
- **2 cups warm milk (about 110°)**
- **2 tablespoons salad oil (or butter or margarine, melted and cooled)**
- **2 teaspoons salt**
- **6 to 6½ cups all-purpose flour**

Pour water into a measuring cup; add yeast and 1 tablespoon of the sugar; stir until dissolved. Let stand until light-colored and bubbly (about 15 minutes); the bubbling tells you that the yeast is active and has not been destroyed by excessively hot water.

Pour milk into a large bowl (about 4-quart size); stir in oil, salt, the remaining 1 tablespoon sugar, and yeast mixture. Sprinkle in 3 cups of the flour, 1 cup at a time, stirring until flour is evenly moistened. Add 4th cup of flour and, with a wooden spoon or heavy-duty mixer, beat until dough is smooth and elastic (about 5 minutes—you can pause if you get tired). Mix in 5th cup of flour to make dough stiff enough to pull away from sides of bowl.

Measure out 6th cup of flour and sprinkle about ¾ cup of it onto a board; turn dough out onto heavily floured area. Sprinkle dough lightly with some of the remaining flour and begin to knead.

To knead, reach over the ball of dough and grasp the edge farthest from you. Pull it toward you in a rolling motion and fold dough almost in half. Then, with the heel of your palm, gently push the ball away from you, lightly sealing the fold and rolling it to top center of dough. Rotate dough a quarter turn and continue this folding-rolling motion, making a quarter turn each time.

Work quickly, adding remaining flour as needed. If dough sticks to board, lift dough, scrape board clean, reflour, and continue. Five minutes of kneading may be long enough, but the longer you spend at it (as long as 20 to 30 minutes) the lighter the loaf will be. When dough is nonsticky, smooth, and satiny, kneading is finished.

Put dough in a greased bowl; turn dough over to grease top. Cover bowl loosely with plastic wrap or a damp cloth. Let rise in a warm place until doubled (45 minutes to 1½ hours). Test by pushing 2 fingers into dough—if indentations remain (see illustration below), dough is ready to shape.

After dough has risen, punch it down with your fist (see illustration below); then turn dough out onto a lightly floured board. Knead dough briefly to release air bubbles, and shape into a smooth oval.

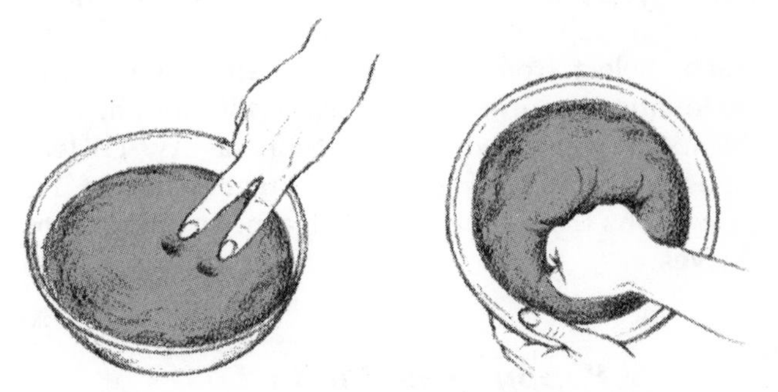

To see if dough has risen long enough, poke it with two fingers; if indentations remain (left), dough is ready. Punch it down with your fist (right); you'll feel it deflate as the air bubbles are released.

With a sharp knife, divide dough in half. Form each half into a loaf by gently pulling top surface toward underside to make top smooth. Turn each loaf over and pinch a seam down center; then turn ends under, and pinch to seal.

Put shaped loaves, seam side down, in greased 9 by 5-inch loaf pans. Cover; let rise in a warm place until almost doubled (about 45 minutes). Loaves should come just to tops of pans—when baked, they'll rise above tops of pans.

Bake in a preheated 375° oven (350° for glass pans) for 35 to 45 minutes or until loaves are nicely browned. Turn loaves out onto a rack to cool. Makes 2 loaves.

Rye Bread

Follow **Basic White Bread** recipe (above), but omit sugar; instead of all milk, use ½ cup light or dark **molasses** with 1½ cups **milk.** Use 3 cups **rye flour** and 3 cups **all-purpose flour** instead of 6 cups all-purpose flour.

(Continued on next page)

Dark Mixed Grain Bread

Follow **Basic White Bread** recipe (page 15), but omit sugar; instead of all milk, use ½ cup **dark molasses** with 1½ cups **milk**. Omit all-purpose flour and use ½ cup **wheat germ,** ½ cup **buckwheat flour,** 1 cup **rye flour,** and 4 cups **whole wheat flour.**

Herb Bread

Follow **Basic White Bread** recipe (page 15). If you want to make 2 kinds, divide dough into 2 parts when you turn it out onto floured board; knead each part separately, kneading a different herb into each. Select from these herbs, using one of the following amounts for *each half* of the dough: 1 tablespoon **dill weed,** 1 tablespoon **savory,** 1½ teaspoons **dry basil,** 1½ teaspoons **oregano leaves,** 1½ teaspoons **thyme leaves,** or 2 teaspoons **marjoram leaves.**

Poppy Seed Bubble Loaf

Follow **Basic White Bread** recipe (page 15), with these changes: After dough is punched down, pinch off pieces of dough to make small balls (about 1 inch in diameter). Melt 4 tablespoons **butter** or margarine. Measure ¼ cup **poppy seeds.** Dip top of each ball first into butter, then into poppy seeds, and pile all the balls, seed side up, in one lightly greased 10-inch tube pan; cover and let rise until almost doubled (about 45 minutes). Bake in a preheated 375° oven for about 55 minutes or until nicely browned.

Cinnamon Swirl Loaf

Pictured on page 11

Follow **Basic White Bread** recipe (page 15). After dough is punched down and divided in half, roll out each half into a rectangle about 6 by 16 inches. Mix 4 tablespoons **sugar** with 4 tablespoons **ground cinnamon;** sprinkle half evenly over top of each rectangle. Beginning with a narrow side, roll each tightly into a loaf; seal ends and bottom by pinching together to make a seam. Let rise in 2 greased 9 by 5-inch loaf pans. Bake in a preheated 375° oven (350° for glass pans) for 30 to 35 minutes or until nicely browned.

Freezer Whole Wheat Bread

What better way to welcome guests than with the aroma of baking bread? But making bread the day company is coming is more than most of us care to undertake. Here's an alternative—a whole wheat dough that's specially formulated (with extra yeast, fat, and sugar) to freeze now and bake later. On the day of your party, all you have to do is let the shaped dough thaw and rise (about 4 hours); then it's ready to bake. For variety, you might want to try the rye version of freezer dough, following the recipe below.

If you want to make this bread without freezing, use only 1 package of yeast; other ingredients remain the same. Instead of freezing, let the shaped loaves rise until almost doubled, then bake as directed.

1½ cups milk
⅓ cup light molasses
2 teaspoons salt
4 tablespoons butter or margarine, cut into pieces
2 packages active dry yeast
½ cup warm water (about 110°)
5½ to 6 cups whole wheat flour
Melted butter or margarine

In a pan, combine milk, molasses, salt, and butter. Heat to about 110° (butter need not melt completely).

In a large bowl, dissolve yeast in water. Stir in warm milk mixture. Beat in about 5 cups of the flour, 1 cup at a time, to make a stiff dough. Turn dough out onto a floured board; knead until smooth and satiny (5 to 20 minutes), adding flour as needed to prevent sticking. Divide dough in half.

Shape into 2 loaves, either standard or round. Place each standard loaf in a well-greased 4½ by 8½-inch loaf pan; wrap and freeze immediately. Place round loaves on a greased 12 by 15-inch baking sheet; cover, freeze until solid, then wrap each loaf separately and return to freezer.

To bake, remove loaves from freezer (place round loaves on greased baking sheets), cover with a cloth, and let thaw at room temperature (about 2 hours). Let rise, covered, in a warm place until almost doubled (about 2 more hours).

Brush loaves with melted butter and bake in a preheated 375° oven (350° for glass pans) for about

30 minutes or until loaves sound hollow when tapped. Transfer to racks and let cool. Makes 2 loaves.

Freezer Rye Bread

Follow directions for **Freezer Whole Wheat Bread,** but substitute ½ cup firmly packed **light brown sugar** for the molasses. Instead of whole wheat flour, measure 3 cups **rye flour** and about 3 cups **all-purpose flour,** and add 1 tablespoon crushed **fennel seeds**. Stir in rye flour, fennel seeds, and about 2 cups all-purpose flour. Knead in remaining all-purpose flour, then shape and freeze. Bake as directed for Freezer Whole Wheat Bread, except just before baking, brush loaves with 1 **egg white** beaten with 1 tablespoon **water,** and sprinkle each loaf with 1 teaspoon **caraway seeds**.

Sponge-method Peasant Rye Bread

Pictured on page 11

To start this bread, you make a "sponge" of yeast, water, and some of the flour. As it stands at room temperature, the sponge ferments, becomes bubbly, and develops a pleasantly tangy flavor. Then you blend in the other ingredients and proceed as usual.

The sponge method works well with whole grain flours, because it allows extra time for the bran to absorb liquid; this helps prevent the dough from getting too stiff later. The stone-ground dark rye flour you'll need is available in some supermarkets and in many health food stores.

This particular recipe makes a rustic, country-style bread, baked as a freeform loaf rather than in a pan. It's crusty and chewy, and it tastes best when eaten still warm from the oven.

Other sponge-method breads include Cracked Wheat Twin-top Bread (page 35), Vanocka (page 70), and Oatmeal Sourdough Bread (page 85).

2½ cups stone-ground dark rye flour
1 package active dry yeast
2½ cups warm water (about 110°)
1½ teaspoons salt
3 tablespoons butter or margarine
About 5 cups all-purpose flour
1 egg beaten with 1 tablespoon milk

To make the sponge, stir together 1½ cups of the rye flour, the yeast, and 1½ cups of the water. Cover with plastic wrap and let stand at room temperature for 6 to 24 hours.

Pour sponge into a large bowl. With a heavy spoon, blend in remaining 1 cup water. Add salt, butter, and remaining 1 cup rye flour; mix well. Gradually mix in 3 to 3½ cups of the all-purpose flour until dough is very stiff. (If dough becomes too heavy to work, mix the flour in with your hands.) Turn dough out onto a floured board; knead until smooth and no longer sticky (about 7 to 10 minutes), adding all-purpose flour as needed.

Place dough in a greased bowl; turn over to grease top. Cover and let rise in a warm place until doubled (about 2 hours).

Punch dough down and divide in half. Knead each piece briefly to release air; then shape each into a smooth ball or fat roll about 10 inches long. Place each loaf on a greased 12 by 15-inch baking sheet. Lightly dust tops of loaves with about 1 tablespoon flour, then cover with wax paper. Let rise in a warm place until almost doubled (about 50 minutes).

Brush loaves lightly with egg mixture. With a razor blade or sharp knife, make ½-inch-deep slashes on surfaces of loaves, as shown in illustrations below.

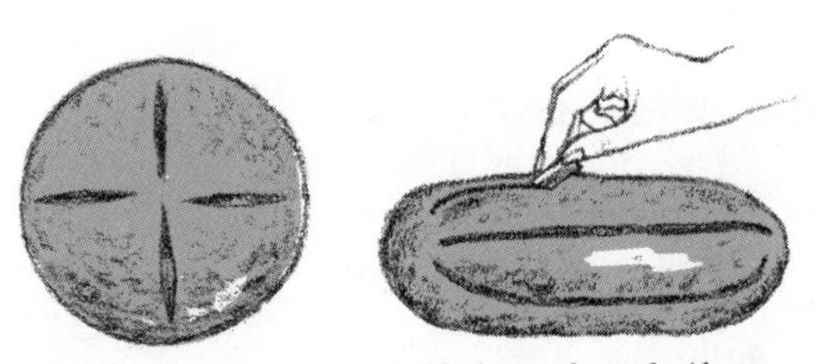

Before baking, use a razor blade or sharp knife to cut 4 or 5 radial slashes or a cross in round loaves, three lengthwise slashes in oblong loaves.

Bake each loaf on middle rack of a preheated 400° oven for about 40 minutes or until crust is a light golden brown. If you have only one oven, position one rack halfway below center and one halfway above center; switch pans halfway through baking.

Use a wide spatula to loosen loaves from pans; slide loaves onto racks to cool. Serve warm or let cool completely, freeze if desired, and recrisp before serving. To recrisp, place loaves (thawed if frozen), uncovered, on baking sheets and heat in a 350° oven until warm (about 20 minutes). Makes 2 loaves.

Rich White Batter Bread

Pictured on page 11

Batter breads are made from very soft yeast doughs—almost like batters, as the name indicates. Vigorous beating takes the place of kneading, and the breads rise only once. We like to bake them in coffee cans, which offer support for the soft dough during rising and also give the breads a distinctive shape—tall, round, and domed.

The plastic lids that come with the coffee cans prove useful at several different stages. First, they seal the batter in the can for freezing if you want to wait and bake the bread another time. Next, the lids tell you when the dough is ready to bake—they pop off! And once the baked loaf is sliced below the top of the can, the lid will seal it in to keep it fresh.

Don't be concerned if the lids pop off before the dough reaches the top of the cans—just put the lids back on until the dough pushes them off.

Other batter breads in this book include Whole Grain Cereal Batter Bread and Three Wheat Batter Bread (page 24), Mushroom Batter Bread and Cheddar-Caraway Batter Bread (page 25), Hot Cross Bread (page 75), and Sourdough Three Wheat Batter Bread and Orange Sourdough Batter Bread (page 89).

- **1 package active dry yeast**
- **½ cup warm water (about 110°)**
- **⅛ teaspoon ground ginger**
- **3 tablespoons sugar**
- **1½ cups milk or 1 large can (13 oz.) evaporated milk**
- **1 teaspoon salt**
- **2 tablespoons salad oil**
- **4 to 4½ cups all-purpose flour**
- **Butter or margarine**

In a large bowl, dissolve yeast in water; blend in ginger and 1 tablespoon of the sugar. Let stand until bubbly (about 15 minutes). Stir in remaining 2 tablespoons sugar, the milk, salt, and oil. Gradually beat in enough of the flour, 1 cup at a time, to make batter very heavy and stiff, but too sticky to knead.

Divide the batter in half and place in 2 well-greased 1-pound coffee cans, or spoon all the batter into 1 well-greased 2-pound coffee can. Cover with well-greased plastic can lids. (Freeze if you wish.)

To continue, let covered cans stand in a warm place until batter rises and pushes off plastic lids (45 to 55 minutes for 1-pound cans, 55 to 60 minutes for a 2-pound can).

If frozen, let batter stand in cans at room temperature until lids are pushed off (4 to 5 hours for 1-pound cans, 6 to 8 hours for a 2-pound can).

Immediately bake, uncovered, on bottom rack of a preheated 350° oven for about 45 minutes for 1-pound cans, about 60 minutes for a 2-pound can; crust will be very brown. Brush tops lightly with butter. Let cool in cans on a rack for about 5 minutes; then loosen crust around edges of cans with a thin knife, slide bread from cans, and let cool in an upright position on rack. Makes 2 small loaves or 1 large loaf.

Light Wheat Batter Bread

Follow **Rich White Batter Bread** recipe, but replace sugar with 3 tablespoons **honey.** Use 1½ cups **whole wheat flour** and 3 cups **all-purpose flour.**

Corn-Herb Batter Bread

Pictured on facing page

Follow **Rich White Batter Bread** recipe, adding to yeast mixture 2 teaspoons **celery seeds**, 1½ teaspoons **ground sage**, and ⅛ teaspoon **marjoram leaves**. Substitute ½ cup **yellow cornmeal** for ½ cup of the flour.

Raisin-Nut Batter Bread

Follow **Rich White Batter Bread** recipe, adding to yeast mixture 1 teaspoon **ground cinnamon** and ½ teaspoon **ground nutmeg**. Stir ½ cup *each* **raisins** and chopped **walnuts** into batter with final addition of flour.

Orange-Rye Batter Bread

Follow **Rich White Batter Bread** recipe, adding to yeast mixture 3 tablespoons **light molasses** instead of the remaining 2 tablespoons sugar, 1 teaspoon **caraway seeds,** and 1 tablespoon grated **orange peel.** Use 1½ cups **rye flour** and 2½ to 3 cups **all-purpose flour** instead of only all-purpose flour. Let rise just until batter pushes up against can lids—not until lids pop off (40 to 45 minutes for 1-pound cans, 55 to 60 minutes for a 2-pound can).

Corn-Herb Batter Bread *(Recipe on facing page)*

1 Gradually beat flour into the batter until it is very heavy and stiff, but still too sticky to knead. Batter breads require vigorous beating, since they're not kneaded.

2 Spoon batter into 2 well-greased 1-pound coffee cans (or into 1 well-greased 2-pound coffee can). Cover with well-greased plastic can lids.

3 Let rise just until dough pushes off can lids. Carefully remove lids and immediately place cans on lowest rack in a 350° oven.

4 After bread has cooled in cans on a rack for about 5 minutes, loosen crust around edges with a thin knife and then slide bread from cans. Let cool on rack in an upright position.

5 Corn-Herb Batter Bread slices into fragrant rounds of moist, rich bread with the earthy flavors of celery, sage, and corn. It's delicious plain or spread with butter.

Buttery Pan Rolls

This recipe shows you a different way to treat batter bread: you let it rise twice, then bake it into pull-apart rolls. There's no kneading, and the rising takes place quickly; when you're finished, you can serve the light, fluffy rolls hot, right out of the baking pan.

2 packages active dry yeast
½ cup warm water (about 110°)
4½ cups all-purpose flour
¼ cup sugar
1 teaspoon salt
10 tablespoons butter or margarine, melted and cooled
1 egg
1 cup warm milk (about 110°)

In a large bowl, dissolve yeast in water; let stand until bubbly (about 15 minutes). Stir together 2 cups of the flour, the sugar, and salt until well mixed. Add 6 tablespoons of the melted butter, the egg, yeast mixture, and milk; beat for about 5 minutes to blend well. Gradually beat in remaining 2½ cups flour. Cover bowl and let batter rise in a warm place until doubled (about 45 minutes).

Pour half of the remaining melted butter into a 13 by 9-inch baking pan, tilting pan to coat bottom. Beat down batter and drop by spoonfuls into buttered pan, making about 15 rolls. Drizzle remaining melted butter over dough. Cover lightly and let rise in a warm place until almost doubled (about 30 minutes).

Bake in a preheated 425° oven (400° for a glass pan) for 12 to 17 minutes or until lightly browned. Serve hot. Makes about 15 rolls.

To bake in muffin cups, make batter and let rise as directed. Then, instead of buttering a large pan, spoon about 1 teaspoon melted butter into each of 15 medium-sized muffin cups. Fill cups about half full; let batter rise until almost doubled. Bake as above.

A traditional gesture of welcome in Russia is to offer visitors a loaf of dark bread and a pile of salt. The guest breaks off a chunk of bread, dips it in the salt, and eats it.

Whole Wheat Onion Buns

Toasted onion flecks and rich wheaty flavor distinguish these crusty sandwich buns. They complement broiled hamburgers and just about anything else you might want to use in a sandwich.

The yeast dough goes together quickly, thanks to this simplified technique: instead of first dissolving the yeast in water, you blend it with some of the dry ingredients, add hot water from the tap, then beat it with an electric mixer. Only very brief kneading is required.

3 tablespoons butter or margarine
¾ cup finely chopped onion
2½ to 3 cups all-purpose flour
3 cups whole wheat flour
3 tablespoons sugar
1½ teaspoons salt
2 packages active dry yeast
2 cups hot tap water

In a small frying pan over medium heat, melt butter; add onion and cook until golden (5 to 7 minutes). Set aside.

In large bowl of an electric mixer, stir together 1 cup of the all-purpose flour, 1 cup of the whole wheat flour, the sugar, salt, and yeast. Measure and set aside about 2 tablespoons onion-butter; then mix remaining onion-butter into yeast mixture. Pour in hot water; beat at low speed for 2 minutes.

Add 1 more cup whole wheat flour and beat at high speed for 2 minutes. Stir in remaining 1 cup whole wheat flour and enough of the all-purpose flour (about 1 cup) to make a soft dough. Sprinkle about ⅓ cup of the remaining all-purpose flour onto a board; turn dough out and knead until smooth (about 5 minutes), adding flour as needed to prevent sticking. Place dough in a greased bowl; turn over to grease top. Cover and let rise in a warm place until doubled (about 1 hour).

Punch dough down, divide into 20 equal pieces, and form each into a ball; place balls about 4 inches apart on greased baking sheets. With greased fingers, flatten each ball into a 4-inch circle. Spread about ¼ teaspoon reserved onion-butter on top of each circle. Cover and let rise until almost doubled (about 50 minutes).

Bake in a preheated 375° oven for 20 to 25 minutes or until brown. Let cool on racks. Makes 20 rolls.

Flours & Grains

Over the ages, bread has been made from a fascinating array of different grains. Here is a list of the most common; look for them in the recipes in this book, or experiment with them to create your own recipes.

All-purpose flour (regular white flour) is a blend of refined wheat flours especially suitable for making bread. It is available either bleached or unbleached—the latter is stronger and creates a better texture. It consists mainly of the starchy interior (called "endosperm") of the wheat kernel, after the bran and germ have been removed and vitamins and minerals added. It is often combined with heavier whole grain flours to improve texture.

Bran (unprocessed) and wheat germ are portions of the wheat kernel sometimes added in small quantities (usually no more than a cup per recipe) to breads for nutritional enrichment, heartiness, and special flavor. Both are much coarser than flour. Bran contributes roughage; wheat germ is rich in food value (B and E vitamins, proteins, iron, and fat).

Bread flour is a high-gluten flour that has also been treated with potassium bromate—a conditioner that gives the dough greater tolerance during kneading and ensures a loaf with good volume and a fine grain.

Cornmeal and oatmeal come, respectively, from coarsely ground white or yellow corn and from rolled or steel-cut oats. In some recipes, one or the other is combined in small quantities (a cup or two per recipe) with wheat flour to create distinctive flavors and textures.

Cracked wheat, also much coarser than flour, results when wheat kernels are cut into angular fragments. In small additions (¼ to ½ cup per recipe), it gives whole grain breads a nutty flavor and crunchy texture.

Gluten flour is wheat flour that has been treated to remove nearly all the starch, leaving a very high gluten content. Since gluten is the protein in wheat that makes dough elastic, you can successfully substitute a higher ratio of nonglutenous flours (such as soy flour) with gluten flour than you could with all-purpose flour. Buy it at health food stores.

Graham flour is practically indistinguishable from regular whole wheat flour. It is stone-ground, and it contains noticeable flecks of coarse bran.

Millet is a nutty-flavored grain that is available, ground or whole, in most stores that sell bulk grain products. It has only a trace of gluten, so it can't replace a very high proportion of the wheat flour in breads; most recipes call for about 1 cup millet to 5 cups wheat flour.

Rye is available in most markets as dark or light flour and in some health food stores as meal. Because it is less glutenous than wheat, the two grains are often combined.

Triticale (trit-i-KAY-lee) is a hybrid grain—a cross between wheat and rye. It has a mild rye flavor and is high in protein, but because it's also low in gluten, it must be combined with at least the same amount of wheat flour to make a bread that rises well. It's available in stores carrying whole grain products, and it comes in two forms: flour and flakes (flattened kernels).

Whole wheat flour, ground from the entire wheat kernel, is heavier, richer in nutrients, and more perishable than all-purpose flour. Unless you use it up quickly, store it in the refrigerator to prevent the wheat germ in it from becoming rancid. Many people prefer stone-ground whole wheat to regularly milled whole wheat, because it is slightly coarser and has a heartier flavor.

Savory Yeast Breads

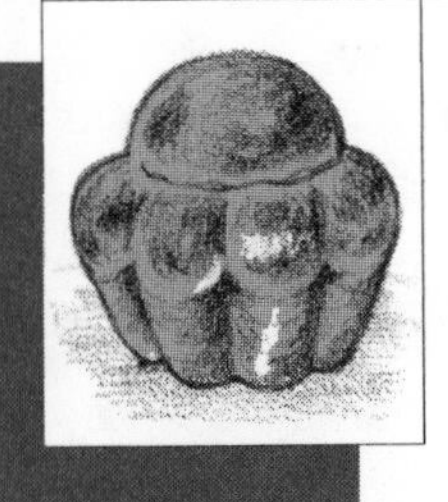

Once you've mastered the basics of yeast baking, there's really no limit to the kinds of bread you can make. From big and hearty country loaves to dainty little dinner rolls, from the coarsest rye to the most silken brioche, there are breads to suit every baker.

If you're new to baking, you'll discover that breads can be made from an unexpected variety of ingredients, and in a wide spectrum of shapes and sizes, ranging from the traditional to the innovative. In this chapter, breads also represent a number of ethnic cuisines: there are croissants from France (pages 54–56), Armenian thin bread (page 44), Swedish *limpa* (page 29), and a Basque sheepherder's bread (page 38).

With experience will come the wish to experiment—with different grains or seasonings, different crust treatments or shaping tricks. After all, bread baking is a creative endeavor—and when you know the basics, the possibilities are endless.

Beautiful breads from near and far include, clockwise from bottom, Zuñi Bread (page 29), Arab Pocket Bread (page 40), Armenian Peda Bread (page 40), Los Angeles Peda Bread (page 41), Armenian Thin Bread (page 44), and Basque Sheepherder's Bread (page 38).

Whole Grain Cereal Batter Bread

This baked-in-a-coffee-can batter bread gets its distinctive flavor and texture from whole grain cereal. For variety, you have a choice of several kinds of cereal—quick-cooking wheat cereal, rolled oats, or a mixed grain cereal. Each gives a slightly different character to the loaf.

1 package active dry yeast
½ cup warm water (about 110°)
2 tablespoons molasses
1 teaspoon salt
1 egg, lightly beaten
1 cup milk
2 tablespoons butter or margarine
1 cup whole grain cereal (see above), uncooked
3½ cups all-purpose flour

In a large bowl, dissolve yeast in water. Stir in molasses, salt, and egg. In a pan, heat milk and butter to about 110° (butter need not melt completely). Add milk mixture to yeast mixture, then blend in cereal. Gradually beat in flour to make a smooth, elastic batter; it will be very stiff, but too sticky to knead.

Spoon batter into 2 well-greased 1-pound coffee cans or into 1 well-greased 2-pound coffee can; cover with well-greased plastic lids. (Freeze if you wish.)

Let covered cans stand in a warm place until batter rises and pushes lids off (40 to 45 minutes for 1-pound cans, 55 to 60 minutes for a 2-pound can). *If frozen,* let batter stand in cans at room temperature until lids are pushed off (4 to 5 hours for 1-pound cans, 6 to 8 hours for a 2-pound can).

Immediately bake, uncovered, on lowest rack in a preheated 350° oven for about 45 minutes for 1-pound cans, about 60 minutes for a 2-pound can; crust will be well browned. Let cool in cans on a rack for 5 minutes; then run a thin knife around edges of cans, slide bread from cans, and let cool, upright, on rack. Makes 2 small loaves or 1 large loaf.

Synonymous with whole wheat flour is graham flour, named for Dr. Sylvester Graham—a 19th century Presbyterian minister who was one of the first to recognize the nourishing quality of whole grain flours.

Three Wheat Batter Bread

Pictured on page 3

Hearty, nutritious ingredients go into this batter bread that bakes in a coffee can. Wheat germ and cracked wheat add a nutty flavor and give the bread a pleasing, crunchy texture.

1 package active dry yeast
½ cup warm water (about 110°)
⅛ teaspoon ground ginger
3 tablespoons honey
1 large can (13 oz.) evaporated milk or 1½ cups fresh milk
1 teaspoon salt
2 tablespoons salad oil
2½ cups all-purpose flour
1¼ cups whole wheat flour
½ cup wheat germ
¼ cup cracked wheat

In a large bowl, combine yeast, water, ginger, and 1 tablespoon of the honey; let stand in a warm place until bubbly (about 20 minutes). Stir in remaining honey, milk, salt, and oil. Stir together all-purpose flour, whole wheat flour, wheat germ, and cracked wheat; add to liquid ingredients, 1 cup at a time, beating well after each addition. Batter will be very stiff, but too sticky to knead.

Spoon batter into 2 well-greased 1-pound coffee cans or into 1 well-greased 2-pound coffee can; cover with well-greased plastic lids. (Freeze if you wish.)

Let covered cans stand in a warm place until batter rises and pushes lids off (55 to 60 minutes for 1-pound cans, 1 to 1½ hours for a 2-pound can). *If frozen,* let batter stand in cans at room temperature until lids are pushed off (4 to 5 hours for 1-pound cans, 6 to 8 hours for a 2-pound can).

Immediately bake, uncovered, on lowest rack in a preheated 350° oven for about 45 minutes for 1-pound cans, about 60 minutes for a 2-pound can; crust will be well browned. Let cool in cans on a rack for 5 minutes; then loosen crust around edges of cans, slide bread from cans, and let cool, upright, on rack. Makes 2 small loaves or 1 large loaf.

Mushroom Batter Bread

Look what mushroomed up for dinner—a savory batter bread, its fanciful shape announcing its surprise ingredient. Baked in a coffee can, the mushroom-flecked batter billows airily over a foil collar attached to the can rim.

After the bread is baked, you slice off the "cap" of the mushroom—you can cut it into thick wedges, and the "stem" into neat round slices. Either shape is delicious.

- **2 tablespoons butter or margarine**
- **¼ pound mushrooms, minced**
- **¾ cup milk**
- **2 tablespoons sugar**
- **1 tablespoon *each* parsley flakes and instant minced onion**
- **¼ teaspoon thyme leaves**
- **1½ teaspoons garlic salt**
- **1 package active dry yeast**
- **⅓ cup warm water (about 110°)**
- **2¾ to 3 cups all-purpose flour**
- **1 egg**
- **Solid vegetable shortening**

In a small frying pan over medium heat, melt butter. Add mushrooms and cook, stirring occasionally, until mushrooms are soft and all liquid has evaporated. Add milk, sugar, parsley flakes, instant minced onion, thyme, and garlic salt. Heat to 110°.

In a large bowl, dissolve yeast in warm water. Add mushroom mixture to yeast mixture. Beat in 1½ cups of the flour and the egg. Gradually beat in more flour (1¼ to 1½ cups) to make a very heavy, stiff batter that is too sticky to knead. Cover and let rise in a warm place until almost doubled (45 minutes to an hour).

While dough rises, prepare pan: Grease a 1-pound coffee can well. Fold an 18 by 22-inch piece of heavy-duty foil in half crosswise. Crumple in edges of foil to form an 8-inch-diameter circle; crimp edges up to make a ½-inch-high rim.

Grease foil with shortening and center the circle over the can opening. With scissors, punch a hole in center of foil, then cut from center to edges of can opening in several places to form triangular flaps. Remove foil from can. Grease foil between the two layers so flaps stick together; then grease all remaining surfaces of flaps. Place foil over top of can and press flaps down around inside of can (see illustration).

Press flaps of foil down around inside of can to secure collar.

After dough has risen, stir down, then spoon into prepared can; top of dough should hold flap tips against inside of can. Place can on a shallow baking pan for easier handling. Let rise in a warm place, uncovered, until mushroom cap measures about 7½ inches across and is about 2½ inches above top of can (30 to 45 minutes).

Bake on lowest rack in a preheated 350° oven for about 50 minutes or until well browned. Immediately remove from can, let cool for 5 minutes, and gently peel off foil collar.

To slice, cut off mushroom loaf's stem near the cap, then slice individual pieces from cap or stem. Makes 1 loaf.

Cheddar-Caraway Batter Bread

This cheesy batter bread and its dill-flavored variation can be baked in a 10-inch tube pan or in regular loaf pans. They're good sliced thinly and served with cold ham or roast beef in sandwiches.

- **1 large can (13 oz.) evaporated milk or 1½ cups fresh milk**
- **3 tablespoons sugar**
- **3 tablespoons butter or margarine, cut into pieces**
- **2 teaspoons *each* salt and caraway seeds**
- **½ teaspoon garlic powder**
- **1½ cups (about 6 oz.) shredded sharp Cheddar cheese**
- **1 package active dry yeast**
- **¼ cup warm water (about 110°)**
- **3¾ cups all-purpose flour**
- **2 eggs**

In a pan, combine milk, sugar, butter, salt, caraway seeds, garlic powder, and cheese. Over medium heat, stir and heat to about 110° (butter and cheese need not melt completely).

(Continued on next page)

In a large bowl, dissolve yeast in warm water. Add milk mixture; beat in 1½ cups of the flour. Add eggs, 1 at a time, beating well after each addition; gradually beat in remaining flour until batter is smooth. Cover and let rise in a warm place until doubled (about 45 minutes).

Stir batter down and spoon into a generously greased 10-inch tube pan or two 4½ by 8½-inch loaf pans. Cover and let rise in a warm place until almost doubled (about 45 minutes).

Bake in a preheated 350° oven (325° for glass pans) for about 55 minutes (45 minutes for loaf pans) or until browned. Let cool in pan on a rack for 5 minutes; then turn out onto rack to cool completely. Makes 1 large loaf or 2 small loaves.

Parmesan-Dill Batter Bread

Follow directions for **Cheddar-Caraway Batter Bread,** but omit Cheddar, caraway seeds, and garlic powder. Instead, use 1 cup grated **Parmesan cheese,** 3 tablespoons **instant minced onion,** and 3 teaspoons **dill seeds.**

Dark Rye Bread

Pictured on facing page and on page 3

Here's the secret to duplicating those dark delicatessen-style rye breads—unlikely as it may seem, professional bakers deliberately scorch some sugar and then use it to color the bread dough.

A word of caution before you start—sugar smokes as it turns black, and when the boiling water is added there will be spattering. Be sure your kitchen is well ventilated (turn on an exhaust fan if available) and protect your hands with oven mitts. When you finish, let the empty pan cool to room temperature, then add hot tap water, soak briefly, and wash as usual. The blackened sugar won't mar the pan.

This recipe also uses stone-ground dark rye flour; it's available in some supermarkets and in health food stores. You can use regular rye flour, but you'll have to use more of it, and the dough will be rather sticky and hard to handle.

½ cup sugar
¾ cup boiling water
2 tablespoons solid vegetable shortening or butter
3 packages active dry yeast
2 cups warm water (about 110°)
¼ cup cocoa
2 teaspoons salt
2 tablespoons caraway seeds
About 4¾ cups all-purpose flour
2 cups stone-ground dark rye flour
2 tablespoons yellow cornmeal

Pour sugar into a heavy 10-inch frying pan. Place over medium-high heat until sugar is melted, stirring constantly. Continue to cook and stir until sugar smokes and is very dark (about 2½ minutes). When all the sugar is black, add boiling water and cook, stirring constantly, until all burnt sugar is dissolved and liquid is reduced to ½ cup. Remove from heat and stir in shortening; let cool to lukewarm.

In a large bowl, dissolve yeast in water. Add cooled caramel liquid, cocoa, salt, caraway seeds, and 2 cups of the all-purpose flour. Beat until smooth. Add rye flour and beat for at least 5 minutes. Stir in 2 more cups all-purpose flour to make a stiff dough.

Turn dough out onto a floured board, cover, and let rest for 10 minutes. Then knead until dough is elastic and feels just tacky to the touch (5 to 10 minutes), adding flour as needed to prevent sticking.

Place dough in a greased bowl; turn over to grease top. Cover and let rise in a warm place until doubled (about 1 hour). Punch dough down, knead briefly on a lightly floured board to release air, and divide in half. Shape each half into a ball, flatten slightly, and place on a greased 12 by 15-inch baking sheet sprinkled with cornmeal (or place both loaves 3 to 4 inches apart on a single larger sheet). Cover and let rise until almost doubled (about 1 hour and 15 minutes).

Bake in a preheated 375° oven for 30 to 35 minutes or until bread sounds hollow when tapped. Transfer to a rack to cool. Makes 2 loaves.

In 1873, Alexandre Dumas invented the following story to explain how pumpernickel got its name: A horseman, riding a steed named Nicol, tasted the coarse, dark bread. Disgusted by the first bite, he fed the remainder to his horse, exclaiming, "Bon pour Nicol!" which, if you say it fast, sounds like "pumpernickel."

Dark Rye Bread *(Recipe on facing page)*

1 *Melt sugar; scrape down undissolved crystals on sides of pan with a wooden spoon. As it cooks, sugar caramelizes and turns amber.*

2 *Continue cooking and stirring until sugar smokes and takes on a very dark color.*

3 *Stirring constantly, pour in hot water (protect hands with mitts—mixture will splatter). Stir to dissolve sugar lumps on pan bottom; reduce mixture to ½ cup.*

4 *Form each half of dough into a round loaf by gently pulling top surface toward underside to make top smooth; pinch underside together. Place on prepared pan.*

5 *Show off your accomplishment with a deli-style picnic—the dark, robust bread partners perfectly with cold cuts for sandwiches.*

European Sour Bread

Flat beer—that's the surprising ingredient used by European bakers to create a distinctive tart flavor in breads.

This European-style dark bread combines the beer with molasses, wheat germ, bran, and whole grain flour. The result is a wholesome, sour-flavored bread with a moist, chewy texture.

2 cups flat beer
About ⅔ cup yellow cornmeal
2 tablespoons butter or margarine
2 teaspoons salt
½ cup dark molasses
½ cup warm water (about 110°)
2 packages active dry yeast
1 tablespoon sugar
½ cup *each* wheat germ and whole bran cereal
2 cups graham flour or whole wheat flour
1 cup gluten flour or all-purpose flour
About 3½ cups all-purpose flour
1 egg yolk beaten with 1 tablespoon water

In a pan over medium heat, heat beer to steaming. Remove from heat and gradually stir in ½ cup of the cornmeal, the butter, salt, and molasses; set aside to cool to lukewarm.

Meanwhile, in a large bowl, combine water, yeast, and sugar; let stand until bubbly (about 15 minutes). Gradually beat in cooled beer mixture, wheat germ, bran cereal, graham flour, and gluten flour. Gradually stir in enough of the all-purpose flour (about 3 cups) to make a stiff dough. Turn dough out onto a board sprinkled with about ¼ cup of the remaining all-purpose flour. Knead until smooth and satiny (10 to 20 minutes), adding flour as needed to prevent sticking.

Place dough in a greased bowl; turn over to grease top. Cover and let rise in a warm place until doubled (about 1 hour). Punch dough down, cover, and let rise again until doubled (about 45 minutes).

Sprinkle 2 greased 12 by 15-inch baking sheets (or 1 larger sheet) evenly with about 2 tablespoons cornmeal. Punch dough down, knead briefly on a lightly floured board to release air, and divide in half. Shape each half into a slightly flattened 8-inch round; place on a baking sheet (or place both loaves 3 to 4 inches apart on a single larger sheet). Cover and let rise until almost doubled (about 40 minutes).

Using a razor blade or a sharp floured knife, make ½-inch-deep slashes on tops of loaves, forming a ticktacktoe design; brush tops and sides with egg yolk mixture. Bake in a preheated 375° oven for 40 minutes or until loaves are well browned. Let cool on a rack. Makes 2 round loaves.

Molasses Pumpernickel Bread

Fine-textured and fragrant, this rustic pumpernickel bread is delicious with hearty winter meals. Its decoratively slashed crust gives it lots of visual appeal, too.

2 tablespoons butter or margarine
2 cups milk
1½ teaspoons salt
½ cup dark molasses
½ cup warm water (about 110°)
2 packages active dry yeast
⅓ cup firmly packed dark brown sugar
1½ cups whole bran cereal
3 cups rye flour
About 4½ cups all-purpose flour
1 egg yolk beaten with 1 tablespoon water

In a small pan, melt butter; stir in milk, salt, and molasses, and set aside.

In a large bowl, combine water, yeast, and sugar; stir until dissolved. Let stand until bubbly (about 15 minutes). Then add milk mixture, bran cereal, rye flour, and 2 cups of the all-purpose flour; beat until well blended.

With a wooden spoon, stir in about 1½ cups more all-purpose flour to make a stiff dough. Turn dough out onto a floured board and knead until smooth and satiny (10 to 15 minutes), adding flour as needed to prevent sticking.

Place dough in a greased bowl; turn over to grease top. Cover with plastic wrap and let rise in a warm place until doubled (about 1½ hours).

Punch dough down, divide into two equal portions, and knead each portion briefly to release air. Then shape each into a smooth ball; flatten slightly.

Place each loaf on a greased baking sheet, at least 10 by 15 inches. Cover and let rise in a warm place until almost doubled (about 40 minutes). With a razor blade or sharp floured knife, make ½-inch-deep slashes on tops of loaves, forming a ticktacktoe design. Brush tops and sides with egg yolk mixture.

Bake in a preheated 350° oven for 30 to 35 minutes or until bread is richly browned and sounds hollow when tapped. Transfer to racks and let cool. Makes 2 round loaves.

Limpa

This rounded, hearty rye bread—a tradition in Sweden—is flavored with fennel and grated orange peel. Wonderful with just butter and a mild cheese, a sliced loaf of limpa could also be turned into a trayful of assorted Scandinavian open-faced sandwiches.

½ cup cracked wheat
2 teaspoons crushed fennel seeds
1 tablespoon grated orange peel
2 teaspoons salt
⅓ cup molasses
3 tablespoons butter or margarine
1 cup boiling water
1 package active dry yeast
¼ cup warm water (about 110°)
1 cup milk, at room temperature
2 cups rye flour
4 to 4½ cups all-purpose flour
Butter or margarine, melted

Put cracked wheat, fennel seeds, orange peel, salt, molasses, and butter in a large bowl; pour boiling water over, and let cool to lukewarm. Meanwhile, dissolve yeast in the warm water; then stir into lukewarm mixture. Beat in milk and rye flour; then gradually stir in about 3½ cups of the all-purpose flour to make a moderately stiff dough.

Turn dough out onto a floured board and knead until smooth and satiny (10 to 20 minutes), adding flour as needed to prevent sticking. Place dough in a greased bowl; turn over to grease top. Cover and let rise in a warm place until doubled (about 2 hours). Punch dough down; knead briefly on a lightly floured board to release air. Divide in half and shape each half into a round loaf about 9 inches in diameter. Place each on a greased 12 by 15-inch baking sheet. Cover and let rise in a warm place until almost doubled (about 1 hour).

Bake in a preheated 350° oven for about 35 minutes (switch pan positions halfway through baking) or until loaves sound hollow when tapped. Brush tops with melted butter. Let cool on racks. Makes 2 loaves.

Zuñi Bread

Pictured on page 22

From the Zuñi people of the Southwest comes this coarse-textured bread, lightly flavored with corn. The village women bake the bread in domed outdoor earth ovens.

1 package active dry yeast
2 cups warm water (about 110°)
¼ cup *each* salad oil and molasses
2 teaspoons salt
1 cup *each* polenta (coarse-ground Italian-style cornmeal) and yellow cornmeal; or 2 cups yellow cornmeal
6½ to 7 cups all-purpose flour

In a large bowl, dissolve yeast in water. Add oil, molasses, salt, polenta, and cornmeal; mix well. Gradually beat in about 6 cups of the flour to make a stiff dough. Turn dough out onto a floured board and knead until smooth and satiny (5 to 20 minutes), adding flour as needed to prevent sticking.

Place dough in a greased bowl; turn over to grease top. Cover and let rise in a warm place until doubled (about 1½ hours). Punch dough down, knead briefly on a lightly floured board to release air, and divide in half. Shape each half into a smooth ball, and flatten the ball into a 9-inch round. Fold the round slightly off-center so top edge is set back about 1 inch from bottom edge. With a razor blade or sharp floured knife, slash through dough from top to bottom, making four equally spaced cuts that extend from curved edge about ⅔ of the way across the loaf.

With a razor blade or floured sharp knife, make four cuts about ⅔ of the way across loaf on curved side.

Place shaped loaves well apart on a greased 14 by 17-inch baking sheet; cover lightly and let rise until almost doubled (about 45 minutes). Bake in a preheated 375° oven for 30 to 35 minutes or until loaves are a rich golden brown. Let cool on racks. Makes 2 large loaves.

Vegetable Breads *(Recipe on facing page)*

1 *For beet bread, steam scrubbed and quartered beets on a rack over boiling water in a covered pan until tender—it will take 25 to 30 minutes.*

2 *Let beets cool until you can handle them comfortably; then remove and discard skins (they'll slip off easily).*

3 *After puréeing beets in a food processor or blender, add to yeast mixture with other ingredients; then stir in flour as for a standard yeast bread dough.*

4 *Thoroughly flour a banneton or other tightly woven basket. Shape each half of dough into a smooth ball and place it in banneton; sprinkle with 1 tablespoon more flour.*

5 *After dough has risen, invert onto a greased baking sheet and carefully lift off banneton before baking.*

6 *Vegetable breads in a rainbow of hues can be baked in bannetons or as freeform loaves. Clockwise from left: spinach, beet, potato, carrot, and tomato bread.*

Vegetable Breads

Pictured on facing page

Puréed vegetables supply the color for these bright loaves. To shape them, you can make freeform loaves or use a *banneton*—the tight-surfaced, round-bottomed basket used by many country bakers in Europe. Bannetons are available in many cookware shops, but if you can't find one, you can use any closely woven, round-bottomed basket that's about 3½ inches deep and 8 inches in diameter.

1 package active dry yeast
¼ cup warm water (about 110°)
2 tablespoons sugar
½ cup milk, at room temperature
¼ cup butter, softened
1 egg
1 teaspoon *each* ground nutmeg and salt
Vegetable purée (choices and directions follow)
About 5½ cups all-purpose flour

In a large bowl, dissolve yeast in warm water. Stir in sugar and let stand until bubbly (about 15 minutes). Add milk, butter, egg, nutmeg, salt, vegetable purée, and 3 cups of the flour. (To make two kinds of bread, measure half the dough into another bowl at this point. To each bowl, add a half-recipe of vegetable purée, then continue as directed, adding half the flour to each bowl.)

With a heavy-duty mixer or wooden spoon, blend ingredients, then gradually mix in about 2 cups more flour to make a soft dough.

Turn dough out onto a floured board and knead until smooth and satiny (10 to 15 minutes); work in as little flour as possible, adding only enough to prevent sticking. Place dough in a greased bowl; turn over to grease top. Cover with plastic wrap and let rise in a warm place until doubled (about 1½ hours).

Punch dough down; knead briefly on a floured board to release air. Divide in half.

To shape in bannetons, shape each half into a smooth ball, then place, smooth side down, in a generously floured banneton or other basket. Dust top of each loaf with about 1 tablespoon flour. Cover with wax paper and let rise in a warm place until almost doubled (about 45 minutes). Invert each loaf onto a greased 12 by 15-inch baking sheet.

To shape freeform loaves, shape each half into a ball or oval. Place each in center of a greased 12 by 15-inch baking sheet and flatten slightly. Dust very lightly with flour, then cover with plastic wrap. Let rise in a warm place until almost doubled (about 45 minutes). With a razor blade or sharp knife, make ½-inch-deep slashes on surface of loaves, if desired; use diagonal slashes for oblong loaves, ticktacktoe pattern for round loaves.

To bake, place in a preheated 350° oven for 30 to 40 minutes or until loaves sound hollow when tapped. Let cool on racks. Makes 2 loaves.

Beet purée. For a full recipe, make 1½ cups purée—you'll need 1½ pounds **beets;** for a half-recipe, make ¾ cup purée from ¾ pound beets. Trim tops from beets; scrub and quarter. Steam on a rack over boiling water in a covered pan until tender (25 to 30 minutes). Let cool; slip off and discard skins. Purée beets in a food processor or blender.

Carrot purée. For a full recipe, make 1½ cups purée—you'll need 1½ pounds **carrots;** for a half-recipe, make ¾ cup purée from ¾ pound carrots. Peel carrots; cut into 2-inch pieces. Steam on a rack over boiling water in a covered pan until tender (15 to 20 minutes). Purée carrots in a food processor or blender.

Potato purée. For a full recipe, use 1 pound medium-size **russet potatoes;** measure 1¼ cups when mashed and mix in ¼ cup **milk.** For a half-recipe, use ½ pound potatoes and 2 tablespoons milk to make ⅔ cup mashed potatoes. Peel potatoes and cut into 2-inch pieces. Steam on a rack over boiling water in a covered pan until tender (about 20 minutes). Let cool, then smoothly mash.

Spinach purée. For a full recipe, make 1½ cups purée—you'll need about 3 pounds **spinach**—and add 1½ teaspoons **dry oregano leaves.** For a half-recipe, use ¾ cup purée—you'll need 1½ pounds spinach and ¾ teaspoon dry oregano leaves. Cut off roots and tough stems, discard tough leaves, and wash spinach well; drain briefly. Place leaves in a 12 to 14-inch frying pan over medium heat. Cover and cook just until spinach wilts (about 3 minutes), stirring often. When cool, squeeze very dry with your hands. Purée spinach in a food processor or blender.

Tomato purée. For a full recipe, stir together 1 large can (12 oz.) **tomato paste** and 1½ teaspoons **Italian herb seasoning.** For a half-recipe, use 1 small can (6 oz.) tomato paste and ¾ teaspoon Italian herb seasoning.

Pebble-top Oatmeal Bread

Pictured on page 3

A crunchy pebble topping of rolled oats adorns this even-textured bread. It makes wholesome breakfast toast, delicious with butter and honey or your favorite jam.

1 package active dry yeast
¼ cup warm water (about 110°)
¼ cup molasses
4 tablespoons butter or margarine
2 teaspoons salt
¼ cup firmly packed brown sugar
2½ cups regular or quick-cooking rolled oats
1 cup *each* boiling water and cold water
4½ to 5 cups all-purpose flour
3 tablespoons milk

In a small bowl, combine yeast, warm water, and 1 tablespoon of the molasses; let stand until bubbly (about 15 minutes). In a large bowl, combine butter, remaining molasses, salt, sugar, 2 cups of the oats, and boiling water; stir until butter has melted; add cold water and yeast mixture. Beat in 4 cups of the flour, 1 cup at a time.

Turn dough out onto a floured board; knead until smooth and satiny (10 to 20 minutes), adding flour as needed to prevent sticking. Place dough in a greased bowl; turn over to grease top. Cover and let rise in a warm place until doubled (about 1 hour).

Punch dough down; knead briefly on a lightly floured board to release air. Divide in half and shape each half into a loaf; place in greased 9 by 5-inch loaf pans. Soften remaining rolled oats in milk; dot over tops. Cover and let rise in a warm place until doubled (about 45 minutes).

Bake in a preheated 350° oven (325° for glass pans) for about 1 hour or until browned. Turn out onto a rack to cool. Makes 2 loaves.

At rough and rowdy medieval banquets, noble diners used thick slabs of bread instead of plates. Leftovers from the slabs—soaked with meat juices—were fed to dogs, servants, or the poor.

Millet Bread

The distinctive flavor of this high-fiber bread comes from ground millet. You can find millet, ground or whole, in most stores that sell bulk grain products. Whirl whole millet in a blender or food processor until finely ground.

One batch of dough gives you three loaves of bread—or three dozen sandwich rolls.

2 packages active dry yeast
4 cups warm water (about 110°)
4 tablespoons butter or margarine, melted
¼ cup honey
1½ teaspoons salt
2 cups ground millet
1 cup unprocessed bran
3 cups whole wheat flour
About 6½ cups all-purpose flour
1 egg beaten with 1 teaspoon water (optional)
Sesame seeds (optional)

In large bowl of an electric mixer, dissolve yeast in warm water. Stir in butter, honey, salt, millet, bran, whole wheat flour, and 1 cup of the all-purpose flour. Beat until mixture pulls away from bowl in stretchy strands. With a heavy-duty mixer or heavy wooden spoon, gradually add 5 more cups of the all-purpose flour to form a stiff dough.

Turn dough out onto a floured board and knead until smooth and satiny (about 15 minutes), adding more flour as needed to prevent sticking. Place dough in a greased bowl; turn over to grease top. Cover and let rise in a warm place until doubled (about 50 minutes).

Punch dough down, divide into 3 equal portions, and knead each one lightly to release air.

For loaves, shape each portion into a smooth loaf and place each in a greased 9 by 5-inch loaf pan; lightly grease tops. Cover and let rise in a warm place until doubled (about 30 minutes).

For sandwich rolls, divide each of the three portions into 12 equal pieces. Roll each piece into a smooth ball; flatten to form 1-inch-thick rounds. Place rolls 3 inches apart on greased baking sheets; lightly grease tops. Cover and let rise in a warm place until light and puffy (about 20 minutes).

To bake, brush loaves or rolls with egg mixture and sprinkle with sesame seeds, if desired. Bake in a preheated 350° oven (325° for glass pans) for 30 minutes or until tops are golden. Transfer to racks to cool. Makes 3 loaves or 3 dozen rolls.

Custom-made Crusts

How do you like your crust—tender to the bite, or thick, chewy, and challenging? Using different glazes and a few baker's tricks, you can achieve a wide spectrum of textures, tastes, and tones.

For a chewy-crisp crust like that of French bread, place a pan of water on the rack below the bread as it bakes. The steam encircling the bread in the hot oven does the trick. Another technique is to spray the bread with a fine mist of water at intervals as it bakes (see Light & Crusty French Bread on page 39).

For a chewy, glossy crust, brush with a simple cornstarch and water mixture. Dissolve 1 teaspoon **cornstarch** in ⅔ cup **water;** heat the mixture in a pan until boiling. Let cool slightly and, with a soft brush, paint all exposed surfaces of the loaf just before baking. After baking it for 10 minutes, remove the bread, paint it again, and finish baking.

For a lustrous crust, try egg glazes. Because they're sticky, they come in handy for keeping poppy or sesame seeds in place. Just before baking, paint the bread with one lightly beaten whole **egg**—or use either one yolk or one white beaten with a tablespoon of cold **water.** If you use yolk, you'll get a deep golden color; the white contributes a sheen, but no extra color. A whole egg gives you a little bit of each.

For a tender crust, brush loaves with melted **butter or margarine** just before baking or as soon as you take them from the oven. Or brush with **milk or cream** before baking.

For a delightfully crunchy and crackled crust, try Dutch crunch—a yeast and rice flour topping. You can find the rice flour in some markets and most health food stores (don't confuse it with Oriental rice flour, which is also called "sweet rice flour").

Here's how to make Dutch crunch topping for two loaves or one and a half dozen rolls: Stir together 1½ tablespoons **sugar,** 4 packages **active dry yeast,** ½ teaspoon **salt,** and ¾ cup **rice flour.** Add 2 tablespoons **salad oil** and ½ cup warm **water** (about 110°); stir to blend well and form a thick paste (if mixture seems very stiff, add a little more water). Cover and let rise in a warm place until doubled and very bubbly (about 30 minutes). Stir down. If necessary, topping can stand, covered, at room temperature for another 15 minutes; then stir again.

Meanwhile, shape dough into loaves or rolls. Spread topping evenly over tops and down sides of rolls or loaves. Cover very lightly with clear plastic wrap. Let rise, remove plastic, and bake as recipe directs.

For a decoratively slashed crust, make ½-inch-deep cuts on tops of loaves, using a single-edged razor blade or a floured sharp knife, just before baking. Traditional patterns include three evenly spaced diagonal cuts on oblong loaves, and a cross, ticktacktoe pattern, or radial slashes on round loaves. Besides making the crusts attractive, the slashes allow steam to escape during baking, preventing the loaves from developing cracks on their sides.

For a seed-studded crust, brush the bread with an **egg glaze** (see "For a lustrous crust," at left), then sprinkle with ¼ to ½ teaspoon of seeds before baking. Seeded crusts give you a double bonus: they deliver extra flavor as well as a tempting appearance. Depending on the flavor of your bread, you might try **poppy or sesame seeds, caraway seeds** (traditionally used with rye breads), **dill seeds, cumin seeds, or fennel seeds.** If you're making an oat-flavored bread, you can dot each loaf with ¼ cup **rolled oats** softened in 1½ tablespoons **milk** before baking; this will give you an attractively pebbled topping (see photo on page 3).

Rosemary Bread

To accompany winter soups or stews, freshly baked rosemary bread is a tasty, nutritious choice. And as if this weren't enough, the bread is particularly delicious for transforming into croutons for salads, soups, or snacks.

1 package active dry yeast
1¾ teaspoons dry rosemary
1 cup warm water (about 110°)
½ teaspoon sugar
1 teaspoon salt
1 cup whole wheat flour
About 2½ cups all-purpose flour
Salad oil
1 egg yolk beaten with 1 tablespoon water

In a large bowl, sprinkle yeast and 1½ teaspoons of the rosemary over warm water and let stand for about 5 minutes. Stir in sugar, salt, whole wheat flour, and about ¾ cup of the all-purpose flour. With a heavy-duty mixer or a wooden spoon, beat until mixture pulls away from bowl in stretchy strands. Gradually beat in enough of the remaining flour (about 1¼ cups) to form a stiff dough.

Turn dough out onto a lightly floured board and knead until smooth and satiny (about 10 minutes), adding flour as needed to prevent sticking. Place dough in a greased bowl; turn over to grease top. Cover and let rise in a warm place until doubled (about 1 hour).

Punch dough down, knead briefly on a lightly floured board to release air, and shape into a smooth loaf. Place in a greased 4½ by 8½-inch loaf pan, and brush top lightly with salad oil. Cover and let rise in a warm place until doubled (about 1 hour).

Brush top with egg yolk mixture, then sprinkle with the remaining ¼ teaspoon rosemary. Bake in a preheated 375° oven (350° for a glass pan) for about 45 minutes or until top is richly browned. Turn out onto a rack to cool. Makes 1 loaf.

Rosemary Croutons

Cut leftover **Rosemary Bread** into ½-inch cubes. Check quantity in a measuring cup; then spread cubes in a single layer on an ungreased rimmed baking pan and bake in a preheated 300° oven for about 15 minutes or until cubes are dry. Reduce oven temperature to 275°. For each cup of bread cubes, melt 2 tablespoons **butter** or margarine. Drizzle butter over bread cubes and toss quickly to coat. Bake for about 45 minutes or until crisp. Let cool completely and store in an airtight container.

Golden Swiss Cheese Loaves

Bread and cheese—a timeless partnership of good flavor—usually greet the palate separately. But in these loaves, they blend in savory harmony.

2 packages active dry yeast
1½ cups warm water (about 110°)
2 tablespoons sugar
¼ cup butter or margarine, melted and cooled
1 teaspoon liquid hot pepper seasoning
¼ cup wheat germ
4½ to 5 cups all-purpose flour
¾ cup shredded Swiss cheese
⅓ cup grated Parmesan cheese
Melted butter or margarine

In large bowl of an electric mixer, dissolve yeast in warm water. Stir in sugar, the ¼ cup melted butter, hot pepper seasoning, wheat germ, and 2 cups of the flour. Beat on medium speed, scraping bowl often, for 4 minutes. Add 1 more cup of the flour and beat on high speed for 4 minutes more.

With a heavy-duty mixer or wooden spoon, beat in enough of the remaining flour (about 1½ cups) to form a dough that is soft but not too sticky to knead. Turn out onto a floured board and knead until smooth and satiny (5 to 20 minutes), adding flour as needed to prevent sticking. Place dough in a greased bowl; turn over to grease top. Cover and let rise in a warm place until doubled (about 1½ hours).

Punch dough down and, with your hands, gradually work in Swiss cheese and all but about 2 tablespoons of the Parmesan cheese. Turn dough out onto a lightly floured board and divide in half. Shape each half into a smooth loaf and place in a greased 4½ by 8½-inch loaf pan. Cover and let rise in a warm place until loaves have risen slightly above pan rims (about 2 hours).

Brush lightly with melted butter and sprinkle with remaining Parmesan cheese. Bake in a preheated 350° oven (325° for glass pans) for 30 to 35 minutes or until loaves are browned. Turn out onto a rack to cool. Makes 2 loaves.

Cracked Wheat Twin-top Bread

This sponge-method bread is distinguished by a light, even texture and a double-domed top.

1 package active dry yeast
2½ cups warm water (about 110°)
1 teaspoon granulated sugar
2 cups graham flour
½ cup cracked wheat
1 cup warm water (about 110°)
2 tablespoons salad oil
1 tablespoon salt
¼ cup firmly packed brown sugar
1 cup wheat germ
1 cup regular or quick-cooking rolled oats
2 tablespoons sesame seeds
5 to 5½ cups all-purpose flour

In a large bowl, dissolve yeast in the 2½ cups water. Add granulated sugar, graham flour, and cracked wheat. Beat until well combined (about 3 minutes). Let stand in a warm place until bubbly (about 20 minutes).

Stir in the 1 cup warm water, the oil, salt, brown sugar, wheat germ, rolled oats, and sesame seeds. Beat in about 4 cups of the all-purpose flour. Turn dough out onto a floured board; knead until smooth and satiny (5 to 20 minutes), adding flour as needed to prevent sticking.

Place dough in a greased bowl; turn over to grease top. Cover and let rise in a warm place until doubled (about 1½ hours). Punch dough down; knead briefly on a lightly floured board to release air. Divide dough into 4 equal portions, shape each into a ball, and place 2 balls side by side in each of 2 greased 9 by 5-inch loaf pans. Cover and let rise until almost doubled (about 45 minutes).

Bake in a preheated 375° oven (350° for glass pans) for 45 minutes or until browned. Let cool in pans for 10 minutes, then turn out onto a rack to cool completely. Makes 2 loaves.

During the American Civil War, ovens were set up in the Senate chamber, and thousands of loaves were baked daily for the Union soldiers.

Triticale Honey Bread

A hybrid grain called triticale (trit-i-*kay*-lee) is rapidly gaining popularity among whole grain enthusiasts. It's a cross between wheat and rye and has a higher amount of complete protein than either. The name comes from the Latin words *triticum* (wheat), and *secale* (rye).

Triticale is available in stores carrying whole grain products, and comes in two forms: flour and flakes (flattened kernels); both can be used for baking bread.

Here's a nutritious bread made with triticale and topped with a sprinkling of sesame seeds.

2 cups boiling water
1 cup triticale flakes
1 package active dry yeast
⅓ cup warm water (about 110°)
½ cup *each* honey and instant nonfat dry milk
¼ cup salad oil
2 teaspoons salt
3½ cups all-purpose flour
About 2½ cups triticale flour
1 egg yolk or white beaten with 1 tablespoon water
2 tablespoons sesame seeds

Pour boiling water over triticale flakes; cool to lukewarm. Set aside.

In large bowl of an electric mixer, dissolve yeast in warm water. Stir in honey, dry milk, oil, salt, all-purpose flour, triticale flake mixture, and ½ cup of the triticale flour. Beat on medium speed for 5 minutes. Gradually stir in enough additional triticale flour to form a soft, nonsticky dough.

Turn dough out onto a floured board and knead until smooth (5 to 10 minutes), adding flour as needed to prevent sticking. Place in a well-greased bowl; turn over to grease top. Cover and let rise in a warm place until doubled (about 1½ hours).

Punch dough down, knead briefly to release air, and divide in half. Shape each half into a smooth loaf and place in a greased 4½ by 8½-inch loaf pan. Cover and let rise in a warm place until almost doubled (about 45 minutes).

Brush loaves with egg mixture and sprinkle with sesame seeds. Bake in a preheated 350° oven (325° for glass pans) for 40 to 45 minutes or until golden brown. Turn out onto a rack to cool. Makes 2 loaves.

Short-cut Bread Mix

This short-cut bread mix will be a real timesaver if you bake yeast breads on a fairly regular basis. You start by mixing a 5-pound bag of flour—either white or whole wheat—with salt, sugar, and instant nonfat dry milk; then you store the mixture until you decide it's time to bake. Since you add the yeast later, there's no worry about its becoming outdated.

When you're ready to bake, measure out some of this mix and add it to the yeast, butter, and egg to get a delicious loaf of bread.

For variety, we've also included a number of other treats you can create from the same recipe. You'll find a pizza crust that you can top with your favorite sauce and toppings; a cinnamon-nut bread drizzled with sugar icing; a round raisin loaf flavored with cardamom, topped with icing, and decorated with almonds; some savory onion-flavored pan rolls; and a fancy ring-shaped bread fragrant with herbs and two cheeses.

If you're unable to decide which of these tempting breads to bake, don't despair; one batch of short-cut bread mix makes enough so that you can try all six.

Short-cut Bread Mix

1 bag (5 lbs.) all-purpose or whole wheat flour
2½ tablespoons salt
1 cup sugar
2 cups nonfat dry milk

In a large bowl, stir together flour, salt, sugar, and dry milk until thoroughly blended. Seal in tightly covered containers or in heavy plastic bags and store in a cool place for 1 month, or refrigerate for up to 6 months. Stir well before each use.

To use stone-ground whole wheat flour: Prepare as directed above, but use 20 cups of the stone-ground whole wheat flour. You'll need to measure total number of cups in the bag, then measure enough additional flour, stone-ground whole wheat *or* all-purpose, to make the 20 cups—you'll need about 4 more cups.

Basic Loaf

1 package active dry yeast
1 cup warm water (about 110°)
2 tablespoons butter or margarine, melted and cooled (or use salad oil)
1 egg
3½ cups Short-cut Bread Mix
About ½ cup all-purpose flour

Dissolve yeast in water; stir in butter and egg. Add bread mix to yeast mixture and stir until well blended. Turn dough out onto a floured board and knead until smooth and satiny (5 to 20 minutes), adding flour as needed to prevent sticking. Place dough in a greased bowl; turn over to grease top. Cover and let rise in a warm place until doubled (about 1½ hours).

Punch dough down and knead briefly on a lightly floured board to release air. Shape into a smooth loaf and place in a greased 9 by 5-inch loaf pan. Cover and let rise in a warm place until almost doubled (30 to 45 minutes).

Bake in a preheated 350° oven (325° for a glass pan) for about 30 minutes or until browned. Turn out onto a rack to cool. Makes 1 loaf.

Pizza Crust

Follow directions for **Basic Loaf,** but increase water to 1¼ cups and omit egg. When time to shape, divide dough in half and roll each to fit a greased 14-inch pizza pan, building up edge slightly. (Or wrap and freeze half the dough; to use, let warm to room temperature.) Do not let dough rise a second time. Adjust oven racks so they are evenly spaced from top to bottom.

Bake crusts in a preheated 450° oven for about 10 minutes or until lightly browned (switch pan positions halfway through baking). Remove from oven and spread with your favorite sauce and toppings. Return to oven and bake for about 10 minutes longer or until topping is bubbly (switch pan positions halfway through baking).

Cinnamon Nut Loaf

Follow directions for **Basic Loaf.** Combine ¼ cup **sugar,** ¼ cup chopped **walnuts,** and 1½ teaspoons **ground cinnamon.** When time to shape, roll dough out into an 8 by 18-inch rectangle. Brush with 1 tablespoon melted **butter** or margarine and sprinkle with cinnamon-nut mixture.

Starting at a narrow end, roll dough up tightly and pinch seam to seal. Place seam side down in a greased 9 by 5-inch loaf pan; cover and let rise until almost doubled (about 1 hour and 15 minutes). Bake as directed for Basic Loaf. While still warm, drizzle with this icing: stir together ½ cup **powdered sugar,** 1 tablespoon **milk,** and ½ teaspoon **orange extract or vanilla.**

Cardamom Raisin Loaf

Follow directions for **Basic Loaf,** but add 1½ teaspoons **ground cardamom** and ½ cup **raisins** with the egg. When time to shape, form dough into a smooth ball and place in a greased 9-inch pie pan. Cover, let rise, and bake as directed for Basic Loaf. While still warm, drizzle with this icing: stir together ½ cup **powdered sugar,** 1 tablespoon **milk,** and ½ teaspoon **orange extract or vanilla.** Decorate with **sliced almonds.**

Onion Pan Rolls

Follow directions for **Basic Loaf,** but add 2 single-serving-size packages **onion soup mix** with the egg. (If using yeast dough mix made with stone-ground whole wheat flour, increase water by 2 tablespoons.) When time to shape, divide dough into 18 equal pieces and shape each into a ball. Arrange balls in 2 greased 8-inch round cake pans. Cover and let rise until almost doubled (about 50 minutes). Bake in a preheated 350° oven for 25 minutes or until browned. Turn out onto racks to cool. Makes 18 rolls.

Herb-Cheese Ring

Follow directions for **Basic Loaf,** but add 2 teaspoons **instant toasted onion** and either 2 teaspoons **dill weed,** *or* 1½ teaspoons **oregano leaves,** *or* 1½ teaspoons **dry basil** with the egg. When time to shape, roll out dough into a 10 by 18-inch rectangle. Sprinkle evenly with 1 cup shredded **Cheddar cheese** (pack into cup) and ¼ cup grated **Parmesan cheese** (see illustration 1).

Starting from a long edge, roll up jelly-roll fashion (see illustration 2); pinch seam to seal. Place roll, seam side down, on a greased 12 by 15-inch baking sheet and shape into a ring; pinch ends together to seal (see illustration 3). With a razor blade or a floured sharp knife, make ½-inch-deep slashes on top of ring, about 2 inches apart (see illustration 4). Cover and let rise until almost doubled (about 50 minutes). Brush ring evenly with 1 **egg yolk** beaten with 2 teaspoons **water;** sprinkle with 1 tablespoon grated **Parmesan cheese;** bake as for Basic Loaf. Let cool on a rack. Makes 1 loaf.

How to Shape Herb-Cheese Ring

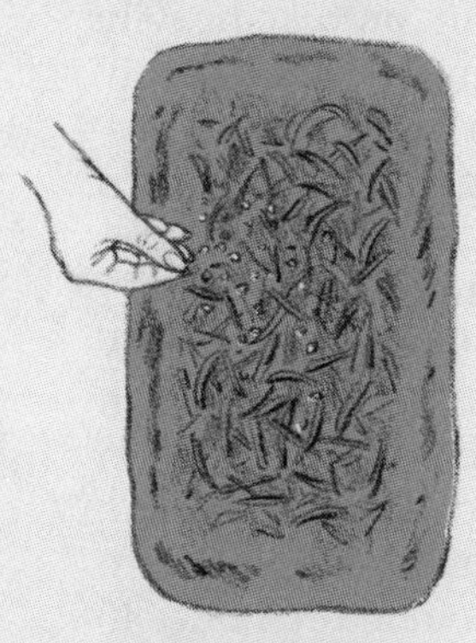

1. Sprinkle Cheddar and Parmesan cheeses evenly over rectangle of dough.

2. Starting from a long edge, roll up jelly-roll fashion; pinch seam.

3. On a greased baking sheet, shape roll into a ring; pinch ends together.

4. Slash top of ring, making cuts ½ inch deep and 2 inches apart.

Basque Sheepherder's Bread

Pictured on page 22

Like most breads, this one freezes well and is good toasted, so don't be deterred by its size.

3 cups very hot tap water
½ cup (¼ lb.) butter or margarine
⅓ cup sugar
2½ teaspoons salt
2 packages active dry yeast
9 to 9½ cups all-purpose flour
Salad oil

In a large bowl, combine hot water, butter, sugar, and salt. Stir until butter has melted; let cool to about 110°. Stir in yeast, cover, and set in a warm place until bubbly (about 15 minutes).

Beat in about 5 cups of the flour to make a thick batter. Stir in enough of the remaining flour (about 3½ cups) to make a stiff dough. Turn dough out onto a floured board; knead until smooth and satiny (10 to 20 minutes), adding flour as needed to prevent sticking. Place dough in a greased bowl; turn over to grease top. Cover and let rise until doubled (about 1½ hours).

Punch dough down and knead briefly on a floured board to release air; shape into a smooth ball. With a circle of foil, cover the inside bottom of a 5-quart cast-iron or cast-aluminum Dutch oven. Grease foil, inside of Dutch oven, and underside of lid with salad oil.

Place dough in Dutch oven and cover with lid. Let rise in a warm place until dough pushes up lid by about ½ inch (about 1 hour—watch closely).

Bake, covered with lid, in a preheated 375° oven for 12 minutes. Remove lid and bake for another 30 to 35 minutes or until loaf is golden brown. Remove from oven and turn out onto a rack to cool (you'll need a helper). Peel off foil and turn loaf upright. Makes 1 very large loaf.

A Basque sheepherder's staff of life is a vast, dome-shaped loaf of bread baked in a kettle in a pit under a campfire. Before serving it, the herder's custom is to slash the sign of the cross in the top of the loaf, then serve the first piece to his invaluable dog.

Bacon & Potato Casserole Bread

Inspired by "old country" potato breads of central Europe, these casserole loaves impart the spirited flavors of bacon and caraway seeds in a typically moist and springy texture. Freeze one loaf for another time, if you like.

1 pound russet potatoes
2 packages active dry yeast
3 tablespoons sugar
½ cup warm water (about 110°)
4 tablespoons butter or margarine, softened
1 large can (13 oz.) evaporated milk or 1½ cups fresh milk
½ cup crisply cooked, drained, and crumbled bacon or bacon-flavored bits
2 tablespoons instant minced onion
1 tablespoon caraway seeds
2 teaspoons garlic salt
1 teaspoon salt
2 eggs
About 6½ cups all-purpose flour

Cook potatoes in 1 inch boiling water, covered, until tender (30 to 40 minutes). Drain, peel, and mash. You should have 2 cups mashed potatoes; place in a large bowl and set aside.

In a measuring cup, dissolve yeast and sugar in warm water; let stand until bubbly (about 10 minutes). Beat butter into mashed potatoes; then gradually beat in milk until blended. Add bacon, onion, caraway seeds, garlic salt, salt, eggs, yeast mixture, and 3 cups of the flour; beat until thoroughly blended.

Gradually stir in an additional 2 to 2½ cups flour, and then turn dough out onto a heavily floured board. Knead until smooth and satiny (about 10 minutes), adding flour as needed to prevent sticking. Place dough in a greased bowl; turn over to grease top. Cover and let rise in a warm place until doubled (1½ to 2 hours).

Punch dough down, knead briefly on a lightly floured board to release air, and divide dough in half. Shape each half into a round and place each in a greased, deep, straight-sided, 2-quart baking dish (such as a soufflé dish). Cover and let rise in a warm place until almost doubled (about 40 minutes).

Bake in a preheated 350° oven for 40 to 50 minutes or until richly browned. Turn out onto a rack to cool. Makes 2 large round loaves.

Light & Crusty French Bread

After delving into the secrets of professional bakers, we've come up with a light and crackly-crusted French bread that rivals the best bakery fare. Until now, it was a near-impossible feat to bake French bread at home that met all the standards of commercial loaves. But the following tricks of the trade make such a feat achievable—if you're willing to take the time.

Professional bakers start with an unusually soft dough, so soft that it needs support from a special canvas cradle while rising. Today, you can buy such cradles in many cookware shops.

Another secret is to let the dough rise slowly, and in three stages, rather than two. Finally, when the loaves are in the oven, you spray them lightly with a mister—the type used for house plants. This duplicates the magical effect that commercial ovens' steam jets have on crusts.

Our recipe makes three standard-size loaves, or four baguettes—the long, slender, crusty loaves seen in French bakeries.

2 packages active dry yeast
2½ cups tepid water (70° to 75°)
2 teaspoons salt
About 6½ cups bread flour or unbleached all-purpose flour
Cornmeal

In large bowl of an electric mixer, dissolve yeast in water; let stand for 5 minutes. Stir in salt and 4 cups of the flour, 1 cup at a time, beating at medium speed until smooth. Continue beating for 10 minutes or until dough begins to pull away from sides of bowl.

With a heavy-duty mixer, gradually beat in another 2 to 2½ cups flour, ¼ cup at a time, until dough begins to clean the sides of the bowl. (*Without a heavy-duty mixer,* add as much of the flour as your mixer can handle, beating as much as possible with the mixer. Then gradually work in the remaining flour, ½ cup at a time, with a wooden spoon or your hands.) Dough should be soft, but not too sticky to knead.

Turn dough out onto a floured board and knead until smooth and satiny (about 15 minutes), adding flour as needed to prevent sticking. Dough is ready when you can slap your hand against it and hold it there for 10 seconds, with the dough just barely sticking to your hand.

Place dough in a large, well-greased bowl; turn over to grease top. Cover with plastic wrap, then a clean cloth. Let rise away from drafts *at room temperature* (65° to 75°—use a room thermometer to check) until doubled (2 to 2½ hours). Do not try to speed rising by setting dough in a warm place; it will cause the dough to become sticky and hard to handle.

Punch dough down, cover, and let rise at room temperature a second time until tripled (about 1½ hours). Meanwhile, assemble bread cradles; use 3 for regular-size loaves, 4 for baguettes. Lightly dust the inside of the canvas with flour.

Punch dough down and turn out onto a floured board. Divide into 3 or 4 pieces; cover and let rest for 15 minutes. For each loaf, shape one portion into a ball (keep others covered), then flatten into a 6-inch round. Fold it in half and flatten again. Repeat folding and flattening process 2 more times, then roll dough into a smooth 15-inch loaf; pinch seam.

Lay loaf, seam side up, in a cradle and cover with a clean cloth; repeat shaping steps with remaining portions of dough. Let rise at room temperature, away from drafts, until very puffy and more than doubled (1½ to 2 hours). Meanwhile, lightly grease two 14 by 17-inch baking sheets and sprinkle each with 2 tablespoons cornmeal. Also have ready a spray bottle of water (set to fine mist setting) and a sharp razor blade.

Turn 2 loaves out onto a baking sheet and, with a razor blade, quickly make 3 diagonal slashes on top of each. Spray loaves with a fine mist and immediately place in a preheated 450° oven. Repeat steps with remaining loaves.

Spray loaves again with a fine mist of water 3 minutes, 6 minutes, and 9 minutes after start of baking. Then reduce oven temperature to 425° and bake 16 to 20 minutes longer (a total of 25 to 30 minutes) or until golden. If you have only one oven, place racks in middle third of oven and stagger pans for better heat circulation (keep pan edges at least an inch from sides of oven); switch pan positions halfway through baking time.

Turn oven off and leave door open for 3 minutes. Then close door and let loaves stand in oven for 15 minutes. Transfer loaves to racks to cool.

Bread is best served freshly baked. If you wish to store, wrap and freeze loaves; unwrap and thaw as needed. To reheat, set loaves directly on racks of a 350° oven for 15 minutes or until crusty and heated through. Let cool slightly before serving. Makes 3 regular loaves or 4 baguettes.

Arab Pocket Bread

Pictured on page 22

These individual-size rounds of Arab bread puff and form pockets as they bake. In the Middle East, they are commonly served as tidy and tasty containers for savory meat fillings and yogurt. To use them this way, just tear or cut them open and fill the pockets.

Depending on the size of your oven and the size of your pans, you can bake three to five breads at a time. You'll need two or three baking sheets, large cloths, and light plastic to cover breads while they rest and rise—a torn piece of sheet or tea towels and a plastic garment bag work well. A large bath towel is a handy surface on which to cool the hot breads.

1 package active dry yeast
1 tablespoon sugar
3 cups warm water (about 110°)
1 tablespoon *each* salt and salad oil
9 cups all-purpose flour

In a small bowl, combine yeast, sugar, and water; let stand until bubbly (about 5 minutes); stir in salt and salad oil. Place all the flour in a large bowl and make a well in center. Pour in about half the yeast mixture at a time. Mix with your hand until flour and liquid hold together.

Turn dough out onto a well-floured board and shape into a log; divide into 20 equal pieces. Place pieces of dough on floured board and keep covered. To shape each loaf, place a piece of dough in a floured palm. With your other hand, pull dough out away from sides, then fold it back toward center and press in middle; continue around edge until dough feels smooth and elastic. Place smooth side up on cloth-lined trays. Cover with a dry cloth, then top with a damp cloth. Let rise at room temperature until puffy (1 to 1½ hours).

One at a time, place a ball on a floured board. Flatten with a rolling pin, then roll out from center with 4 strokes each way to make a 6-inch round. Shake off excess flour and place rounds at least ½ inch apart on a dry cloth. Cover with another dry cloth, then top with a damp cloth. Cover all with plastic. Let rest at room temperature until slightly puffy (about 1 hour).

Carefully lift and transfer 3 to 5 breads to an ungreased 14 by 17-inch baking sheet, placing them about ½ inch apart. Place one oven rack 2 inches from oven bottom, and second rack 4 inches below broiler. While baking, open oven only when necessary—it's important to maintain an even, hot oven temperature.

Bake in a preheated 475° oven until pockets form and bottoms brown lightly (about 5 minutes). Immediately switch oven to broil and move baking sheet to rack below broiler. Broil until tops are lightly browned (about 1 minute). Slide loaves off baking sheet onto a towel and let cool thoroughly; return oven to 475° before baking next batch. After loaves cool, you can gently flatten each, package airtight, and refrigerate or freeze. Thaw frozen loaves and reheat, uncovered, in a 300° oven for 5 to 10 minutes. Makes 20.

Whole Wheat Arab Pocket Bread

Prepare **Arab Pocket Bread** as directed, but reduce all-purpose flour to 5 cups and add 3½ cups **whole wheat flour** and ½ cup **wheat germ.**

Armenian Peda Bread

Pictured on page 22

The Armenian bread called *peda* looks like an oversized doughnut baked by someone too frugal to discard the hole in the center. Our version of this flat sesame-seeded loaf is simpler to make than most other yeast breads. After mixing and shaping the dough, you can refrigerate it for 2 to 24 hours and then bake it just before serving.

2 packages active dry yeast
½ cup warm water (about 110°)
1¾ cups warm milk (about 110°)
2 tablespoons sugar
1 teaspoon salt
3 tablespoons olive oil
6 to 6½ cups all-purpose flour
Olive oil
1 egg yolk beaten with 1 tablespoon water
4 tablespoons sesame seeds

In a large bowl, dissolve yeast in water. Stir in milk, sugar, salt, and the 3 tablespoons olive oil. Gradually beat in about 5½ cups of the flour to make a stiff dough. Turn dough out onto a floured board and knead until smooth and satiny (5 to 20 minutes), adding flour as needed to prevent sticking.

Cover dough and let rest at room temperature for 20 minutes. Knead on a lightly floured board to release air, then pinch off 2 small portions of dough (each about ½-cup size) and set aside. Divide large piece of dough in half, and shape each portion into a smooth ball.

To make each loaf, place a large piece of dough on a greased 12 by 15-inch baking sheet and flatten dough into a round cake. Poke a hole in the center and, with your fingers pulling in opposition, make a 4-inch-diameter hole; flatten dough ring to make it 10 inches in diameter. Place 1 of the small balls of dough in center and flatten gently to fill hole; brush lightly with olive oil. Repeat to make second loaf. Cover dough with clear plastic wrap and refrigerate for 2 to 24 hours.

When ready to bake, remove loaves from refrigerator, uncover, and let stand at room temperature for 10 minutes. Brush each loaf with egg yolk mixture and sprinkle with 2 tablespoons sesame seeds.

Bake in a preheated 350° oven for 35 minutes or until crust is a deep golden color. Let cool on racks. Makes 2 large loaves.

To bake freshly made dough, shape, oil, and let stand at room temperature, lightly covered, for 20 minutes; then brush with egg yolk mixture, top with sesame seeds, and bake as directed.

Los Angeles Peda Bread

Pictured on page 22

There are many versions of *peda.* This one closely resembles the flat, chewy loaves made in Armenian bakeries in Los Angeles. Delicious with meat, this peda can be adapted several ways—even to make hamburger buns (see variations following recipe, on page 43).

2 packages active dry yeast
2 cups warm water (about 110°)
2 tablespoons sugar
1 tablespoon salt
3 tablespoons butter or margarine (melted) or salad oil
5½ to 6 cups all-purpose flour
Flour glaze (recipe follows)
About 2 teaspoons toasted sesame seeds or poppy seeds (optional)

In a large bowl, dissolve yeast in water. Stir in sugar, salt, and butter. With a heavy wooden spoon, gradually beat in about 5 cups of the flour to make a stiff dough.

Turn dough out onto a floured board and knead until smooth and satiny (5 to 20 minutes), adding flour as needed to prevent sticking. Place dough in a greased bowl; turn over to grease top. Cover and let rise in a warm place until doubled (about 1 hour).

Lightly grease two 12 by 15-inch baking sheets and dust with flour. Punch dough down, divide into 2 equal parts, and shape each into a smooth ball. Set each ball on a baking sheet, cover lightly, and let rest at room temperature for 30 minutes. Then press, pull, and pound with your fist to shape each loaf into an oval about 11 by 14 inches (if too elastic to hold shape, let rest a few minutes longer). Cover and let rise in a warm place until doubled (45 to 60 minutes).

Using a soft brush dipped in cool water, brush top and sides of each loaf. Then dip finger tips in water and, with the 4 finger tips of each hand lined up, mark bread like this: press down to metal pan, marking first a 1½-inch-wide border around edge, then lines crosswise and lengthwise, about 2 inches apart.

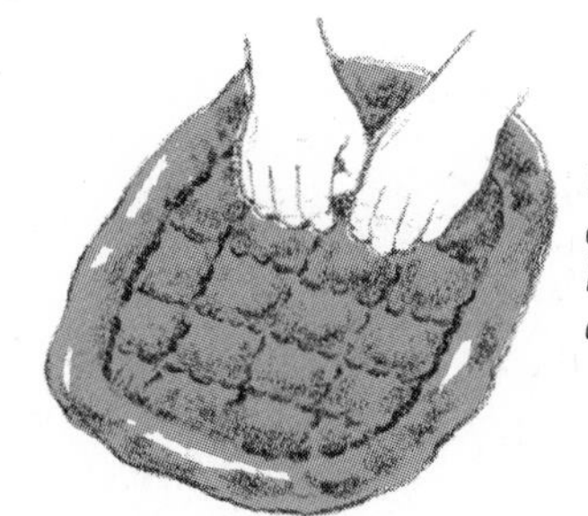

Using your finger tips, mark crosswise and lengthwise lines in bread, pressing down to pan.

Let rise, uncovered, until almost doubled (about 45 minutes). Meanwhile, prepare flour glaze.

Bake 1 loaf at a time in center of a preheated 450° oven for about 15 minutes or until golden brown. As each loaf comes from oven, apply glaze lightly over sides and top with a soft brush. To add seeds, repaint each loaf lightly and immediately sprinkle with seeds (toast sesame seeds in a small frying pan over medium heat, shaking pan frequently, until golden—about 2 minutes). Let cool on racks. Makes 2 large loaves.

Flour glaze. In a small pan, blend 2 teaspoons **all-purpose flour** with ½ cup cold **water** until smooth. Place over medium heat and cook, stirring, until mixture boils and thickens. Remove from heat and cover until ready to use.

(Continued on page 43)

Tricolor Braid *(Recipe on facing page)*

1 *After the first rising, punch down doughs and divide each in half; then roll each portion into a smooth 15-inch rope.*

2 *Place a white, a whole wheat, and a pumpernickel rope on a greased 14 by 17-inch baking sheet. Pinch ropes together at top; tuck ends underneath.*

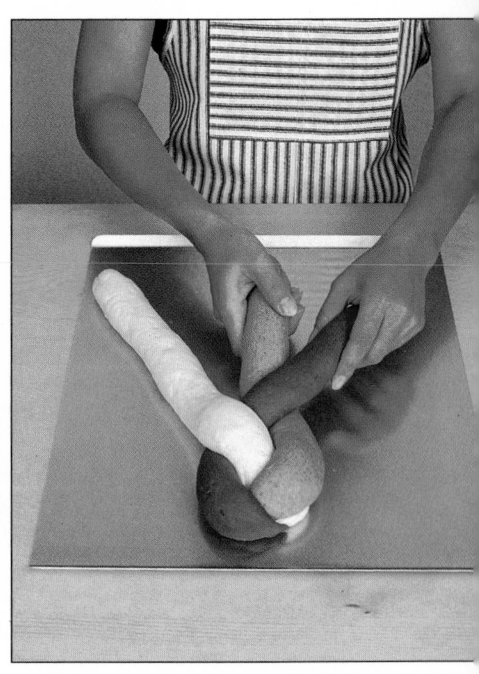

3 *Braid the three ropes together; then pinch ends and tuck under loaf. Repeat braiding for remaining dough.*

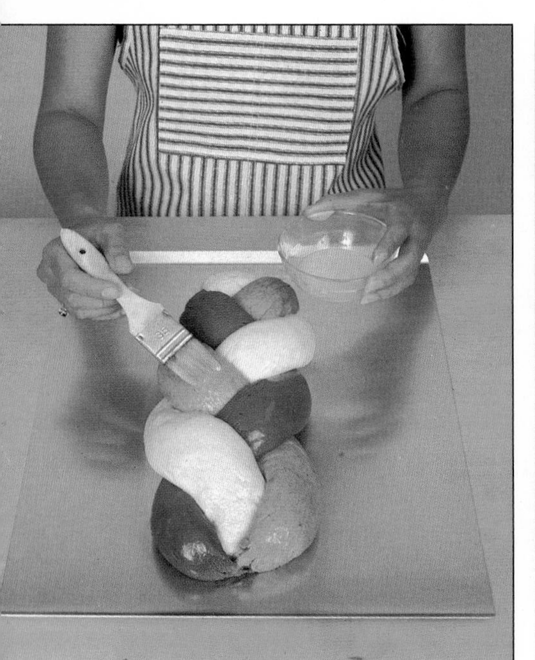

4 *When loaves have risen until almost doubled, brush all exposed surfaces with egg yolk mixture for a glossy, golden crust.*

5 *Tricolor Braid's three-in-one personality adds interest to even the simplest meal. With its hearty, down-to-earth flavor, it's perfect with soup or stew on a wintry night.*

Whole Wheat Peda

Follow directions for **Los Angeles Peda Bread** (page 41), using 2½ cups **whole wheat flour,** ½ cup **wheat germ,** and only about 2½ cups **all-purpose flour.** Add all the whole wheat flour and wheat germ and 1 cup of the all-purpose flour in first mixing stage. Mix in remaining all-purpose flour and finish as directed.

Mini-loaves of Peda

Prepare regular or whole wheat **Los Angeles Peda Bread** (page 41), as directed in preceding recipes, but after dough rises the first time, divide it into 12 equal pieces. Shape each into a smooth ball and place on greased and floured 12 by 15-inch baking sheets (6 rolls on each sheet). Let rest for 30 minutes, then flatten each ball to about 4½ inches in diameter. Omit brushing with water and marking. After loaves have risen until almost doubled, bake in a preheated 425° oven for about 15 minutes or until golden brown. Remove from oven and immediately brush on flour glaze; if desired, repaint and sprinkle with seeds. Makes 12 mini-loaves.

Tricolor Braid

Pictured on facing page

No two slices of this handsome braided loaf look alike. Each is a colorful twist of whole wheat, dark pumpernickel, and white bread.

Though it looks complicated, the bread is not difficult to make. You start with one simple yeast dough, divide it in thirds, then add different ingredients to each portion.

2 packages active dry yeast
2⅓ cups warm water (about 110°)
2 tablespoons honey
1 tablespoon salt
4 tablespoons butter or margarine, softened
About 5 cups all-purpose flour
4 tablespoons dark molasses or dark corn syrup
2 tablespoons wheat germ
1⅓ cups whole wheat flour
2 tablespoons cocoa
1½ teaspoons caraway seeds
1⅓ cups rye flour
1 egg yolk beaten with 1 tablespoon water

In large bowl of an electric mixer, dissolve yeast in water. Stir in honey, salt, butter, and 2⅓ cups of the all-purpose flour and beat on high speed for 4 minutes. Divide batter into thirds (about 1¼ cups each) and put into 3 bowls.

For whole wheat bread: To dough in one bowl, add 2 tablespoons of the molasses, the wheat germ, and the whole wheat flour. Turn out onto a floured board and knead until smooth (about 5 minutes), adding all-purpose flour as needed to prevent sticking. Place dough in a greased bowl; turn over to grease top.

For pumpernickel bread: To dough in another bowl, stir in the remaining 2 tablespoons molasses, the cocoa, caraway seeds, and rye flour. Turn dough out onto a floured board and knead until smooth (about 5 minutes), adding all-purpose flour as needed to prevent sticking. Place dough in a separate greased bowl; turn over to grease top.

For white bread: To dough in last bowl, stir in 1⅓ cups of the remaining all-purpose flour. Turn dough out onto a floured board and knead until smooth (about 5 minutes), adding all-purpose flour as needed to prevent sticking. Place dough in a separate greased bowl; turn over to grease top.

To continue, cover bowls and let dough rise in a warm place until doubled (about 1 hour).

Punch doughs down and divide each in half. Roll each portion into a smooth 15-inch rope. For each loaf, place a white, a wheat, and a pumpernickel rope on a greased 14 by 17-inch baking sheet; braid loosely and pinch ends to seal, tucking them underneath. Cover lightly and let rise in a warm place until doubled (about 1 hour).

Brush both loaves with egg yolk mixture. Bake in a preheated 350° oven for about 35 minutes or until well browned. To bake both loaves in one oven, place oven racks in middle of oven, stagger pans, and switch pan positions halfway through baking. Cool on racks. Makes 2 loaves.

Tricolor Pan Loaves

Prepare the three doughs as directed. Punch down and divide each into 4 pieces. Roll each into an 11-inch rope. For each loaf, loosely braid a white, wheat, and pumpernickel rope. Pinch ends to seal and place each in a greased 4½ by 8½-inch loaf pan, tucking ends under. Cover and let rise in a warm place until doubled (about 45 minutes). Brush with egg mixture and bake in a preheated 350° oven for 25 to 30 minutes or until browned. Turn out onto racks to cool. Makes 4 loaves.

Challah

Pictured on front cover

This festive, seed-studded braid with its glossy brown crust and delicate flavor is called *challah* (sometimes spelled "hallah"). Now a popular delicatessen item, challah has long-standing religious significance for the Jewish people, who enjoy it at Friday night Sabbath suppers, and sometimes adorn it with a sugar glaze and candied fruit or candies for special holidays.

- **1 package active dry yeast**
- **1¼ cups warm water (about 110°)**
- **1 teaspoon salt**
- **¼ cup *each* sugar and salad oil**
- **2 eggs, lightly beaten**
- **Pinch of saffron (optional)**
- **5 to 5½ cups all-purpose flour**
- **1 egg yolk beaten with 1 tablespoon water**
- **About 1 tablespoon sesame seeds or poppy seeds**

In a large bowl, dissolve yeast in water. Stir in salt, sugar, oil, eggs, and saffron (if used). Gradually beat in about 4½ cups of the flour to make a stiff dough.

Turn dough out onto a floured board and knead until smooth and satiny (5 to 20 minutes), adding flour as needed to prevent sticking. Place dough in a greased bowl; turn over to grease top. Cover and let rise in a warm place until doubled (about 1½ hours). Punch dough down; knead briefly on a lightly floured board to release air. Set aside about ¾ cup dough and cover it.

Divide remaining dough into 4 equal portions; roll each between your hands to form a strand about 20 inches long. Place the 4 strands lengthwise on a large greased baking sheet (at least 14 by 17 inches, or put two sheets together, overlapping ends and wrapping the overlap with foil). Pinch tops together, and braid as follows: pick up strand on right, bring it over next one, under the third, and over the fourth (see illustration below). Repeat, always starting with strand on right, until braid is complete. Pinch ends together and tuck underneath loaf.

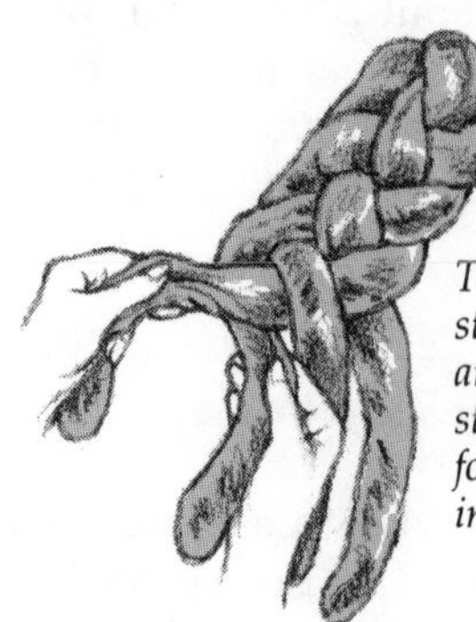

To make four-strand braid, start with right-hand strand and place it over second strand, under third, over fourth; repeat, always starting at right.

Roll reserved dough into a strand about 15 inches long; cut into 3 pieces and make a small 3-strand braid (see photo 3 on page 42). Lay on top center of large braid (see illustration below). Cover and let rise in a warm place until almost doubled (about 1 hour).

Make small three-strand braid and place over center of large loaf.

Using a soft brush or your fingers, spread egg yolk mixture evenly over braids; sprinkle with seeds. Bake in a preheated 350° oven for 30 to 35 minutes or until loaf is golden brown. Let cool on a rack. Makes 1 loaf.

On Rosh Hashanah—the Jewish New Year—a custom is to dip a slice of challah into honey, symbolizing sweetness to be hoped for in the year to come.

Armenian Thin Bread

Pictured on page 22

Thin and crackly, these big, bubbly rounds snap apart into serving-size pieces. Sesame seeds, whole wheat flour, and wheat germ give them a delicious, nutty flavor. Serve them with cheese, or with Middle Eastern dips such as hummus.

Each of the rounds must be rolled until very thin, but the dough is easy to handle.

2 packages active dry yeast
2 cups warm water (about 110°)
2 tablespoons sugar
1 tablespoon salt
½ cup (¼ lb.) butter or margarine, melted and cooled
2½ cups whole wheat flour
½ cup wheat germ
3 to 3½ cups all-purpose flour
1 egg beaten with ¼ cup cold water
About ¾ cup sesame seeds

In a large bowl, dissolve yeast in warm water. Stir in sugar, salt, and butter. Add whole wheat flour, wheat germ, and 1 cup of the all-purpose flour; beat until well blended and stretchy. Then stir in about 1½ cups of the remaining all-purpose flour to make a stiff dough.

Turn dough out onto a floured board and knead until smooth and satiny (5 to 20 minutes), adding flour as needed to prevent sticking. Place dough in a greased bowl; turn over to grease top. Cover and let rise in a warm place until doubled (1 to 1½ hours).

Punch dough down, knead briefly on a lightly floured board to release air, then divide into 12 equal pieces. Shape each piece into a smooth ball and place balls about 1 inch apart on a lightly floured board or baking sheet. Cover and let rest at room temperature for at least 45 minutes.

Arrange oven racks so that one is at lowest level and the other at highest level of your oven.

On a lightly floured board, roll out 1 ball of dough at a time to form a 10 by 12-inch oval—it will be almost paper thin. Carefully transfer to an ungreased 12 by 15-inch baking sheet. Brush lightly with egg-water mixture and sprinkle with about 1 tablespoon sesame seeds. Prick surface 3 or 4 times with a fork.

Bake on lowest rack of a preheated 400° oven for about 4 minutes, then move to top rack and bake for another 4 minutes or until golden brown and puffy. As you move first bread to top rack, place another bread on bottom rack. Continue in this way until all are baked. Let cool briefly on racks, then stack. Makes 12 breads.

White Flour Thin Bread

Follow recipe for **Armenian Thin Bread,** but instead of mixture of flours, use about 6 cups **all-purpose flour,** adding 4 cups in first addition and remaining flour as directed.

Onion Boards

These puffy-rimmed, rectangular breads have a bagel-like chewy texture and an authoritative flavor from onion bits that are liberally strewn on their flat tops. When they're served warm, their aroma is irresistible.

Served whole or broken apart, onion boa are good companions to a soup or salad for a lig satisfying meal.

1 package active dry yeast
2 cups warm water (about 110°)
2 tablespoons sugar
2 teaspoons salt
5½ to 6 cups all-purpose flour
¾ cup instant minced onion
Water
1 egg yolk beaten with 1 tablespoon water

In a large bowl, dissolve yeast in warm water. Stir in sugar, salt, and about 2 cups of the flour. Beat in 2 to 3 cups more flour to make a stiff dough. Turn out onto a floured board; knead until smooth and satiny (5 to 20 minutes), adding flour as needed to prevent sticking. Place dough in a greased bowl; turn over to grease top. Cover and let rise in a warm place until doubled (about 1½ hours).

Punch dough down; knead briefly on a lightly floured board to release air. Divide into 6 equal parts, cover lightly, and let rest for 10 minutes. Soak onion in enough water to cover for 5 to 10 minutes; then squeeze out excess moisture.

On a lightly floured board, roll and stretch each portion of dough into a rectangle about 7 by 11 inches; edges should be slightly raised. Lightly brush with egg yolk mixture and then transfer to a lightly greased 12 by 15-inch baking sheet. Distribute onion evenly over top.

Bake 1 or 2 at a time in a preheated 375° oven for 20 to 25 minutes or until golden brown; let cool on racks. Unbaked boards can stand, uncovered, until placed in oven. Makes 6 boards.

An old Slavic proverb: "Without bread, even a palace would be sad, but with it a pine tree is paradise."

Bagels

Pictured on facing page

Bagels are dense, chewy little ring-shape breads that are boiled before they're baked; and if you've never had a fresh one, you're in for a treat! Split and toast them, then spread with butter or cream cheese for a satisfying breakfast. Or use bagels for open-faced sandwich rolls—the classic combination is cream cheese and lox (smoked salmon), perhaps with a bit of sliced red onion or tomato and a squeeze of lemon.

2 packages active dry yeast
2 cups warm water (about 110°)
3 tablespoons sugar
3 teaspoons salt
5½ to 6 cups all-purpose flour
1 tablespoon sugar in 3 quarts water
Cornmeal
1 egg yolk beaten with 1 tablespoon water

In a large bowl, dissolve yeast in warm water. Stir in sugar and salt; gradually mix in 4 cups of the flour. Beat well to make a smooth batter. Mix in about 1¼ cups more flour to make a stiff dough.

Turn dough out onto a floured board and knead until smooth and satiny (10 to 20 minutes), adding flour as needed to prevent sticking—dough should be firmer than for most other yeast breads. Place dough in a greased bowl; turn over to grease top. Cover and let rise in a warm place until doubled (about 40 minutes).

Punch dough down; knead briefly on a lightly floured board to release air, then divide into 18 equal pieces. Form each piece into a smooth ball by gently kneading. Holding ball with both hands, poke your thumbs through center. With one thumb in the hole, work around perimeter, shaping bagel like a doughnut, 2½ to 3 inches across. Place shaped bagels on a lightly floured board, cover lightly, and let stand in a warm place for 20 minutes.

Bring sugar-water mixture to boiling in a 4 or 5-quart pan; adjust heat to keep it boiling gently. Lightly grease 2 baking sheets (at least 12 by 15 inches) and sprinkle with cornmeal. With a slotted spatula, lift one bagel at a time and lower into water; boil 5 or 6 at a time, turning often, for 5 minutes. Lift out of pan, drain briefly on a towel, and place on baking sheet.

Brush bagels with egg yolk mixture. Bake in a preheated 400° oven for 25 to 30 minutes or until well browned and crusty. Let cool on a rack. Makes 18 bagels.

Like many traditional breads, the bagel has a long, romantic history. According to legend, a Viennese baker invented it in 1683 as a tribute to Polish Prince John Soviesky, who had rescued the city from invading Turks. Originally called a "beugal," it was shaped like the prince's stirrup.

Whole Wheat Bagels

Follow directions for **Bagels,** but omit the 3 tablespoons sugar; use 3 tablespoons **honey** instead. In place of the flour use 2 cups **whole wheat or graham flour,** ½ cup **wheat germ,** and about 2¾ cups **all-purpose flour.** Mix in all the whole wheat flour and wheat germ and 1¼ cups of the all-purpose flour before beating dough. Then mix in about 1½ cups more all-purpose flour; knead and finish as directed.

Pumpernickel Bagels

Follow directions for **Bagels,** but omit the 3 tablespoons sugar; use 3 tablespoons **dark molasses** instead. In place of the flour use 2 cups **rye flour,** 2 cups **whole wheat flour or graham flour,** and about 1¾ cups **all-purpose flour.** Add all the rye and 1 cup *each* of the whole wheat and all-purpose flour before beating dough. Then add remaining 1 cup whole wheat and about ¾ cup more all-purpose flour; knead and finish as directed.

More Bagel Variety

Add ½ cup **instant toasted onion** to **Bagels or Whole Wheat Bagels**—add it to yeast mixture along with the sugar and salt. Or sprinkle ½ teaspoon **poppy seeds or sesame seeds or** ¼ teaspoon **coarse salt** on each glazed bagel before baking. Or add 1 tablespoon **caraway seeds** to **Pumpernickel Bagels,** then sprinkle each glazed bagel with ¼ teaspoon more **caraway seeds** before baking.

Bagels *(Recipe on facing page)*

1 *Divide dough into 18 equal pieces. Working with one piece at a time, shape into a smooth ball by gently kneading and rolling between your palms.*

2 *Holding ball with both hands, poke your thumbs through center. Then, with one thumb in the hole, work around perimeter, shaping like a doughnut.*

3 *Lower bagels into boiling sugar-water and cook, turning often, for 5 minutes to develop a chewy crust. Lift out and drain on a towel.*

4 *Transfer bagels to greased and cornmeal-sprinkled baking sheets. Brush with egg yolk mixture to make crust glossy and golden. Then, if desired, sprinkle with seeds or salt.*

5 *A basket of bagels, a platter of lox, and a pot of cream cheese mean good eating for breakfast, brunch, or snacks. The basket contains whole wheat, pumpernickel, and plain bagels.*

Dinner Rolls

This is a good basic roll dough that can take many shapes—ranging from plain pan rolls to something as fancy as butterhorns or fan-tans.

- **1 package active dry yeast**
- **¼ cup warm water (about 110°)**
- **2 eggs, lightly beaten**
- **Milk**
- **½ cup (¼ lb.) butter or margarine, melted and cooled**
- **1½ teaspoons salt**
- **½ cup sugar**
- **About 6 cups all-purpose flour**

In a large bowl, dissolve yeast in warm water. Combine eggs with enough milk to make 2 cups liquid; add to yeast mixture along with butter, salt, and sugar, stirring until well blended. Stir in 5 cups of the flour, 1 cup at a time, beating until smooth after each addition; dough will be stiff.

Turn dough out onto a heavily floured board and knead until smooth and satiny (5 to 10 minutes), adding flour as needed to prevent sticking. Place dough in a greased bowl; turn over to grease top. Cover and let rise in a warm place until almost doubled (1½ to 2 hours).

Punch dough down and divide into four equal portions. For easier handling, wrap each in plastic wrap and chill for 30 minutes. To shape, work with one portion of dough at a time, following directions below and referring to the illustrations. Let shaped rolls rise in a warm place until almost doubled (30 to 40 minutes). Bake in a preheated 425° oven (400° for glass pans) for about 10 minutes or until golden. Transfer to racks to cool.

For pan rolls, divide each portion of dough into 16 pieces (each about 1 inch in diameter) and form into smooth balls. Arrange 16 balls of dough, about 1 inch apart, in a greased round or square 8 or 9-inch baking pan. Repeat with remaining dough. Let rise and bake as directed at left. Makes 64 rolls.

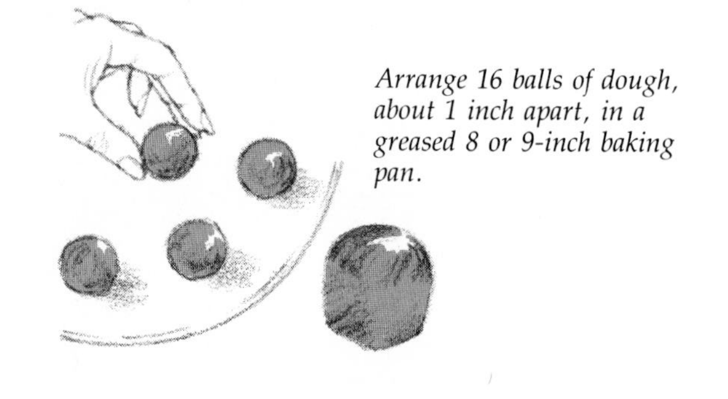

Arrange 16 balls of dough, about 1 inch apart, in a greased 8 or 9-inch baking pan.

For butterhorns, roll each portion of dough into two 8-inch circles, ¼ inch thick. Brush with melted butter. Cut each circle into 6 wedges and roll up each wedge, starting with wide end and rolling toward point. Place, point down, about 2 inches apart on greased baking sheets (at least 12 by 15 inches). Let rise and bake as directed at left. Makes 48 rolls.

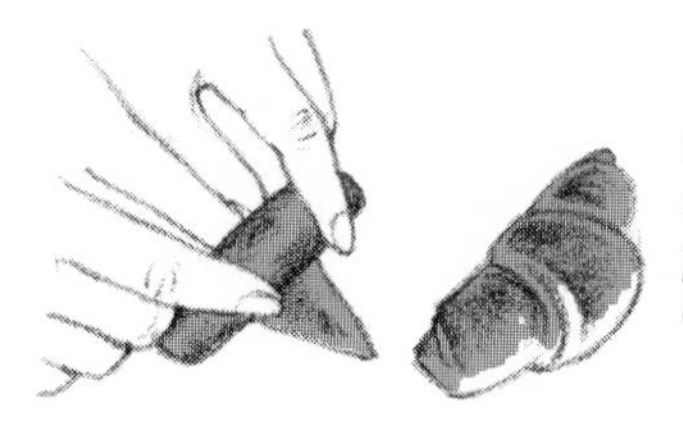

Starting with wide end, roll up each wedge; place, point down, on greased baking sheets.

For fan-tans, roll each portion of dough into an 8 by 15-inch rectangle, ¼ inch thick. Brush with melted butter; cut lengthwise into 5 strips. Stack strips evenly on top of each other; cut into 10 squares. Place squares, cut side up, in greased muffin pans. Let rise and bake as directed at left. Makes 40 rolls.

Place each square, cut side up, in a greased muffin cup.

For cloverleaf rolls, pinch off pieces of dough and use fingertips to shape each into a ¾-inch ball, tucking edges under to make smooth tops. Place in greased 2½-inch muffin pans, arranging 3 balls in each muffin cup. Let rise and bake as directed at left. Makes 48 rolls.

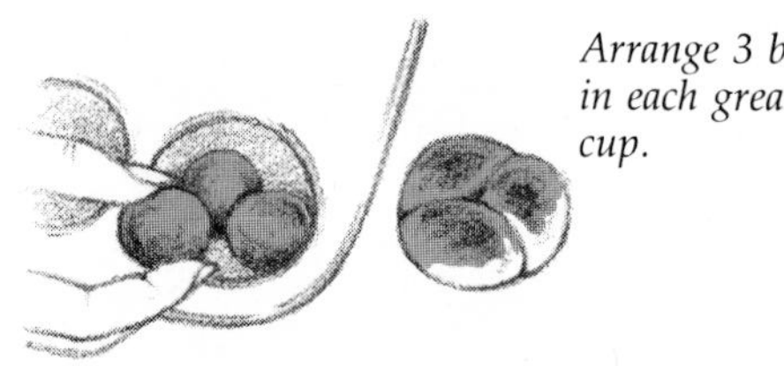

Arrange 3 balls of dough in each greased muffin cup.

For Parker House rolls, roll each portion of dough out ¼ inch thick; cut into 2½-inch circles. With the dull edge of a knife, crease each circle just off center. Brush with melted butter, then fold each circle along the crease, folding large part over small. Press folded edge firmly. Reroll scraps and repeat. Place about 2 inches apart on greased baking sheets (at least 12 by 15 inches). Let rise and bake as directed at far left. Makes 64 rolls.

Crease each circle just off center. Brush with melted butter, then fold along crease, bringing large part over small.

Crusty Water Rolls

These crusty glazed rolls have a soft, moist interior and a crunchy cornmeal bottom crust. Sharing the oven with a shallow pan of hot water is the secret of their special crust.

1 cup warm water (about 110°)
1 tablespoon sugar
1½ teaspoons salt
1 package active dry yeast
3½ to 4 cups all-purpose flour
2 tablespoons salad oil
2 egg whites
Cornmeal
1 egg yolk beaten with 1 tablespoon water

In a large bowl, combine water, sugar, salt, and yeast; let stand until bubbly (about 15 minutes). Then add 1 cup of the flour and the oil; beat until smooth. In small bowl of an electric mixer, beat egg whites until stiff but not dry; fold into batter. Gradually beat in about 2 cups more flour to make a stiff dough. Turn dough out onto a floured board; knead until smooth and satiny (5 to 20 minutes), adding flour as needed to prevent sticking.

Place dough in a greased bowl; turn over to grease top. Cover and let rise in a warm place until doubled (about 1 hour). Punch dough down, cover, and let rise 15 minutes longer. Punch dough down again, knead briefly on a lightly floured board to release air, divide into 18 pieces, and shape each into a ball. Dip bottoms in cornmeal and place balls, about 1½ inches apart, on a greased baking sheet (at least 12 by 15 inches). Cover and let rise until almost doubled (about 50 minutes).

Brush rolls with egg yolk mixture. Place a rimmed baking sheet on lowest rack of a preheated 400° oven and pour in boiling water to a depth of ¼ inch. Bake rolls on rack just above pan of water for 15 to 20 minutes or until richly browned. Let cool on racks. Makes 18 rolls.

Whole Wheat Biscuit Buns

Crunchy seeds and wheat germ give these wholesome little breads a nutty flavor and robust texture. If you don't have a biscuit cutter or round cookie cutter, use an inverted drinking glass to cut the buns. Serve them warm or split and toasted, spread with butter, jam, or peanut butter.

2 packages active dry yeast
2 cups warm water (about 110°)
½ cup soy oil or salad oil
¼ cup *each* molasses and honey
1 tablespoon salt
¼ cup *each* sesame seeds, hulled sunflower seeds, and wheat germ
6½ to 7 cups whole wheat flour

In a large bowl, dissolve yeast in ½ cup of the water. Add oil, molasses, honey, salt, sesame seeds, sunflower seeds, wheat germ, and 4 cups of the flour. Beat to blend well. Stir in remaining 1½ cups water. Beat in about 2 more cups flour to form a stiff dough.

Turn dough out onto a floured board; knead until smooth and satiny (10 to 20 minutes), adding flour as needed to prevent sticking. Place dough in a greased bowl; turn over to grease top. Cover and let rise in a warm place until doubled (about 1½ hours).

Punch dough down. On a lightly floured board, knead briefly to release air, then roll dough into a ½-inch-thick rectangle on floured board. Cut with a floured 2-inch biscuit cutter. Place about 1 inch apart on greased baking sheets (at least 12 by 15 inches); cover and let rise until very puffy (about 40 minutes).

Bake in a preheated 375° oven for 20 minutes or until golden. Let cool on racks. Makes about 4 dozen buns.

Whole Wheat Pretzels *(Recipe on facing page)*

1 *Roll each piece of dough into a rope about 24 inches long and as thick as a pencil; cut in half.*

2 *To shape into a pretzel, pick up one end of rope in each hand and curve into a circle, crossing ends at top.*

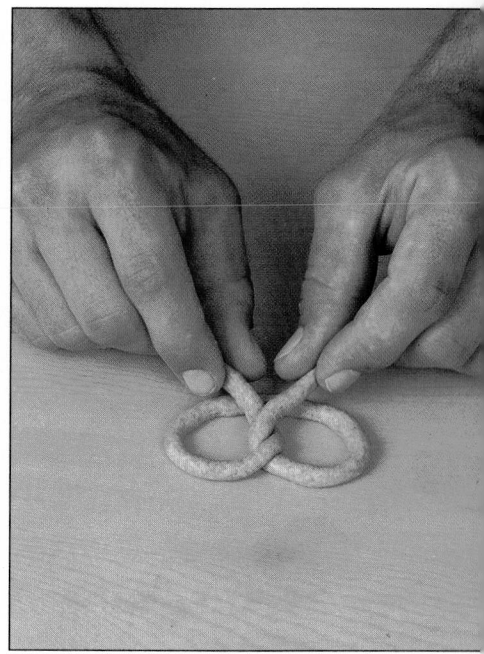

3 *Twist ends once and lay down over bottom of circle.*

4 *Inverting pretzels so ends are underneath, place slightly apart on well-greased baking sheets. Then brush with beaten egg and sprinkle lightly with coarse salt.*

5 *After pretzels are baked, pile them all onto 2 ungreased baking sheets and set in turned-off oven for 2 to 3 hours or overnight. They should be dry and crunchy—break one to test.*

6 *Crisp, wheaty pretzels and a big stein of beer make a welcome reward for a tired softball player. Armchair athletes love them, too.*

Whole Wheat Pretzels

Pictured on facing page

Here's a sure cure for rainy-day doldrums—home-twisted pretzels. Our recipe makes a whopping 8 dozen of the crunchy little treats from an easy-to-work-with whole wheat dough. They can provide an afternoon of happy twisting for the whole family—with lots of happy, wholesome snacking later on.

1 package active dry yeast
¼ cup warm water (about 110°)
1¾ cups warm milk (about 110°)
3 tablespoons *each* honey and solid vegetable shortening
¼ cup wheat germ
About 5¼ cups whole wheat flour
¾ teaspoon baking powder
1¾ teaspoons salt
2 eggs, lightly beaten
Coarse salt

In a large bowl, dissolve yeast in warm water. Stir in milk, honey, shortening, and wheat germ. Using a wooden spoon or electric mixer, gradually mix in 3½ cups of the flour. Beat until dough pulls away from sides of bowl in stretchy strands. Cover and let stand in a warm place until light and bubbly (about 40 minutes).

Meanwhile, combine 1½ cups of the flour with baking powder and the 1¾ teaspoons salt; set aside. Punch dough down and stir in flour mixture. Turn onto a lightly floured board and knead until smooth (about 5 minutes), adding flour as needed to prevent sticking.

Divide kneaded dough into 4 equal portions. Cut each quarter into 12 equal pieces and roll each piece into a rope about 24 inches long. Cut in half and twist each half into a pretzel (see photos 2 and 3 on facing page). Place pretzels, slightly apart and with loose ends turned under, on well-greased baking sheets (at least 12 by 15 inches).

Brush pretzels with beaten egg and sprinkle lightly with coarse salt. Bake in a preheated 400° oven for 10 to 12 minutes or until golden; transfer to a rack.

After all pretzels have been baked, turn oven off. Pile baked pretzels onto 2 ungreased baking sheets and set in turned-off oven for 2 to 3 hours or overnight, until thoroughly dried (break one to test). Makes 8 dozen.

German Soft Pretzels

German soft pretzels are crusty and have a bread-like interior—quite different from packaged crisp pretzels. Though they're best the day you bake them, you can freeze extras, then reheat to serve. Try them warm with butter or your favorite spicy mustard.

1 package active dry yeast
1 cup warm water (about 110°)
2½ to 3 cups all-purpose flour
2 tablespoons salad oil
1 tablespoon sugar
6 tablespoons baking soda in 6 cups water
Coarse salt

In a bowl, dissolve yeast in water. Add 1½ cups of the flour, the oil, and sugar. Beat for about 3 minutes to make a smooth batter. Gradually stir in enough of the remaining flour (about 1 cup) to form a soft dough. Turn out onto a floured board and knead until smooth and satiny (about 5 minutes), adding flour as needed to prevent sticking. Place dough in a greased bowl; turn over to grease top. Cover and let rise in a warm place until doubled (about 1 hour).

Punch dough down, turn out onto floured board, and divide into 12 pieces. Shape each into a smooth ball by gently kneading. Then roll each into a smooth rope about 18 inches long, and twist into a pretzel shape (see photos 2 and 3 on facing page). Place slightly apart on a greased baking sheet (at least 12 by 15 inches), turning loose ends underneath. Let rise, uncovered, until puffy (about 25 minutes).

Meanwhile, in a 3-quart stainless steel or enameled pan (don't use aluminum), bring soda-water mixture to boiling; adjust heat to keep water boiling gently. With a slotted spatula, lower 1 pretzel at a time into pan. Let simmer for 10 seconds on each side, then lift from water, drain briefly on spatula, and return to baking sheet. Let dry briefly, then sprinkle with coarse salt and let stand, uncovered, until all have been simmered.

Bake in a preheated 425° oven for 12 to 15 minutes or until golden brown. Transfer to racks; serve warm with butter or mustard. Or let cool completely, wrap airtight, and freeze. To reheat, place frozen pretzels on ungreased baking sheets and bake in a preheated 400° oven for about 10 minutes or until hot. Makes 1 dozen pretzels.

Party Bread Sticks

This recipe makes dramatically long bread sticks—16 or 20 inches—to add spectacle to a simple spaghetti dinner. Or you can make 12-inch sticks—served with sweet butter, they're a delicious accompaniment to aperitif wines.

The length of the sticks is limited only by the dimensions of your oven. You can bake them on heavy-duty foil placed directly on the oven rack, or on a large rimless baking sheet. You might put two sheets together end to end, wrapping them around the middle with foil; or use the bottom of a large roasting pan, inverted. For good heat circulation in the oven, always allow at least an inch on all sides of the foil or pan.

3 to 3½ cups all-purpose flour
1 tablespoon sugar
1 teaspoon salt
2 packages active dry yeast
¼ cup olive oil or salad oil
1¼ cups hot water (120° to 130°)
1 egg white beaten with 1 tablespoon water
Coarse salt, toasted sesame seeds, or poppy seeds (optional)

In large bowl of an electric mixer, stir together 1 cup of the flour, the sugar, salt, and yeast. Add oil, then gradually stir in hot water. Beat at medium speed for 2 minutes. Add ½ cup more flour and beat at high speed for 2 minutes. With a heavy-duty mixer or wooden spoon, mix in 1½ to 2 cups of the remaining flour to make a soft dough.

Turn dough out onto a well-floured board and, with well-floured hands, work it into a smooth ball. With a sharp knife, cut into 20 equal pieces for 16-inch sticks—or 16 pieces for 20-inch sticks. Roll each piece of dough into a 16 or 20-inch rope, and arrange ropes about 1 inch apart on oiled baking sheets or oiled heavy-duty foil placed on oven racks, rolling to grease all sides of dough before placing in oven.

Set bread sticks in a warm place, cover, and let rise until puffy (about 15 minutes). With a soft brush, paint each stick with egg mixture. Sprinkle lightly with coarse salt or either of the seeds, or leave plain. Bake in a preheated 375° oven for 15 to 20 minutes or until lightly browned all over. Let cool slightly on racks before serving, or let cool completely, then wrap airtight and freeze. To recrisp frozen bread sticks, unwrap and allow to thaw at room temperature; then bake, uncovered, in a preheated 300° oven for 5 minutes. Makes 16 to 20 extra-large bread sticks.

For appetizer bread sticks, divide dough into 40 equal pieces and roll each to about 12 inches long. Proceed as directed for larger sticks. Bake in a preheated 375° oven for 10 to 15 minutes or until golden brown.

Chewy Bread Sticks

A breeze to make, even on a busy day, these chewy, hand-rolled bread sticks give a pleasing nibble. Choose from three flavor options: onion, garlic, or seasoned salt. Freeze what you don't want to serve right away, then thaw and recrisp when you need last-minute appetizers or dinner accompaniments.

1 package active dry yeast
1½ cups warm water (about 110°)
1 tablespoon honey
5 to 5¼ cups all-purpose flour
Melted butter
Onion salt, garlic salt, or seasoned salt

In large bowl of an electric mixer, dissolve yeast in warm water. On medium speed, beat in honey, then gradually add 3 cups of the flour, beating well until mixture pulls away from bowl in stretchy strands.

With a heavy-duty mixer or wooden spoon, gradually add enough of the remaining flour (1½ to 2 cups) to make a soft dough. Knead on a lightly floured board until smooth and satiny (about 10 minutes), adding flour as needed to prevent sticking. With a knife, cut dough into 32 equal pieces (quarter the dough, then cut each quarter into 8 pieces). Roll each piece into a 10-inch rope, and arrange ropes about 1 inch apart on greased baking sheets (at least 12 by 15 inches). Let rise in a warm place for about 15 minutes or until slightly puffy.

Brush each rope lightly with butter, then sprinkle lightly with seasoning salt. Bake in a preheated 400° oven for 15 minutes or until golden. Let cool slightly on racks before serving. Or let cool completely, then wrap airtight and freeze. To recrisp frozen bread sticks, unwrap and allow to thaw at room temperature; then bake, uncovered, in a preheated 300° oven for 5 minutes. Makes 32 bread sticks.

Baking in Quantity

How can you serve your family homemade bread all week without baking every day? One way is to mix up enough dough to bake a week's worth of bread at one time.

That's the idea behind this expandable bread recipe. With it, you can prepare up to six loaves of bread at once, using individual loaf pans or one big foil roasting pan. Use all-purpose flour to make white bread, or substitute whole wheat flour to get a darker, heartier loaf. You can also choose between sugar and honey to sweeten the dough.

Other advantages are that the dough requires little kneading, and it rises in the refrigerator, so you can mix it up one day and bake it up to two days later.

Quantity Refrigerator Bread

Following the chart below, gather the ingredients for the number of loaves you wish to make. In a large mixing bowl, thoroughly combine ⅓ of the flour called for, sugar (if used), salt, and yeast. Add oil (and honey, if used); then gradually stir in water. Add another ⅓ of the flour, a little at a time, stirring vigorously after each addition. With your hands or a heavy wooden spoon, work in remaining flour, 1 cup at a time.

Turn dough out onto a floured board and knead until smooth and satiny (about 5 minutes); dough should be soft. Place dough in a greased bowl; turn over to grease top. Cover with plastic wrap and refrigerate for at least 2 hours or as long as 48 hours.

For 2 or 4 loaves, punch dough down and divide into 2 or 4 equal portions (about 1½ lbs. *each*). On a floured board, knead each portion about 40 times and shape into a smooth loaf. Place each loaf in a greased 4½ by 8½-inch loaf pan. Cover and let rise in a warm place until doubled (2 to 2½ hours). Bake in a preheated 375° oven (350° for glass pans) for 35 to 40 minutes or until well browned. Turn out onto racks to cool.

For 6 loaves, punch dough down and divide into 6 equal portions (about 1½ lbs. *each*). On a floured board, knead each portion about 40 times and shape into a smooth loaf. Place all the loaves side by side in a greased 13 by 17-inch foil roasting pan (or in individual greased 4½ by 8½-inch loaf pans). Cover and let rise in a warm place until doubled (2 to 2½ hours). Bake in a preheated 350° oven (325° for glass pans) for about 55 minutes or until well browned (if baking in separate pans, allow at least 1 inch around and between pans for heat circulation).

Let the 6-section loaf cool in roasting pan for about 10 minutes; then turn out onto a rack to cool (you may need a helper). After about 10 more minutes, gently pull to separate loaves. (If baking in separate pans, immediately turn out onto racks to cool.)

When loaves are completely cool, wrap airtight and refrigerate or freeze. Makes 2, 4, or 6 loaves.

Number of loaves	All-purpose or whole wheat flour	Sugar or honey	Salt	Active dry yeast	Salad oil or melted butter or margarine	Warm water (about 110°)
2	6 cups	¼ cup	1 tablespoon	1 package	2 tablespoons	2¼ cups
4	12 cups	½ cup	2 tablespoons	2 packages	¼ cup	4½ cups
6	18 cups	¾ cup	3 tablespoons	3 packages	6 tablespoons	6¾ cups

Croissants

Pictured on facing page

Making croissants at home isn't as difficult as you might think. The secret to achieving a really flaky product is in the folding and rolling process, in which you insert thin sheets of butter between layers of dough. You'll have best results if you keep the butter and dough cold while working with them, so use a cool surface, if possible—marble or plastic laminate, for example, rather than a wooden board.

We've also found that the best croissants are made with a combination of bread flour and gluten flour, rather than the usual all-purpose flour.

- **1 package active dry yeast**
- **¼ cup warm water (about 110°)**
- **¾ cup warm milk (about 110°)**
- **1 tablespoon sugar**
- **½ teaspoon salt**
- **⅓ cup gluten flour**
- **2¼ cups bread flour**
- **2 sticks (½ lb. *total*) firm unsalted butter**
- **Fillings (optional; suggestions follow)**
- **1 egg yolk beaten with 1 tablespoon milk**

In a large bowl, dissolve yeast in warm water. Stir in milk, sugar, salt, and gluten flour. Gradually add 2 cups of the bread flour and beat with a heavy-duty mixer for 5 minutes on high speed (or beat vigorously by hand for 15 minutes) until dough is elastic and pulls away from sides of bowl in stretchy strands. Cover and let rise in a warm place until doubled (about 1½ hours).

Scrape dough out onto a lightly floured baking sheet; cover with plastic wrap and refrigerate until very cold (about 30 minutes). Meanwhile, cut butter sticks crosswise into thin slices, place on wax paper, and refrigerate until very cold.

Sprinkle about 1 tablespoon flour on a cool surface. Roll out dough to form a rectangle about ¼ inch thick. Arrange butter slices, slightly overlapping, in center ⅓ of dough rectangle. Fold each extending side over butter and roll out again until rectangle is about ⅜ inch thick. If necessary while rolling, turn dough over occasionally, flouring surface lightly to prevent sticking; use as little flour as possible. Fold dough in thirds again to make a squarish rectangle. Roll and fold dough again the same way. Wrap dough in plastic wrap and refrigerate for 30 minutes.

Roll and fold again 2 more times, exactly as directed before; then wrap and refrigerate for 15 to 30 minutes.

Roll dough into a rectangle ⅛ inch thick. Cut in triangles about 6 inches at base and 8 inches long. If desired, place filling in center of 6-inch side of each triangle. Roll triangles up from base to point and place, point down, on 2 ungreased 14 by 17-inch baking sheets; croissants should be about 1½ inches apart all around. Curve ends inward to form a crescent shape. Cover lightly and let rise in a warm place until very puffy and doubled (about 2 hours).

Brush each croissant gently with egg yolk mixture. Bake in a 400° oven for 20 to 25 minutes or until golden brown. Serve hot, or transfer to racks and let cool. Makes about 16 croissants.

Almond filling. In a blender or food processor, whirl ⅓ cup unblanched whole **almonds** until finely ground. Stir in ⅓ cup *each* **all-purpose flour** and **powdered sugar.** Using food processor or a fork, work in ⅓ cup firm **unsalted butter** and ¼ teaspoon **almond extract.**

Fill each croissant with 1 tablespoon filling rolled into a 3-inch log. After brushing croissants with egg yolk mixture, sprinkle with **sliced almonds.** Bake as directed; if desired, sift **powdered sugar** over tops while still hot.

Chocolate filling. Break each of 4 **semisweet chocolate bars** (about 1½ oz. *each*) into 12 small rectangles; fill each croissant with 2 or 3 rectangles, slightly overlapping. Bake as directed; if desired, sift **powdered sugar** over tops while still hot.

Chocolate-almond filling. Prepare the **almond filling** as directed. Press 2 small rectangles of **semisweet chocolate** (see chocolate filling, above) into each 3-inch log. Proceed as for almond filling.

Fruit filling. Fill each croissant with 1 tablespoon **canned fruit pie filling** (such as apple, cherry, blueberry, or peach). Bake as directed; if desired, sift **powdered sugar** over tops while still hot.

Chile & cheese filling. Fill each croissant with 2 tablespoons shredded **jack cheese** and 1 teaspoon **diced green chiles.** Bake as directed.

Ham & cheese filling. Fill each croissant with 1 tablespoon thin julienne strips of **ham** (or use turkey or roast beef) and 2 teaspoons shredded jack, Cheddar, or Swiss **cheese.** Bake as directed.

Croissants *(Recipe on facing page)*

1 *To create flaky croissants, work on a cool surface such as marble, and be sure dough and butter are chilled. Arrange butter slices in center 1/3 of dough rectangle; fold each extending side over butter.*

2 *Roll dough out again into a 3/8-inch-thick rectangle. If necessary while rolling, turn dough over occasionally, flouring surface lightly to prevent sticking; use as little flour as possible.*

3 *Fold dough in thirds again to make a squarish rectangle. Roll and fold dough again the same way.*

4 *After completing the rolling and folding process, roll dough into a rectangle about 1/8 inch thick. Cut in triangles 6 inches at base and 8 inches long.*

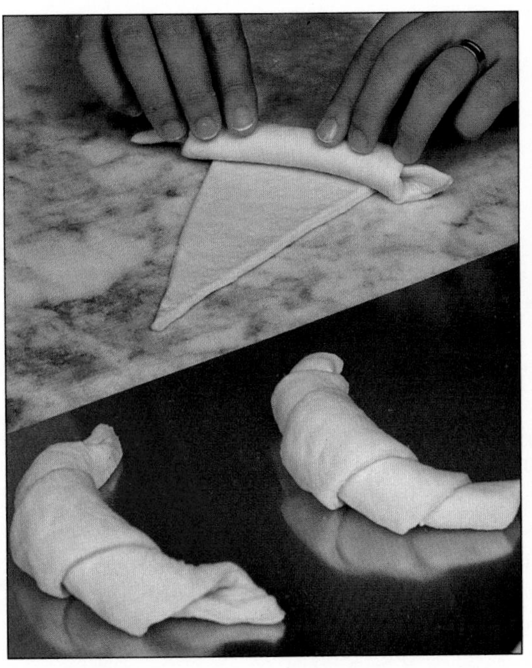

5 *Roll croissants up from base to point and place, point down, on baking sheets; curve ends inward to form a crescent.*

6 *In Parisian boulangeries and American bakeshops alike, the croissant has ardent admirers. When you make croissants at home, you'll garner a fan club of your own.*

Quick Butter Croissants

We've discovered a remarkably simple method of making croissants that closely resemble the traditional ones the French serve for breakfast. You cut firm butter into flour (as you would when making baking powder biscuits), then blend this mixture with a yeast batter. The resulting dough is marbled with pockets of butter that form flaky layers when the croissants are baked.

1 package active dry yeast
1 cup warm water (about 110°)
¾ cup evaporated milk
1½ teaspoons salt
⅓ cup sugar
1 egg
5¼ to 5½ cups all-purpose flour
4 tablespoons butter or margarine, melted and cooled
1 cup (½ lb.) firm butter or margarine, cut into pieces
1 egg beaten with 1 tablespoon water

In large bowl of an electric mixer, dissolve yeast in water. Add milk, salt, sugar, egg, and 1 cup of the flour. Beat on medium speed until smooth. Stir in the 4 tablespoons melted butter; set aside.

Put 4 cups of the remaining flour in another large bowl. Using a pastry blender or 2 knives, cut in the 1 cup firm butter until particles are the size of peas. Pour in yeast batter and fold in just until flour is evenly moistened. Cover tightly and refrigerate for at least 4 hours or up to 4 days.

Turn dough out onto a floured board, press into a compact ball, and knead for about 5 minutes. Divide dough into 4 equal parts. Shape 1 part at a time, leaving remaining dough, wrapped in plastic wrap, in refrigerator.

On a floured board, roll 1 part of dough into a circle 17 inches in diameter. Using a sharp knife, cut circle into 8 equal wedges.

For each croissant, loosely roll wedge from base to point. Shape each roll into a crescent and place, point down, on an ungreased baking sheet; keep croissants 1½ inches apart all around. Cover lightly and let rise at room temperature in a draft-free place. (Do not speed rising by placing rolls in a warm spot.)

When almost doubled (about 2 hours), brush with egg mixture. Bake in a preheated 325° oven for about 35 minutes or until lightly browned. Serve warm. Makes 32 croissants.

Whole Wheat Croissants

These croissants are made the same way as Quick Butter Croissants (at left), but with whole wheat flour and honey instead of white flour and sugar. They're perfect for the health-conscious pastry lover.

1 package active dry yeast
1 cup warm water (about 110°)
¾ cup evaporated milk
1½ teaspoons salt
⅓ cup honey
1 egg
3 cups whole wheat flour
4 tablespoons butter or margarine, melted and cooled
About 3 cups all-purpose flour
1 cup (½ lb.) firm butter or margarine, cut into pieces
1 egg beaten with 1 tablespoon water

In large bowl of an electric mixer, dissolve yeast in water. Add milk, salt, honey, egg, and 2 cups of the whole wheat flour. Beat on medium speed until smooth. Stir in the 4 tablespoons melted butter; set aside.

In another large bowl, stir together 3 cups of the all-purpose flour and remaining 1 cup whole wheat flour. Using a pastry blender or 2 knives, cut in the 1 cup firm butter until particles are the size of peas. Pour in yeast batter and fold in just until flour is evenly moistened. Cover tightly and refrigerate for at least 4 hours or up to 4 days.

Turn dough out onto a well-floured board, press into a compact ball, and knead for about 5 minutes. Divide dough into 4 equal parts. Shape 1 part at a time, leaving remaining dough, wrapped in plastic wrap, in refrigerator.

On a floured board, roll 1 part of dough into a circle 17 inches in diameter. Using a sharp knife, cut circle into 8 equal wedges.

For each croissant, loosely roll wedge from base to point. Shape each roll into a crescent and place, point down, on an ungreased baking sheet; keep croissants 1½ inches apart all around. Cover lightly and let rise at room temperature in a draft-free place. (Do not speed rising by placing rolls in a warm spot.)

When almost doubled (about 2 hours), brush with egg mixture. Bake in a preheated 325° oven for about 35 minutes or until lightly browned. Serve warm. Makes 32 croissants.

Brioches

Eggy and rich with butter, French *brioches* come in many different shapes and sizes. We offer you the two best-known: the *petite brioche* (little brioche), a roll with a fluted rim and a topknot, and the *brioche à tête* (brioche with a head), which is a grand-scale version of a petite brioche.

Settle "topknot" securely on top of brioche so that it doesn't pop off at an angle during baking.

- **1 package active dry yeast**
- **½ cup warm water (about 110°)**
- **2 teaspoons sugar**
- **1¼ teaspoons salt**
- **3 eggs**
- **½ cup (¼ lb.) butter or margarine, at room temperature**
- **3½ to 4 cups all-purpose flour**
- **1 egg yolk beaten with 1 tablespoon milk**

In a large bowl, blend yeast with warm water; let stand until bubbly. Stir in sugar, salt, and eggs. Cut butter into small pieces and add to yeast mixture along with 3⅓ cups of the flour.

Stir with a wooden spoon until flour is evenly moistened and dough holds together; then shape into a ball and place on a floured board. Knead until smooth and velvety (about 5 minutes), adding flour as needed to prevent sticking.

Place dough in a greased bowl; turn over to grease top. Cover with plastic wrap and let rise in a warm place until doubled (1 to 2 hours).

Turn dough out onto a lightly floured board; knead to release air. Return to greased bowl, cover with plastic wrap, and refrigerate for at least 12 hours or up to 24 hours.

Stir, or knead on floured board to release air. Shape dough and bake according to directions for brioche à tête or petites brioches, following.

For brioche à tête, pinch off a sixth of the brioche dough and set it aside. Shape large portion into a smooth ball by pulling surface of dough to underside of ball.

Set ball, smooth side up, in a well-buttered 9-inch-diameter fluted brioche pan or a 2-quart round baking pan. Press dough down to fill pan bottom evenly.

Shape small piece of dough into a teardrop shape that is smooth on top. With your finger, poke a hole in center of large dough portion through to pan. Nest pointed end of small piece into hole—settle it securely (see illustration at top right), or topknot will pop off at an angle during baking.

Cover with plastic wrap and let stand in a warm place until doubled (1 to 2 hours).

With a very soft brush, paint surface of brioche with egg yolk mixture; do not let mixture accumulate in joint of topknot. Bake in a preheated 350° oven (325° for glass pan) for about 1 hour or until well browned and bread begins to pull away from sides of pan. Let stand for 5 minutes; then carefully invert to remove from pan. Turn upright and serve warm, or let cool on a rack and serve at room temperature. Makes 1 brioche.

For petites brioches, divide brioche dough into 12 equal portions. Set slightly apart on a baking sheet, cover with plastic wrap, and refrigerate while you shape brioches one at a time.

To shape each brioche, pinch off about a sixth of a portion and set aside. Shape larger section into a smooth ball by pulling surface of dough to underside of ball—this is very important if you want to achieve a good-looking brioche.

Set ball, smooth side up, in a well-buttered 3 or 4-inch petite brioche pan or fluted tart pan, or in a 3-inch muffin cup. Press dough down to fill pan bottom.

Shape small piece of dough into a teardrop shape that is smooth on top. With your finger, poke a hole in center of brioche dough through to pan, and insert pointed end of small piece into hole—settle it securely, or topknot will pop off at an angle during baking. Repeat until all brioches are shaped. (If you work quickly you can leave pans at room temperature when filled; otherwise, return filled pans, lightly covered, to refrigerator.)

Cover filled pans lightly with plastic wrap and let stand in a warm place until doubled (1 to 2 hours).

With a very soft brush, paint tops of brioches with egg yolk mixture; do not let mixture accumulate in joints of topknots. Bake in a preheated 425° oven for about 20 minutes or until richly browned. Remove from pans and serve warm, or let cool on racks and serve at room temperature. Makes 12 brioches.

Sweet & Festive Yeast Breads

Here you'll find a delectable array of yeast rolls, coffee cakes, and breads—all sweetened just enough to make them something really special. Many, with their rich fillings and glazes, spicy fragrances and elegant shapes, would make a festive centerpiece at a holiday buffet, or a distinctive gift for a lucky friend. Others in this selection of sweet treats will add gaiety to the breakfast table or irresistible temptation to brunch. You might also serve them for tea or a late evening snack.

Because sweet yeast breads are so often holiday showpieces, they're prime candidates for elaborate and festive shaping techniques. You'll discover various braids, rings, wreaths, and twists in this chapter, as well as more fanciful shapes such as fish, a dove, and a special coiled basket for Easter (page 74). And if your creative impulses still aren't satisfied, see page 79 for a recipe designed with sculpture in mind—you can use it to shape almost anything that strikes your fancy.

Make sweet breads ahead of time, if you like—then freeze them, and reheat to serve later (see page 9).

Sweet treats for holiday indulgence or everyday enjoyment are, clockwise from top, Maple Wheat Swirls (page 65), Dresden-style Stollen (page 72), Buttery Almond Bear Claws (page 69), and Streuselkuchen (page 62).

Danish Coffee Cake

This buttery Danish coffee cake—a heart or a butterfly—can be filled with either of two fillings.

- **⅓ cup milk**
- **3 tablespoons sugar**
- **½ teaspoon salt**
- **¼ cup butter or margarine, cut into pieces**
- **1 package active dry yeast**
- **¼ cup warm water (about 110°)**
- **3 to 3½ cups all-purpose flour**
- **2 eggs**
- **½ teaspoon almond extract**
- **1 teaspoon grated lemon peel**
- **Cinnamon-nut or apricot-nut filling (recipes follow)**

In a small pan, combine milk, sugar, salt, and butter. Heat, stirring, to about 110° (butter need not melt completely). In a large bowl, dissolve yeast in water; blend in milk mixture. Add 1½ cups of the flour and stir to moisten evenly. Beat in eggs, almond extract, and lemon peel until smoothly blended. Then stir in 1 cup of the remaining flour.

Turn dough out onto a floured board; knead until smooth and satiny (5 to 20 minutes), adding flour as needed to prevent sticking. Place dough in a greased bowl; turn over to grease top. Cover and let rise until doubled (about 1½ hours).

Punch dough down, knead briefly on lightly floured board to release air, and roll into a 12 by 18-inch rectangle. Cover with your choice of filling to within 1 inch of edges.

Starting with a long side, roll up jelly-roll fashion; pinch seam along top to seal. Then fold the roll in half, bringing one end over the other; tightly pinch ends together, tuck them under, and place on a large, lightly greased baking sheet. Slash and shape the roll for either the butterfly or the heart, as shown below.

Cover lightly and let rise until almost doubled (about 45 minutes). Bake in a preheated 350° oven for 25 minutes or until golden brown. Let cool on a rack. Makes 1 large coffee cake.

Cinnamon-nut filling. Brush dough rectangle with 3 tablespoons melted **butter** or margarine. Combine ¼ cup *each* **granulated sugar** and firmly packed **brown sugar** and 1½ teaspoons **ground cinnamon;** distribute evenly over buttered area as directed; sprinkle with ¾ cup sliced **almonds.**

Apricot-nut filling. In a small pan over medium-high heat, combine 1 cup **moist-pack dried apricots** (chopped), ½ cup **raisins,** and ¼ cup *each* **water** and **sugar.** Bring to a boil; then cover, reduce heat, and simmer, stirring occasionally, until mixture is thick and fruits are soft (about 10 minutes). Spread over dough as directed; sprinkle with ½ cup chopped **pecans or walnuts.**

How to Shape Danish Coffee Cake

To shape heart, *cut through folded roll from center to one end; then (as shown at left) begin 1 inch from other end and make a shallow slash to meet first cut. Lift, pull, and spread out each side (as shown at right). Pinch end into a slight point.*

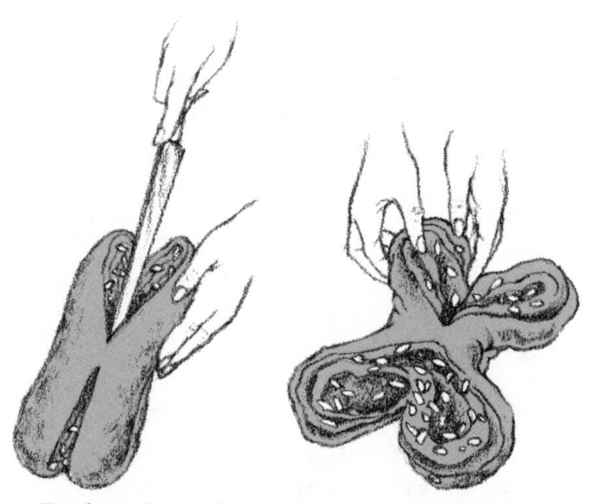

To shape butterfly, *start near center and cut to each end of folded roll, leaving 1 inch uncut in center (as shown at left). Lift, pull, and spread out "wings" (as shown at right).*

Anise Bread

For festive occasions in northeastern New Mexico, it's a tradition to bake a sweet yeast bread with the flavor of anise. Serve this tender treat warm or toasted to enhance its spicy fragrance.

- **1 package active dry yeast**
- **½ cup warm water (about 110°)**
- **½ cup warm milk (about 110°)**
- **2 tablespoons sugar**
- **1½ tablespoons anise seeds**
- **½ cup (¼ lb.) butter or margarine, melted and cooled**
- **2 eggs**
- **½ teaspoon salt**
- **4½ to 5 cups all-purpose flour**
- **⅔ cup firmly packed brown sugar mixed with ½ teaspoon ground cinnamon**
- **Sugar glaze (recipe follows)**

In a large bowl, dissolve yeast in water. Add milk, sugar, anise seeds, 3 tablespoons of the butter, eggs, salt, and 1½ cups of the flour. Beat for about 5 minutes, then gradually beat in about 2½ cups more flour to make a soft dough.

Turn dough out onto a floured board; knead until smooth and satiny (5 to 20 minutes), adding flour as needed to prevent sticking. Place dough in a greased bowl; turn over to grease top. Cover and let rise in a warm place until doubled (about 1½ hours). Punch dough down, knead briefly on a lightly floured board to release air, and roll out into a 12 by 22-inch rectangle. Brush remaining 5 tablespoons butter over dough to within ½ inch of edges. Sprinkle brown sugar–cinnamon mixture evenly over butter. Starting with a wide side, roll up tightly jelly-roll fashion, pinching edge to seal.

Being careful not to stretch roll, place it seam side down in a greased 10-inch tube pan; pinch ends together to close circle. With a razor blade or floured sharp knife, make 7 evenly spaced slashes, ½ inch deep, on top. Cover and let rise in a warm place until almost doubled (about 45 minutes).

Bake in a preheated 350° oven for 50 to 60 minutes or until loaf is lightly browned. Let cool in pan for 5 minutes; then turn out onto a rack. While still warm, spoon on sugar glaze, letting it drizzle down sides. Makes 1 loaf.

Sugar glaze. Blend ½ cup **powdered sugar** with 1 tablespoon **water** until smooth.

Potica

In Yugoslavia, the autumn harvest of nuts signals the time to bake this rich, lavishly nut-filled coffee bread (pronounced poh-TEE-tsa). Our recipe treats it as a batter bread—you spoon alternate layers of dough and ground nut filling into two large ring molds or tube pans. The fine-grained loaves that result have a honey and cinnamon-flavored walnut filling that compactly rings their interior.

- **2 packages active dry yeast**
- **½ cup warm water (about 110°)**
- **1½ cups warm milk (about 110°)**
- **¾ cup butter or margarine, melted and cooled**
- **½ cup sugar**
- **2 teaspoons *each* salt and grated lemon peel**
- **2 eggs**
- **5 cups all-purpose flour**
- **Walnut filling (recipe follows)**
- **Powdered sugar**

In a large bowl, dissolve yeast in water. Add milk, butter, sugar, salt, lemon peel, and eggs; blend well. Beat in flour, 1 cup at a time, beating well after each addition, to make an elastic dough.

Cover bowl and let dough rise in a warm place until doubled (about 1 hour). Meanwhile, prepare walnut filling and generously grease two 10-cup plain or fancy tube pans or ring molds.

Beat dough down; spoon about ¼ of it into each pan, spreading in a thin, even layer. Spoon ½ the filling in an even ring over dough in each pan; filling should not touch pan sides or center tube. Top each with ½ the remaining dough, smoothing it over filling and against pan sides. Cover and let rise until puffy (about 20 minutes).

Bake in a preheated 350° oven for about 45 minutes or until golden brown. Let cool in pans for 5 minutes; then turn out onto racks. Serve warm, dusting with powdered sugar just before serving. Makes 2 loaves.

Walnut filling. In a blender or food processor, whirl 2¾ cups (about ¾ lb.) **walnuts,** about ¼ at a time, until finely ground; transfer to a bowl. In a pan, bring ⅓ cup **half-and-half** (light cream) to simmering, then stir into nuts. Gradually stir in ¼ cup **sugar,** 2 teaspoons **ground cinnamon,** 1 tablespoon **vanilla,** and ½ cup **honey.** Separate 1 **egg** and stir yolk into nut mixture. Beat egg white until stiff peaks form; fold into nut mixture.

Poppy Seed Coffee Cake

Pictured on facing page

Bakers throughout eastern Europe are famous for their artistry with poppy seeds in cakes and breads. This breakfast loaf is one delicious example. The slate-colored seeds contribute an intriguing nutlike flavor and crunchy texture.

Because of the large amount of poppy seeds required, you may want to buy a half pound (about 1½ cups) at a health food store. Or check stores that specialize in spices, coffee, and nuts.

1 package active dry yeast
¼ cup warm water (about 110°)
¼ cup warm milk (about 110°)
½ teaspoon salt
¼ cup sugar
1 egg
¼ cup butter or margarine, softened
3 to 3½ cups all-purpose flour
Poppy seed filling (recipe follows)
1 egg white beaten with 1 teaspoon water
2 tablespoons sliced almonds

In a large bowl, dissolve yeast in water. Blend in milk, salt, sugar, egg, and butter. Gradually beat in about 2½ cups of the flour to make a soft dough.

Turn dough out onto a floured board; knead until smooth and satiny (5 to 20 minutes), adding flour as needed to prevent sticking. Place dough in a greased bowl; turn over to grease top. Cover and let rise in a warm place until doubled (1 to 1½ hours). Meanwhile, prepare poppy seed filling.

Punch dough down; knead briefly on a lightly floured board to release air, and roll into a 10 by 15-inch rectangle. Place on a lightly greased 14 by 17-inch baking sheet; mark dough to indicate 3 lengthwise sections. Spread filling in center ⅓ of dough. With a sharp knife, cut 10 diagonal strips in each of the 2 outer sections of dough, cutting in almost as far as the filling. As shown at right (see photo 4), overlap strips; first one from right side, then one from left, alternating until all strips are folded over. If there is excess dough at the end, tuck it underneath loaf.

Brush loaf with egg white mixture and sprinkle almonds evenly over top. Let rise, uncovered, in a warm place until almost doubled (about 30 minutes). Bake in a preheated 350° oven for 25 to 30 minutes or until richly browned. Let cool on a rack. Makes 1 large loaf.

Poppy seed filling. In a blender or food processor, combine ¾ cup **poppy seeds** and ¾ cup blanched whole **almonds;** whirl until mixture is consistency of cornmeal. In a small pan, combine seed-nut mixture with ½ cup **sugar,** ⅓ cup **milk,** ¾ teaspoon grated **lemon peel,** 1 tablespoon **lemon juice,** and 3 tablespoons **butter** or margarine. Cook over low heat, stirring, until mixture boils and thickens (about 10 minutes). Let cool.

Streuselkuchen

Pictured on page 58

German bakers often tuck a luscious filling under the crumbly streusel toppings on their breakfast breads and pastries. This super-size *streuselkuchen,* baked in a 14-inch pizza pan or a jelly-roll pan, is constructed on a sweet, eggy yeast dough; you have a choice of poppy seed, apple, or cream cheese filling.

½ cup milk
2 tablespoons granulated sugar
¾ teaspoon salt
¼ cup butter or margarine
1 package active dry yeast
¼ cup warm water (about 110°)
2 eggs
About 3¼ cups all-purpose flour
Poppy seed, apple, or cheese filling (recipes follow)
Streusel topping (recipe follows)
Powdered sugar (optional)

In a small pan, heat milk, sugar, salt, and butter until butter has melted; let cool to lukewarm. In large bowl of an electric mixer, dissolve yeast in water. Blend in cooled milk mixture and eggs, then add 2 cups of the flour. Beat at medium speed for 3 minutes or until batter pulls away from sides of bowl in stretchy strands. Using a wooden spoon, stir in 1 cup more flour to make a soft dough. Turn dough out onto a floured board and knead until smooth and satiny (10 to 15 minutes), adding flour as needed to prevent sticking.

Place dough in a greased bowl; turn over to grease top. Cover and let rise in a warm place until almost doubled (about 1 hour). Prepare filling of your choice, and streusel topping.

Punch dough down and knead briefly on floured board to release air. Place on a greased

(Continued on page 64)

Poppy Seed Coffee Cake *(Recipe on facing page)*

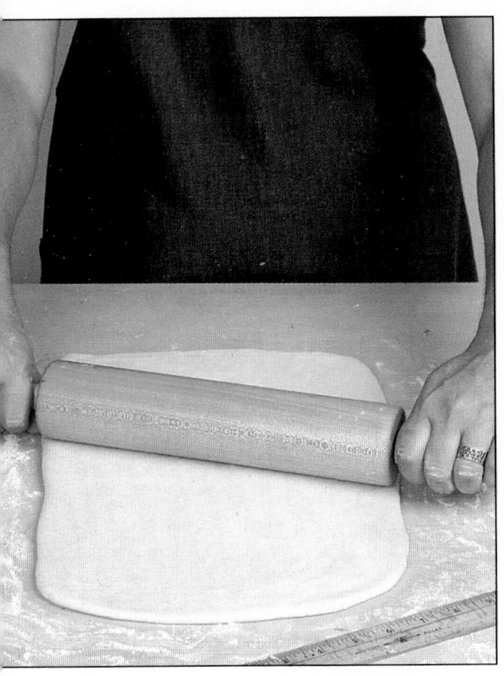

1 *On a lightly floured board, roll out dough to make a 10 by 15-inch rectangle.*

2 *Place rectangle on a lightly greased baking sheet. Mark into three lengthwise sections and spread filling down center ⅓ of dough.*

3 *With a sharp knife, cut 10 diagonal strips in each of the 2 outer sections of dough, cutting in almost to the filling.*

4 *Fold strips over filling, alternating one from the right side, one from the left, and so on, overlapping strips in center. Then brush with egg white and sprinkle with sliced almonds.*

5 *Like something from Grandma's kitchen, Poppy Seed Coffee Cake looks old-fashioned and fancy. It's perfect when company's expected for brunch, a midmorning break, or an afternoon snack.*

14-inch pizza pan or 10 by 15-inch jelly-roll pan; cover and let rest for 5 to 10 minutes. Pat dough out to fit pan. Cover evenly with filling and then with streusel topping. Let rise until puffy (about 20 minutes).

Bake in a preheated 375° oven for 25 minutes or until golden brown. Let cool on a rack for 20 minutes. If desired, dust with powdered sugar before serving. Makes 12 to 16 servings.

Poppy seed filling. In a blender or food processor, combine 1 cup **poppy seeds** and ⅓ cup whole blanched **almonds.** Whirl until mixture is consistency of cornmeal. Transfer mixture to a small pan and add ⅔ cup **sugar,** ¼ teaspoon **ground nutmeg,** ½ cup **milk,** ½ teaspoon grated **lemon peel,** 1 tablespoon **lemon juice,** and 2 tablespoons **butter** or margarine. Cook over low heat, stirring, until mixture boils and thickens (10 to 15 minutes); let cool to room temperature.

Apple filling. In a 2-quart pan, combine 5 cups peeled and chopped tart **cooking apples,** 2 tablespoons **lemon juice,** and 1 tablespoon **water.** Bring to boiling over medium heat; cover and simmer, stirring occasionally, until apples are just tender (8 to 10 minutes). Stir together ¾ cup **sugar,** 2 tablespoons **all-purpose flour,** ½ teaspoon **ground cinnamon,** and ¼ teaspoon **ground nutmeg;** stir sugar mixture into apples and cook, stirring, until thickened. Remove from heat and let cool to room temperature.

Cheese filling. In small bowl of an electric mixer, beat 1 large package (8 oz.) **cream cheese** (softened) until fluffy; beat in ½ cup **sugar,** 1 **egg,** and 1 teaspoon *each* grated **lemon peel** and **vanilla.** Stir in ½ cup **golden raisins.**

Streusel topping. In a bowl, stir together 1¼ cups **all-purpose flour,** ½ cup **powdered sugar,** 1 teaspoon **baking powder,** and ½ teaspoon **ground cinnamon.** Cut in ½ cup cold **butter** or margarine until mixture forms coarse, moist crumbs that begin to clump together. Mix in ½ teaspoon **vanilla.**

Chalk dust was one of many bizarre bleaching agents used in processing 19th century white flour before the Food & Drug Administration began to regulate the industry.

Fish-shaped Almond Loaves

You bake this golden bread from Switzerland in metal fish-shaped molds—the kind often used for gelatin salads. A core of rich almond filling runs through the bread, and sliced almonds contribute the scaly surface.

You can use the variation following this recipe to make the traditional Alsatian loaf called *kugelhof.* It bakes in one large, decorative tube pan, and has no filling. A dusting of powdered sugar highlights the surface pattern.

- **¾ cup raisins**
- **1½ tablespoons kirsch (cherry brandy) or lemon juice**
- **1 package active dry yeast**
- **¼ cup warm water (about 110°)**
- **½ cup (¼ lb.) butter or margarine, softened**
- **½ cup sugar**
- **1 teaspoon *each* grated lemon peel, vanilla, and salt**
- **3 eggs**
- **3 cups all-purpose flour**
- **½ cup milk**
- **Almond filling (recipe follows)**
- **About 6 tablespoons sliced almonds**
- **Granulated or powdered sugar**

Mix raisins with kirsch and set aside. In a small bowl, dissolve yeast in water. In a large bowl, beat butter with sugar, lemon peel, vanilla, and salt until well blended; then add eggs, one at a time, mixing thoroughly after each. Stir in yeast, then add flour alternately with milk, mixing well. Beat dough very well for 5 minutes. Stir in raisin mixture. Cover and let rise in a warm place until doubled (about 2 hours). Meanwhile, prepare and chill almond filling.

Generously butter 3 fish-shaped molds suitable for baking—each should have 2½-cup capacity and be about 10 inches long. In bottom of each pan, overlap sliced almonds like fish scales, starting just behind the head; you'll need about 2 tablespoons almonds for each mold.

Beat dough down, then spoon about ⅙ of the dough into each mold; gently press out evenly with buttered fingers.

Lay a roll of almond filling on dough in each mold, pressing gently so dough oozes up against filling. Spoon remaining dough equally into each mold, covering filling; with buttered fingers, press dough out to fill mold evenly and seal in filling.

Cover and let rise until almost doubled (about 45 minutes).

Bake on lowest rack in a preheated 350° oven for about 35 minutes or until loaves are well browned. Let cool in pans for about 10 minutes, then invert each onto a serving dish or rack. Sprinkle with granulated or powdered sugar. Makes 3 small loaves; each serves 4.

Almond filling. Smoothly blend ¼ cup **butter** or margarine (softened) and ⅔ cup **powdered sugar.** Add ⅓ cup **all-purpose flour** and ½ cup **almond paste;** stir until crumbly and evenly mixed. Beat in 1 **egg white.** Cover and chill until easy to handle (about 30 minutes). Shape into 3 rolls, each about 8 inches long; cover rolls of filling and keep cold until ready to use.

Alsatian Kugelhof

Prepare dough as directed for **Fish-shaped Almond Loaves,** omitting almond filling and adding ⅓ cup coarsely chopped blanched **almonds** to dough along with raisins. Generously butter a 10-cup decorative tube pan or mold, and arrange only ¼ cup of the sliced almonds in bottom. After dough has risen once, beat down and pour into prepared pan. Cover and let rise in a warm place until dough almost reaches top of pan (about 1 hour).

Bake on lowest rack in a preheated 350° oven for about 40 minutes or until loaf is well browned. Let cool in pan for about 15 minutes; invert onto dish or rack to cool. Sprinkle with granulated or powdered sugar. Makes 1 loaf.

Maple Wheat Swirls

Pictured on page 58

Sweet yeast breads are most often made from white flour, which gives them a fine, even texture. Current interest in whole grain baking, however, has led to the creation of many sweet breads made with whole wheat flour. They have a heartier texture and are often less sweet than their white-flour counterparts.

This slightly sweet whole wheat dough bakes into tempting rolls that have a light texture and maple flavor. Swirled inside the rolls are toasted sesame seeds and spices, their flavors further enhanced with a maple glaze.

1 package active dry yeast
2 tablespoons sugar
1½ cups warm water (about 110°)
⅓ cup maple or maple-blended syrup
⅓ cup molasses
⅓ cup salad oil
1 teaspoon salt
3½ cups all-purpose flour
About 4 cups whole wheat flour
1 cup raisins (optional)
6 tablespoons butter or margarine
¼ cup sesame seeds
⅔ cup sugar
2 tablespoons ground cinnamon
2 teaspoons ground nutmeg
1 cup finely chopped walnuts or almonds
Maple glaze (recipe follows)

In large bowl of an electric mixer, dissolve yeast and sugar in warm water; let stand until bubbly (5 to 15 minutes). Blend in syrup, molasses, oil, and salt. At medium speed, beat in the all-purpose flour, 1 cup at a time, and continue beating for 10 to 15 minutes, until dough pulls away from bowl in stretchy strands. With a heavy-duty mixer or wooden spoon, gradually add 3 cups of the whole wheat flour to make a stiff dough.

Turn dough out onto a lightly floured board; knead until smooth (10 to 15 minutes), adding flour as needed to prevent sticking. Knead in raisins, if desired. Place dough in a greased bowl; turn over to grease top. Cover and let rise in a warm place until doubled (about 2 hours).

In a small frying pan, melt butter; add sesame seeds and stir until golden; set aside. Combine sugar, cinnamon, nutmeg, and nuts; set aside.

Punch dough down; knead briefly on floured board to release air, then divide in half. Roll each half into a rectangle, about 12 by 16 inches. Brush evenly with sesame seed mixture; sprinkle with sugar mixture. Starting with a long edge, roll each rectangle up snugly, jelly-roll fashion; slice into 12 equal pieces. Lay rolls flat, ½ inch apart, on two greased 12 by 15-inch baking sheets. Cover and let rise until doubled (about 45 minutes).

Bake in a preheated 375° oven for 20 minutes or until golden brown. Let cool on baking sheets for about 5 minutes, then transfer to a rack. Separate rolls, if desired. Prepare maple glaze and drizzle it over warm rolls. Makes 2 dozen rolls.

Maple glaze. In a small bowl, blend 1½ cups **powdered sugar,** 2 tablespoons **water,** and ½ teaspoon **maple flavoring** until smooth.

Pan Dulce *(Recipe on facing page)*

1 *To make a shell (concha): Pat dough into a 3-inch round. Top with ¼ cup streusel, either patted to a smooth layer and slashed, or piled on in lumps.*

2 *To make a horn (cuerno): Roll dough to a 4 by 8-inch oval. Top with 3 tablespoons streusel. Roll from one end, stop halfway and fold in sides, then finish rolling and curve ends in.*

3 *To make an ear of corn (elote): Roll dough to a 4 by 8-inch oval. Top with 3 tablespoons streusel. Roll up from one end to other; with a sharp knife, slash top, cutting halfway through roll.*

4 *A bounty of sweet Mexican breads makes a special breakfast treat. For extra authenticity, serve Pan Dulce with cinnamon-flavored Mexican hot chocolate.*

Pan Dulce

Pictured on facing page

Like other Mexican artisans, south-of-the-border bakers have a talent for creating fanciful designs. In their hands, a simple ball of dough plus some sweet crumb topping can become a seashell, a horn, or some other imaginatively shaped treat. All of these egg-rich yeast buns are called *pan dulce* (pronounced pahn DOOL-seh), which simply means sweet bread.

1 cup milk
6 tablespoons butter or margarine, cut into pieces
1 package active dry yeast
1 teaspoon salt
⅓ cup sugar
5 to 5½ cups all-purpose flour
2 eggs
Plain and chocolate egg streusel (recipes follow)
1 egg beaten with 2 tablespoons milk

In a small pan, heat milk and butter until very warm (120° to 130°; butter need not melt completely). In large bowl of an electric mixer, combine yeast, salt, sugar, and 2 cups of the flour. Pour in milk mixture and beat on medium speed for 2 minutes, scraping bowl often. Blend in eggs and 1 cup more flour; beat on high speed for 2 minutes. With a heavy-duty mixer or wooden spoon, gradually beat in enough of the remaining flour (about 1½ cups) to make a stiff dough.

Turn dough out onto a floured board; knead until smooth and satiny (5 to 20 minutes), adding flour as needed to prevent sticking. Place dough in a greased bowl; turn over to grease top. Cover and let rise in a warm place until doubled (about 1½ hours).

Meanwhile, prepare both plain and chocolate egg streusel mixtures.

Punch dough down; knead briefly on floured board to release air. Divide into 14 equal pieces and shape each into a smooth ball; then shape buns (see photos 1, 2, and 3 at left), making 7 round buns (shells) and 7 long shapes (horns and ears of corn). Lightly pack streusel into cup or spoon when measuring amount indicated; for shells, squeeze streusel firmly into a ball, then either pat out smooth or break into lumps.

Place buns about 2 inches apart on greased baking sheets, placing streusel-topped buns on 1 sheet and filled buns on another; lightly cover filled buns only. Let buns rise in a warm place until almost doubled (about 45 minutes).

Brush filled buns with egg mixture.

Bake in a preheated 375° oven for 17 to 20 minutes or until tops are lightly browned. Makes 14 buns.

Plain egg streusel. In a bowl, mix ½ cup **sugar** with ⅔ cup **all-purpose flour.** Cut in 3½ tablespoons **butter** or margarine with a pastry blender or by rubbing mixture between your fingers until fine, even crumbs form. With a fork, stir in 2 **egg yolks** until well blended.

Chocolate egg streusel. Follow directions for plain egg streusel, but add 2 tablespoons **unsweetened cocoa** with the sugar and flour.

Giant Upside-down Pecan Rolls

These sweet pecan rolls are so generously proportioned that just one or two will feed a small family.

⅔ cup milk
1¾ cups sugar
1 teaspoon salt
½ cup (¼ lb.) butter or margarine, cut into pieces
2 packages active dry yeast
½ cup warm water (about 110°)
5½ to 6 cups all-purpose flour
2 eggs
¼ cup butter or margarine, melted and cooled
1 tablespoon ground cinnamon
1 cup coarsely chopped pecans
Water
Brown sugar–nut syrup (recipe follows)

In a small pan, combine milk, ¾ cup of the sugar, salt, and the ½ cup butter. Heat, stirring, to about 110° (butter need not melt completely).

In a large bowl, dissolve yeast in water. Blend in milk mixture. Gradually mix in 3 cups of the flour, then beat for 5 minutes. Beat in 1 whole egg and 1 egg yolk (reserve remaining egg white), then gradually beat in enough of the remaining flour (about 2 cups) to make a stiff dough.

Turn dough out onto a floured board; knead until smooth and satiny (10 to 20 minutes), adding flour as needed to prevent sticking. Place dough in a greased bowl; turn over to grease top. Cover and let rise in a warm place until doubled (about 2 hours).

Punch dough down. Knead briefly on a lightly floured board to release air; let rest for 10 minutes. Then roll and stretch dough into an 18 by 24-inch rectangle. Brush evenly with the ¼ cup melted butter.

Combine the remaining 1 cup sugar with cinnamon; sprinkle evenly over butter, then sprinkle with pecans. Starting with a narrow side, roll up jelly-roll fashion. Moisten edge of dough with water and pinch it snugly against roll to seal. With a sharp knife, cut roll into 6 equal parts. Prepare brown sugar–nut syrup, pour into pan, and arrange slices, cut side up, in pan. Cover; let rise in a warm place until almost doubled (about 1½ hours).

Beat reserved egg white with 1 teaspoon water, and brush on surfaces of rolls. Bake, uncovered, in a preheated 350° oven (325° for a glass pan) for 30 to 35 minutes or until well browned. Immediately invert onto a serving tray. Rolls will be very hot; let cool slightly before serving. Makes 6 large rolls, about 12 servings.

Brown sugar–nut syrup. Boil together ¼ cup **butter** or margarine, 2 tablespoons **water,** and 1 cup firmly packed **dark brown sugar** for 1 minute. Immediately pour into a 9 by 13-inch baking pan; tilt pan so syrup forms an even layer. Arrange 1 cup **pecan halves,** flat side up, on syrup.

Giant Cinnamon Rolls

Following recipe for **Giant Pecan Rolls,** prepare dough, roll out, and top with the melted butter and the cinnamon and sugar mixture. Instead of chopped nuts, use ½ to 1 cup **currants** or raisins. Roll and cut as directed. Omit brown sugar–nut syrup. Arrange sections, cut side up, in a well-greased 9 by 13-inch baking pan; cover and let rise in a warm place until almost doubled (about 1½ hours).

Brush rolls with reserved egg white beaten with 1 teaspoon water. Bake, uncovered, in a preheated 350° oven (325° for a glass pan) for 30 to 35 minutes or until well browned.

With a large spatula, transfer rolls from pan to racks. Drizzle with **powdered sugar glaze** (recipe at top right) while still warm. Makes 6 large rolls, about 12 servings.

Powdered sugar glaze. Beat together until smooth 1½ cups **powdered sugar,** 1 tablespoon **butter** or margarine (softened), ⅛ teaspoon **vanilla,** and 2 to 3 tablespoon hot **water.**

Sweet Cinnamon Pretzels

Unlike their salty cousins, these big cinnamon-swirled pretzels make a tempting breakfast treat. Prepare and chill the dough up to two days ahead, then shape and bake the pretzels when time allows.

1 package active dry yeast
½ cup warm water (about 110°)
½ cup warm milk (about 110°)
⅓ cup granulated sugar
⅓ cup butter or margarine, softened
½ teaspoon salt
1 egg
3½ to 4 cups all-purpose flour
2 tablespoons butter or margarine, softened
3 tablespoons firmly packed brown sugar
½ teaspoon ground cinnamon
Sugar glaze (recipe follows)

In a large bowl, dissolve yeast in water. Add milk, granulated sugar, the ⅓ cup butter, salt, egg, and 2 cups of the flour. Beat with an electric mixer or wooden spoon until smooth. Gradually beat in enough of the remaining flour to make a soft dough (about 1½ cups).

Turn dough out onto a floured board and knead until smooth (about 5 minutes), adding flour as needed to prevent sticking. Place dough in a greased bowl; turn over to grease top. Cover and let rise in a warm place until doubled (about 1½ hours) or in the refrigerator for at least 8 hours or up to 2 days.

Punch dough down, knead briefly on floured board to release air, then roll out into a 12 by 14-inch rectangle. Spread with the 2 tablespoons butter. Combine brown sugar and cinnamon; sprinkle over half the rectangle (crosswise). Fold plain half onto sugared half and press gently to seal.

Cut rectangle lengthwise into 12 strips and roll each strip into a smooth 20-inch rope. Place ropes on a greased baking sheet and twist like pretzels (see page 50), tucking ends under; pretzels should be about 2 inches apart. Cover lightly with plastic wrap; let rise in a warm place until puffy (about 25 minutes—about 35 minutes if cold).

Bake in a preheated 350° oven for about 12 minutes or until golden brown. Prepare glaze and drizzle over pretzels while still warm. Makes 12.

Sugar glaze. In a small bowl, beat ¾ cup **powdered sugar,** 1 tablespoon **butter** or margarine (softened), and 1 tablespoon hot **water** until smooth. Use at once.

Buttery Almond Bear Claws

Pictured on page 58

Rich and almondy, bear claws are usually considered a bakery specialty. But with our easy refrigerator dough and streamlined technique, you'll find yourself making bear claws that rival the best you can buy. With hot coffee and fresh fruit, they make an appealing breakfast.

1 cup (½ lb.) butter or margarine
1 package active dry yeast
¼ cup warm water (about 110°)
3 eggs
¼ cup sugar
½ teaspoon salt
1 small can (5⅓ oz.) evaporated milk
About 3⅓ cups all-purpose flour
Almond filling (recipe follows)
About ¾ cup sliced almonds
Sugar

Melt butter, then let cool to 110°. In a bowl, dissolve yeast in water. Separate eggs, reserving 2 of the whites in a bowl and remaining white in another bowl. Stir egg yolks into yeast mixture, along with the ¼ cup sugar, salt, evaporated milk, and cooled butter.

Place 3⅓ cups of the flour in a large bowl, pour in yeast mixture, and beat well. Cover and refrigerate for at least a day or up to 3 days. Prepare almond filling and refrigerate as directed; also refrigerate remaining egg whites.

To shape bear claws, punch dough down and knead briefly on a well-floured board to release air. Roll into a 13½ by 27-inch rectangle, using a ruler to straighten edges. Cut dough lengthwise into 3 strips, each 4½ inches wide. Divide filling into 3 portions; on a floured board, roll each portion into a 27-inch rope. Lay an almond rope in center of each dough strip; then flatten rope slightly with your fingers.

Fold long sides of each strip over filling as shown in illustration below. Cut each filled strip into 6 pieces, each 4½ inches long (see illustration below). Arrange, seam side down, on 3 greased 12 by 15-inch baking sheets.

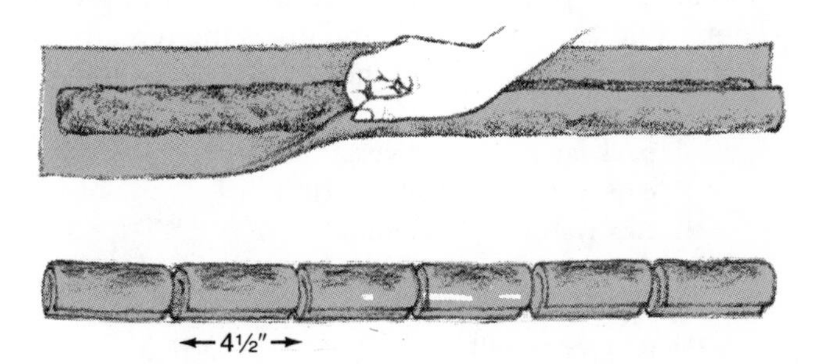

Fold long sides of each strip over filling (top); then cut each strip into 6 pieces, each 4½ inches long (bottom).

Using a floured sharp knife, make a row of cuts ¾ inch apart halfway across each piece; curve each bear claw so cut pieces fan out (see illustrations below).

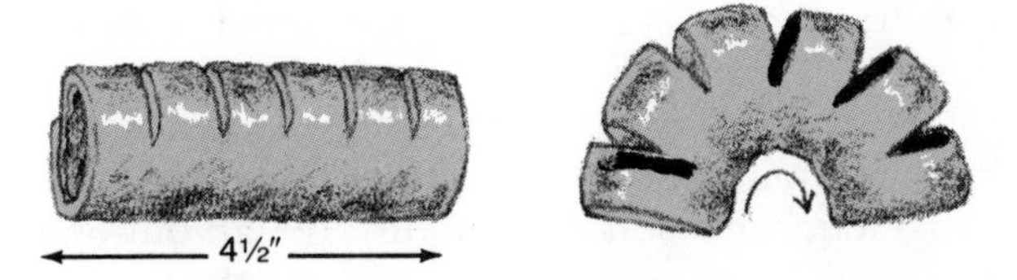

Make a row of cuts ¾ inch apart halfway across each piece (left); curve each bear claw so it fans (right).

Lightly beat remaining egg white and brush over bear claws; top with sliced almonds and sprinkle lightly with sugar. Let rise, uncovered, in a warm place until puffy (about 20 minutes).

Bake in a preheated 375° oven for 15 minutes or until golden brown. Transfer to racks to cool. Makes 18 bear claws.

Almond filling. In a bowl, smoothly blend ½ cup (¼ lb.) **butter** or margarine (softened) with 1⅓ cups **powdered sugar.** Add ⅔ cup **all-purpose flour** and 1 can (8 oz.) **almond paste.** Stir until crumbly and evenly mixed; then beat in 1 teaspoon grated **lemon peel** and 2 of the reserved egg whites. Stir in ¾ cup finely chopped **almonds.** Cover and refrigerate until firm (several hours, or up to 3 days).

Cherry-Almond Christmas Wreath

Pictured on facing page

A new twist makes this breakfast wreath a colorful treat for Christmas morning. The special cutting and shaping procedure exposes the red and green cherry and almond filling, and gives the wreath its distinctive swirled appearance.

- **1 package active dry yeast**
- **¼ cup warm water (about 110°)**
- **½ cup warm milk (about 110°)**
- **3 tablespoons sugar**
- **4 tablespoons butter or margarine, softened**
- **1½ teaspoons salt**
- **½ teaspoon ground cardamom**
- **2 eggs**
- **1 teaspoon grated lemon peel**
- **About 3½ cups all-purpose flour**
- **Cherry-almond filling (recipe follows)**
- **Sugar glaze (recipe follows)**

In large bowl of an electric mixer, dissolve yeast in water. Stir in milk, sugar, butter, salt, cardamom, eggs, and lemon peel. Beat in 2 cups of the flour, a cup at a time. Then beat on medium speed for 3 minutes, scraping bowl frequently.

With a heavy-duty mixer or wooden spoon, beat in enough of the remaining flour (about 1¼ cups) to make a soft dough. Turn dough out onto a floured board and knead until smooth (5 to 10 minutes), adding flour as needed to prevent sticking. Place dough in a greased bowl; turn over to grease top. Cover and let rise in a warm place until doubled (about 1½ hours).

Meanwhile, prepare cherry-almond filling and refrigerate.

Punch dough down, knead briefly on floured board to release air, then roll into a 9 by 30-inch rectangle. Crumble filling and scatter it over dough to within 1 inch of edges. Starting with a long side, roll dough up tightly, jelly-roll fashion. Moisten edge with water; pinch to seal.

Using a floured sharp knife, cut roll in half lengthwise; carefully turn cut sides up, and loosely twist these ropes around each other, keeping cut sides up. Carefully transfer to a greased and flour-dusted 12 by 15-inch baking sheet and shape into a 10-inch circle; pinch ends together firmly to seal. Let rise, uncovered, in a warm place until puffy (45 to 60 minutes).

Bake in a preheated 375° oven for 20 minutes or until lightly browned. Run wide spatulas under wreath to loosen; then transfer to a rack.

Prepare sugar glaze and drizzle over wreath while still warm. Serve plain or spread with butter. Makes 1 large wreath.

Cherry-almond filling. In large bowl of an electric mixer, beat 4 tablespoons **butter** or margarine (softened), ¼ cup **all-purpose flour,** and 2 tablespoons **sugar** until smooth. Stir in ⅔ cup finely chopped **blanched almonds,** ¼ cup *each* **red and green candied (glacé) cherries,** ½ teaspoon grated **lemon peel,** and ¾ teaspoon **almond extract.** Cover and refrigerate.

Sugar glaze. In a small bowl, blend ⅔ cup **powdered sugar,** 1½ teaspoons **lemon juice,** and 3 teaspoons **water** until smooth.

Vanocka

For many families, a holiday morning means a special holiday breakfast bread. For a Czechoslovakian family, this might be *vanocka*—a plump and glossy braided loaf, filled with chopped candied fruit and nuts, and flavored with lemon.

- **2 packages active dry yeast**
- **1 cup warm water (about 110°)**
- **About 5 cups all-purpose flour**
- **½ cup *each* raisins and water**
- **2 tablespoons rum or brandy (optional)**
- **1 cup (½ lb.) butter or margarine, softened**
- **½ cup sugar**
- **2 eggs**
- **1 teaspoon *each* salt and grated lemon peel**
- **½ cup *each* chopped blanched almonds and mixed chopped candied (glacé) fruit**
- **1 egg beaten with 1 tablespoon water**

In a large bowl, dissolve yeast in the 1 cup water. Stir in 1 cup of the flour and beat until well blended. Cover and let stand in a warm place until bubbly (about 1 hour).

Meanwhile, in a small bowl, soak raisins in the ½ cup water for 1 hour. Pour off and discard water; add rum, if desired, and set aside.

In a large bowl, beat butter until creamy. Gradually add sugar, beating until light and fluffy. Add eggs, one at a time, beating well after each addi-

(Continued on page 72)

Cherry-Almond Christmas Wreath *(Recipe on facing page)*

1 *To shape wreath, roll dough out to a 9 by 30-inch rectangle and sprinkle with filling to within 1 inch of edges. Then roll dough up jelly-roll fashion, starting with a long edge.*

2 *With a floured sharp knife, cut roll in half lengthwise; carefully turn halves so that cut side faces up.*

3 *Loosely twist ropes of dough around each other, keeping cut sides up so filling is visible.*

4 *Carefully transfer to a greased and flour-dusted baking sheet and shape into a circle; pinch ends together firmly to seal.*

5 *In the glow of holiday candlelight, Cherry-Almond Christmas Wreath welcomes guests to a festive yuletide brunch.*

tion. Stir in salt and lemon peel. Add butter mixture to yeast mixture, stirring until blended.

Gradually beat in 2 cups of the remaining flour. Stir in raisins, almonds, and candied fruit. Gradually beat in enough of the remaining flour (about 1½ cups) to make a stiff dough.

Turn dough out onto a floured board and knead until smooth and satiny (about 10 minutes), adding flour as needed to prevent sticking. Place dough in a greased bowl; turn over to grease top. Cover and let rise in a warm place until doubled (about 1½ hours).

Punch dough down; knead briefly on floured board to release air. Divide into 6 equal portions and roll each into a 10-inch-long rope. For each loaf, arrange 3 ropes side by side on a greased 12 by 15-inch baking sheet. Pinch together at top and braid loosely; pinch ends together and tuck underneath. Cover and let rise in a warm place until almost doubled (30 to 40 minutes).

Brush loaves with egg mixture and bake in a preheated 350° oven for 30 minutes or until browned. Transfer to racks to cool. Makes 2 loaves.

Belgian Cramique

This egg-rich raisin bread with its glossy, golden crust is so beautiful you might like to serve it at holiday time—or give it as a gift. It owes its festive shape to a wreath of topknotted brioche-type rolls.

1 cup milk
¼ cup butter or margarine, cut into pieces
⅓ cup sugar
1 teaspoon salt
2 packages active dry yeast
½ cup warm water (about 110°)
3 eggs
5½ to 6 cups all-purpose flour
1 cup seedless raisins
1 egg yolk beaten with 1 tablespoon water

In a pan, combine milk, butter, sugar, and salt. Heat, stirring, to about 110° (butter need not melt completely). Dissolve yeast in warm water, then stir yeast and eggs into milk mixture. Gradually beat in 5 cups of the flour to make a soft dough.

Add raisins and turn dough out onto a floured board; knead until smooth and satiny (5 to 20 minutes), adding flour as needed to prevent sticking. Place dough in a greased bowl; turn over to grease top. Cover and let rise in a warm place until doubled (about 45 minutes).

Punch dough down, knead briefly on floured board to release air, then divide into 12 equal parts. Pinch off about ⅕ of each part and set aside to shape topknots. Shape each larger piece into a smooth ball; place, smooth side up, around edges of 2 greased 9-inch round cake pans (each pan will hold 6 balls). Shape each smaller piece into a teardrop that is smooth on top. With your finger, poke a hole in center of each large ball and insert pointed end of teardrop in hole—settle securely or it may pop off at an angle while baking. Cover and let rise in a warm place until almost doubled (about 45 minutes).

Brush loaves with egg yolk mixture, being careful not to let it accumulate in joints of topknots. Bake in a preheated 350° oven for about 45 minutes or until richly browned. Let cool in pans for 5 minutes, then turn out onto racks. Makes 2 wreaths.

Dresden-style Stollen

Pictured on page 58

Almost every country has a favorite sweet bread traditionally served during the holidays. In Germany, it's *stollen,* laden with fruit and nuts. Though there are many versions of stollen, one of the most popular is this one from Dresden. Its rich, buttery dough, studded with candied orange peel, almonds, raisins, and currants, is folded a special way to form an ellipse-shaped loaf, then baked and dusted with powdered sugar.

½ cup milk
1 cup (½ lb.) butter or margarine
½ cup granulated sugar
2 packages active dry yeast
½ cup warm water (about 110°)
½ teaspoon salt
1 teaspoon *each* grated lemon peel and almond extract
About 5¼ cups all-purpose flour
2 eggs
⅓ cup finely chopped candied orange peel
½ cup *each* raisins, golden raisins, currants, and slivered almonds
1 egg white beaten with 1 teaspoon water
4 tablespoons butter or margarine, melted
⅓ cup powdered sugar

In a small pan over medium-low heat, combine milk, the 1 cup butter, and granulated sugar. Heat to scalding (120°), stirring to dissolve sugar and melt butter. Set aside; let cool to lukewarm.

In a large bowl, dissolve yeast in warm water. Add cooled milk mixture, salt, lemon peel, almond extract, and 3 cups of the flour; beat until well blended. Add eggs, one at a time, beating well after each addition. Gradually stir in orange peel, raisins, currants, almonds, and 2 cups of the remaining flour.

Turn dough out onto a floured board and knead until smooth and satiny (about 10 minutes), adding flour as needed to prevent sticking. Place dough in a greased bowl; turn over to grease top. Cover and let rise in a warm place until doubled (about 1½ hours).

Punch dough down. Knead briefly on floured board to release air, then divide in half. Place each portion on a lightly greased 12 by 15-inch baking sheet and shape into a 7 by 9-inch oval about ¾ inch thick. Brush surface with some of the egg white mixture. Crease each oval lengthwise, slightly off center, and fold so top edge lies about an inch back from bottom edge. Brush evenly with remaining egg white mixture. Cover and let rise in a warm place until puffy and almost doubled (35 to 45 minutes).

Bake in a preheated 375° oven for 25 minutes or until richly browned. Brush with the 4 tablespoons melted butter and sift powdered sugar over top. Return to oven and bake for 3 more minutes. Transfer to racks and let cool. Makes 2 loaves.

Swedish Letter Buns (Lussekätter)

In Sweden during the holiday season, sweet little S-shaped rolls are typically served with the hot wine punch called *glögg*. They're made from a light, buttery dough flavored with cardamom or saffron, and then adorned with raisins. This dough is a popular one in Sweden; in different regions of the country, it's likely to be formed into different shapes. Some people know it best as Lucia buns.

Early on the morning of December 13, Lucia—Queen of Light—begins the Christmas season in many Swedish homes. Dressed in white, wearing a crown of evergreen leaves and lighted candles, the oldest daughter awakens her family with song and a tray of coffee and sweet, golden buns.

½ cup (¼ lb.) butter or margarine
¾ cup whipping cream or milk
⅓ cup sugar
½ teaspoon salt
1 teaspoon ground cardamom or 1/16 teaspoon ground saffron
1 package active dry yeast
¼ cup warm water (about 110°)
1 egg
About 4 cups all-purpose flour
About ⅓ cup raisins
1 egg yolk beaten with 1 tablespoon water

In a small pan, melt butter; remove from heat and stir in cream, sugar, salt, and cardamom. Let cool to lukewarm.

In large bowl of an electric mixer, dissolve yeast in warm water. Add cooled cream mixture, egg, and 2 cups of the flour. Mix until well blended, then beat at medium speed 2 minutes longer. With a heavy-duty mixer or wooden spoon, gradually beat in about 1½ cups more flour to make a stiff dough.

Turn dough out onto a floured board and knead until smooth and satiny (about 10 minutes), adding flour as needed to prevent sticking. Place dough in a greased bowl; turn over to grease top. Cover and let rise in a warm place until doubled (about 1½ hours).

Punch dough down; knead briefly on floured board to release air. To shape rolls, divide dough into 24 equal pieces; roll each piece on a flat surface with your palm to make a rope about 9 inches long, and coil ends of each in opposite directions to form an S shape. Push a raisin deep into center of each coil.

Place rolls about 2 inches apart on 2 greased 14 by 17-inch baking sheets. Cover and let rise in a warm place until puffy and almost doubled (about 45 minutes). Brush rolls with egg yolk mixture. With racks placed in the upper and lower middle of a preheated 375° oven, bake buns for 15 minutes or until golden brown on bottoms and lightly browned around edges (switch pan positions halfway through baking, if necessary for even browning). Makes 2 dozen rolls.

Scandinavian legend claims that if a boy and a girl eat from the same loaf, they're sure to fall in love.

Golden Basket Bread

Served upside down, this bread resembles a beehive. Turned over, it's a basket ready to hold Easter eggs. Either way, it makes a handsome edible centerpiece.

To create the beautifully textured exterior, you roll dough into thin ropes, twist them, coil them around a bowl, then bake until golden. Because of the twist, it's easy to pull off small servings of the slightly sweet, golden egg bread to eat.

Golden Basket Bread

- **1 package active dry yeast**
- **¼ cup warm water (about 110°)**
- **½ cup (¼ lb.) butter or margarine, softened**
- **½ cup sugar**
- **1 tablespoon grated lemon peel**
- **⅓ cup warm milk (about 110°)**
- **½ teaspoon salt**
- **5 eggs**
- **5½ to 6 cups all-purpose flour**
- **1 egg beaten with 1 tablespoon milk**

In a large bowl, dissolve yeast in warm water. Blend in butter, sugar, lemon peel, milk, salt, and eggs. Gradually beat in 5 cups of the flour to make a stiff dough. Turn out onto a floured board and knead until smooth and satiny (10 to 15 minutes), adding flour as needed to prevent sticking. Place dough in a greased bowl; turn over to grease top. Cover and let rise in a warm place until doubled (about 2 hours).

Punch dough down, then knead briefly on floured board to release air. Return to greased bowl; turn dough over. Cover with plastic wrap and refrigerate for at least 1 hour, or as long as 24 hours.

Select a 2 to 2½-quart mixing bowl of ovenproof glass or metal (about 9 inches in diameter and 4 inches deep). Wrap the outside with foil, folding excess foil inside bowl. Grease foil generously and invert bowl on a greased 12 by 15-inch baking sheet.

Punch dough down, knead briefly on a floured board, and divide into 20 equal pieces. Working with 2 pieces at a time (keep remaining dough covered and refrigerated), roll each portion into a rope about ⅜ inch thick and 18 to 20 inches long. Pinch ends of 2 ropes to seal, and twist ropes together. Starting at bowl rim, wrap twists around bowl, pinching ends together to join whenever you add a new twist (see illustration below). Keep bowl in refrigerator to prevent uneven rising as you roll more ropes. With a 2½-quart bowl, dough may not quite cover entire bowl, but you can leave a small opening at top.

Wrap dough twists around inverted bowl from bottom to top, pinching ends together to join as you add each new twist.

Lightly cover shaped dough with plastic wrap and let rise in a warm place until puffy (20 to 30 minutes). Gently brush with egg mixture. Bake in a preheated 350° oven for 25 to 30 minutes or until well browned. Let cool on bowl on a rack for about 10 minutes.

Crumple a large piece of foil into a loose ball with same diameter and depth as bowl; set foil ball in center of a rack. Gently remove bread from bowl, using a small spatula if needed to free bread; set bread over foil so that foil supports top of loaf (bread is fragile when hot) until bread is almost cool. Invert to form basket, if desired. To eat, tear off serving-size pieces. Makes 1 large loaf.

Hot Cross Bread

We've captured the sweet, lightly spiced flavor of hot cross buns in this easy batter bread.

1 package active dry yeast
½ cup warm water (about 110°)
½ cup sugar
1 large can (13 oz.) evaporated milk
1 teaspoon salt
2 tablespoons salad oil
1½ teaspoons ground cinnamon
½ teaspoon ground nutmeg
¼ teaspoon ground cloves
1 egg, lightly beaten
4½ to 5 cups all-purpose flour
½ to ¾ cup *each* currants and finely diced candied orange peel or citron
Butter or margarine, softened
Sugar frosting (recipe follows)

In a large bowl, dissolve yeast in water, then blend in 1 tablespoon of the sugar. Let stand in a warm place until bubbly (about 15 minutes). Stir in remaining sugar, the milk, salt, oil, cinnamon, nutmeg, cloves, and egg. Gradually beat in the flour, 1 cup at a time, to make a batter that is very heavy and stiff but too sticky to knead. Stir in currants and orange peel.

Spoon batter into a well-greased 2½ to 3-quart round casserole or soufflé dish. Lightly coat top of dough with butter; cover with plastic wrap. Let rise in a warm place until doubled (about 1 hour).

Bake in a preheated 350° oven for 60 to 65 minutes or until loaf is very brown. Brush top with more butter. Let cool in dish on a rack for 20 minutes, then turn out onto rack. Prepare sugar frosting (at top right); paint a 2-inch-wide cross of frosting across top. Makes 1 large loaf.

Sugar frosting. In a small bowl, blend ¾ cup **powdered sugar** with 1½ tablespoons **orange juice or milk** until smooth.

Before the evangelizing of England around A.D. 600, the Anglo-Saxon pagans baked small breads as part of the jollity of welcoming spring. Early missionaries from Rome despaired of breaking this ritual, so they blessed the buns with a Christian cross. Hot cross buns have been an Easter tradition ever since.

Kulich

Towering loaves of a fragrant, sweet yeast bread called *kulich* are an important part of the traditional Russian Easter meal. Our recipe is simpler and less rich in eggs and butter than strictly traditional ones; to add a traditional crowning touch, though, you can decorate the top of the bread with a delicate rosebud in place of the cherries and almonds.

2 packages active dry yeast
½ cup warm water (about 110°)
¾ cup milk
½ cup sugar
1 teaspoon ground cardamom
2 teaspoons salt
4 tablespoons butter or margarine
About 5 cups all-purpose flour
2 eggs, lightly beaten
2 teaspoons grated lemon peel
½ cup chopped blanched almonds
¼ cup *each* raisins and chopped candied citron, orange peel, and cherries
Sugar glaze (recipe follows)
Candied cherries and whole blanched almonds

In a measuring cup, dissolve yeast in warm water. In a small pan, heat milk to steaming, then pour into large bowl of an electric mixer. Stir in sugar, cardamom, salt, and butter. Let cool to lukewarm.

Add 3 cups of the flour and beat on medium speed until dough pulls away from sides of bowl in stretchy strands. Add yeast, eggs, lemon peel, chopped almonds, raisins, citron, orange peel, and cherries. With a heavy-duty mixer or wooden spoon, gradually mix in 2 cups more flour to make a soft dough.

Turn dough out onto a lightly floured board and knead until smooth and satiny (about 10 minutes), adding flour as needed to prevent sticking. Place dough in a greased bowl; turn over to grease top. Cover and let rise in a warm place until doubled (about 2 hours).

Generously butter three 1-pound coffee cans. Punch dough down and knead briefly on floured board to release air. Divide dough into thirds; shape each portion into a smooth oval and place each oval in a prepared can. Cover cans with well-greased plastic lids and let rise in a warm place until dough pushes lids off cans (1 to 1½ hours).

Bake on lowest rack in a preheated 350° oven for about 35 minutes or until well browned and loaves begin to pull away from sides of cans. Let stand on a rack for 10 minutes, then remove loaves from cans and let cool on their sides on a towel-covered rack. Meanwhile, prepare sugar glaze.

Before serving, stand loaves upright and drizzle tops with sugar glaze. Decorate tops with candied cherries and whole almonds. Makes 3 loaves.

Sugar glaze. In a small bowl, beat 1 cup **powdered sugar** and 5 teaspoons **milk** until smooth.

Christopsomo

Decorated with a sculptured cross modeled from ropes of dough, this round Greek holiday loaf is rich with eggs and pleasantly flavored with anise.

- **2 packages active dry yeast**
- **½ cup warm water (about 110°)**
- **½ cup warm milk (about 110°)**
- **1 cup (½ lb.) butter or margarine, melted and cooled**
- **4 eggs, lightly beaten**
- **¾ cup sugar**
- **2 teaspoons crushed anise seeds**
- **1 teaspoon salt**
- **7 to 7½ cups all-purpose flour**
- **9 candied cherries or walnut halves**
- **1 egg white beaten with 1 tablespoon water**

In a large bowl, dissolve yeast in water. Blend in milk, butter, eggs, sugar, anise seeds, and salt. Gradually beat in about 7 cups of the flour to make a stiff dough.

Turn dough out onto a floured board; knead until smooth and satiny (10 to 20 minutes), adding flour as needed to prevent sticking. Place dough in a greased bowl; turn over to grease top. Cover and let rise in a warm place until doubled (about 2 hours).

Punch dough down; knead briefly on floured board to release air. Then pinch off 2 balls of dough, each about 3 inches in diameter; set aside. Shape remaining dough into a smooth ball. Place on a greased 12 by 15-inch baking sheet and flatten into a 10-inch round.

Gently roll each of the 3-inch balls between your hands to make a 15-inch-long rope. With a razor blade or a sharp floured knife, cut a 5-inch-long slash into each end of the ropes. Cross ropes on center of loaf; *do not press down.* Curl slashed sections of each rope as shown in illustration below; then place a candied cherry or walnut half in each curl and one in center of cross.

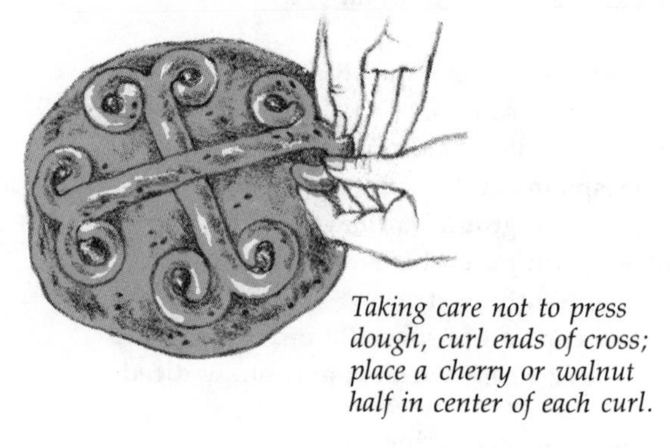

Taking care not to press dough, curl ends of cross; place a cherry or walnut half in center of each curl.

Brush loaf with beaten egg white. Cover lightly and let rise in a warm place until almost doubled (about 1 hour). Bake in a preheated 350° oven for about 45 minutes or until loaf is richly browned. Let cool on a rack. Makes 1 large loaf.

Greek Easter Egg Braid

This festive braid called *tsoureki* (pronounced TOO-reki) wraps around colorful hard-cooked eggs. The Greeks favor bright red eggs—but because the dye seeps into the dough, you may prefer pastel shades that tinge it less.

- **½ teaspoon salt**
- **¼ cup sugar**
- **¼ cup butter or margarine**
- **½ cup milk**
- **2½ to 3 cups all-purpose flour**
- **1 package active dry yeast**
- **2 eggs**
- **1 teaspoon vanilla**
- **1½ teaspoons grated lemon peel**
- **5 hard-cooked eggs, colored, at room temperature**
- **1 egg yolk beaten with 1 tablespoon water**

In a pan combine salt, sugar, butter, and milk; warm over low heat to about 125°. In large bowl of an electric mixer, combine 1 cup of the flour with yeast. Add warm milk mixture, eggs, vanilla, and lemon peel. Beat at low speed, scraping bowl, until moistened. Then beat at high speed for 3 minutes (or beat by hand for 5 minutes). With a wooden spoon, beat in enough of the remaining flour (about 1⅓ cups) to make a stiff dough.

Turn dough out onto a floured board; knead until smooth and satiny (10 to 20 minutes), adding flour as needed to prevent sticking. Place dough in a greased bowl; turn over to grease top. Cover and let rise in a warm place until doubled (about 45 minutes).

Punch dough down, knead briefly on lightly floured board to release air, and divide into 3 equal portions. Gently roll each with your hands to make a rope about 28 inches long. Place ropes side by side on a greased 12 by 15-inch baking sheet; pinch tops together. Braid, then curve braid to form a ring, pinching ends together.

At equal intervals, press colored eggs upright between ropes of dough. Cover and let rise until almost doubled (about 30 minutes). Press eggs into dough again if necessary.

Brush egg yolk mixture evenly over braid, without touching eggs. Bake in a preheated 350° oven for 25 to 35 minutes or until richly browned. Let cool on a rack. Makes 1 loaf.

Colomba di Pasqua

During the season when Easter and the coming of spring share festivities, breads take on special shapes and flavors in Italy. One very handsome loaf is shaped like its name—Easter dove, or *colomba di Pasqua* (pronounced PAH-squaw).

1 package active dry yeast
¼ cup warm water (about 110°)
½ cup (¼ lb.) butter or margarine, softened
10 tablespoons (½ cup plus 2 tablespoons) sugar
2 tablespoons grated lemon peel
2 teaspoons vanilla
½ teaspoon salt
3 whole eggs
3 egg yolks
½ cup warm milk (about 110°)
5 to 5½ cups all-purpose flour
About 4 ounces (4 to 5 tablespoons or half an 8-oz. can) almond paste
About 27 whole blanched almonds
1 egg white, lightly beaten
Sugar

In a small bowl, dissolve yeast in water. In a large bowl, beat together butter, sugar, lemon peel, vanilla, and salt until fluffy. Beat in eggs and egg yolks, 1 at a time. Mix in milk and dissolved yeast; then gradually beat in 4½ cups of the flour to make a soft dough.

Turn dough out onto a floured board; knead until smooth and satiny (10 to 20 minutes), adding flour as needed to prevent sticking. Place dough in a greased bowl; turn over to grease top. Cover and let rise in a warm place until doubled (about 1½ hours).

Punch dough down; knead briefly on lightly floured board to release air. Divide in half and shape each half into a smooth ball. In center of a greased 14 by 17-inch baking sheet, flatten 1 dough ball and roll out across narrow dimension of pan to make an oval about 11 inches long and 6 inches wide. On a floured board, roll out other ball of dough to make a softly outlined triangle about 16 inches tall and 8 inches across the base. As shown in illustration below, lay triangle across oval; fold over narrow end to make head, and pinch firmly to form beak. Fold wide end in opposite direction to make tail; gently pull tail into fan shape and cut into 5 strips to simulate feathers.

Pinch off 26 pieces of almond paste and roll each into a ball. Press a whole almond into each; then arrange 13 balls on each of dove's wings, pressing balls into dough. Press another whole almond into dough to form dove's eye.

Let rise in a warm place until puffy (about 25 minutes). Brush dove gently with beaten egg white and sprinkle wings generously with sugar. Bake in a preheated 350° oven for about 40 minutes or until bread is richly browned—cover loosely with foil for the last 15 minutes to prevent sugared portion from scorching. Let cool on a rack. To serve, cut slices from either body or wings of dove. Makes 1 large loaf.

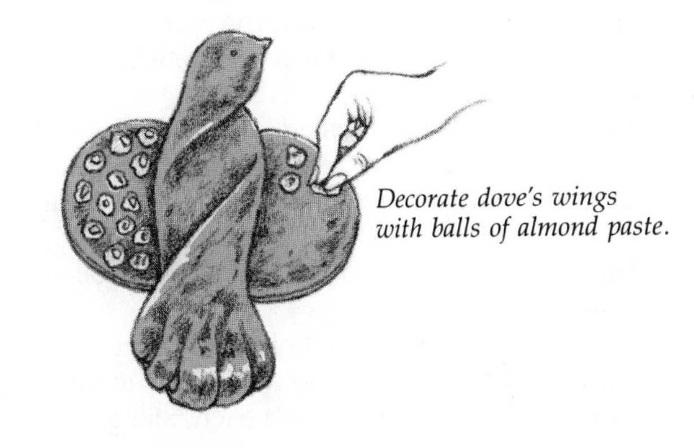

Decorate dove's wings with balls of almond paste.

Pumpkin Spice Bubble Loaf

As Thanksgiving approaches, get your family in the mood by serving them this festive breakfast bread. To make it, you roll spicy pumpkin yeast dough into balls, dip them in melted butter and spiced sugar, and layer them in a tube pan to bake.

- **2 teaspoons ground cinnamon**
- **1 teaspoon *each* ground cloves, ginger, and nutmeg**
- **2 packages active dry yeast**
- **1 cup warm water (about 110°)**
- **1¼ cups sugar**
- **½ cup (¼ lb.) butter or margarine, melted**
- **1 teaspoon salt**
- **½ cup instant nonfat dry milk**
- **1 cup canned pumpkin**
- **About 5½ cups all-purpose flour**
- **½ cup finely chopped walnuts**

In a small bowl, stir together cinnamon, cloves, ginger, and nutmeg; set aside.

In large bowl of an electric mixer, dissolve yeast in warm water. Stir in ½ cup of the sugar, 3 tablespoons of the butter, the salt, dry milk, and pumpkin. Add 2 teaspoons of the spice mixture; also add 2½ cups of the flour. Beat on low speed for 3 minutes, scraping bowl often.

With a heavy-duty mixer or wooden spoon, gradually beat in enough remaining flour (about 2½ cups) to make a stiff dough. Turn out onto a floured board and knead until smooth (about 5 minutes), adding flour as needed to prevent sticking. Place dough in a greased bowl; turn over to grease top. Cover and let rise in a warm place until doubled (about 1½ hours).

Lightly grease a 10-inch tube pan—if pan has a removable bottom, first line the bottom and halfway up the sides with foil, then grease foil. Stir together remaining spice mixture and remaining ¾ cup sugar.

Punch down dough. Knead briefly on floured board to release air; divide into thirds. Shape each third into a smooth 18-inch rope, cut into 18 equal pieces, and shape pieces into smooth balls. Dip each ball in remaining melted butter, and roll in sugar mixture.

Arrange 18 balls in a single layer in bottom of pan so they just touch; sprinkle with ⅓ of the nuts. Top with 2 more layers of 18 balls each, staggering balls; sprinkle each layer with some of the remaining nuts. Cover lightly and let rise in a warm place until very puffy (about 45 minutes).

Bake in a preheated 350° oven for about 55 minutes or until golden brown. Let cool on a rack for 20 minutes, then invert onto a plate. To serve, break apart with forks. Makes 12 servings.

Sally Lunn

Controversy has raged for many a year over how this bread got its name. Some say that Sally Lunn was an English pastry cook who made and served the light, eggy yeast cake at her refreshment house in the town of Bath around 1680. Others insist that the bread was sold on the streets by a girl crying "*soleil-lune*!" or "sun and moon"—French words used to describe the golden tops and lighter bottoms of the breads. Whichever theory is true, you're sure to enjoy eating the slightly sweet golden bread.

- **1 package active dry yeast**
- **½ cup warm water (about 110°)**
- **1 cup milk**
- **½ cup (¼ lb.) butter or margarine, cut into pieces**
- **⅓ cup sugar**
- **1 teaspoon salt**
- **3 eggs**
- **5½ to 6 cups all-purpose flour**

In a large bowl, dissolve yeast in water. In a pan, heat milk with butter, sugar, and salt to about 110° (butter need not melt completely). Add to yeast mixture; stir in eggs and 3 cups of the flour; beat until smooth.

Beat in enough of the remaining flour (2½ to 3 cups) to make a dough that is heavy and stiff but too sticky to knead. Cover; let rise in a warm place until doubled (about 1½ hours). Stir dough down and turn into a well-buttered 10-inch tube pan with removable bottom. Push and punch dough to cover pan bottom evenly. Cover and let rise in a warm place until level with pan top (about 1 hour).

Bake in a preheated 375° oven for about 35 minutes or until well browned. Run a long spatula around pan sides; lift out tube and bread. Loosen bottom of loaf with spatula; invert and twist tube gently to remove. Let cool standing upright on a rack. Cut into thin wedges. Makes 1 large loaf.

Fanciful Bread Sculpture

A great big loaf designed to create a great big smile—that can be the effect when you put a little whimsy into the shape of your bread. For instance, as a personalized gift, you might present a teddy bear to a family with a new baby, or a mermaid to someone who loves to fish. Or, for a fanciful Easter treat, why not serve a fat, fragrant hen complete with golden egg? All three sculpture possibilities are shown below right.

The golden dough recipe offered here is enough for one large (about 2-pound) loaf. In deciding on your design, choose a form that you can put together with simple geometric shapes—ropes, rounds, ovals, and oblongs of dough. Keep the outline bold, the detail simple. For a really big sculpture, you can overlap two rimless baking sheets, adjusting them to fit your oven (leave a 1-inch space all around for heat circulation), and wrap them with foil. It might help to draw a full-size pattern on a sheet of paper first.

Golden Sculpture Dough

1 package active dry yeast
¼ cup warm water (about 110°)
¾ cup butter or margarine, softened
½ cup sugar
⅓ cup warm milk (about 110°)
½ teaspoon salt
5 eggs
5 to 5½ cups all-purpose flour
1 egg beaten with 1 tablespoon water

In a large bowl, dissolve yeast in water. Stir in butter, sugar, milk, salt, and eggs until thoroughly blended. Gradually beat in about 4¾ cups of the flour to make a stiff dough—do not knead. Cover and let rise until doubled (about 1½ hours).

Beat down to release air; then knead on a lightly floured board until smooth and satiny (10 to 20 minutes), adding flour as needed to prevent sticking.

Divide dough into portions to fit your design, saving a small piece for decorative detail. Build sculpture on the greased, foil-covered, overlapped baking sheets.

For a solid area, shape dough into a ball and place smooth side up on the foil; then pat or roll out to achieve desired form (make no thicker than about 1 inch, or bread may crack during baking). Because dough expands as it rises, keep shapes about half as plump as you want them to be in the end.

Butt pieces of dough close together if they are to be joined. Leave at least 2 inches of space between parts you don't want to join. To attach small, round details (such as eyes), shape them into teardrops and set, points down, into holes poked into background dough. To create surface detail, such as mermaid's scales, or to separate areas like fingers or feathers, snip dough with scissors. Roll pieces of dough between your hands to make strands for arms, legs, or hair (try twisting, curling, or braiding strands).

Cover sculpture lightly and let rise in a warm place until puffy (about 30 minutes). Brush gently with egg mixture.

Bake in a preheated 350° oven for about 30 minutes or until bread is richly browned. Let cool on pan for 10 minutes; then slip a spatula beneath loaf and gently slide onto a rack to cool completely. Makes 1 large loaf.

Give whimsical loaves as gifts: from left, a bear, a mermaid, and a laying hen.

Bath Buns

Hot cross buns, scones, and crumpets are all familiar to fans of British baked goods. Those who dig deeper into England's breadbasket will find other treats as well, and here's an example. Bath buns, made from a rich yeast dough, are large buns full of currants or candied fruit and sprinkled with crushed sugar. They are equally good with afternoon tea or morning coffee.

2 packages active dry yeast
½ cup warm water (about 110°)
1 cup milk
⅔ cup butter or margarine, cut into small pieces
½ cup sugar
1 teaspoon salt
2 eggs
6½ to 7 cups all-purpose flour
1 cup currants or chopped candied fruit
1 egg yolk beaten with 1 tablespoon milk
About ½ cup coarsely crushed sugar cubes

In a large bowl, dissolve yeast in warm water. In a small pan, heat milk, butter, sugar, and salt to about 110° (butter need not melt completely). Add to dissolved yeast; also stir in eggs and 2 cups of the flour. Gradually beat in another 3 cups flour; then stir in currants.

With a wooden spoon, beat in enough additional flour (about 1¼ cups) to make a soft dough. Turn out onto a floured board and knead until smooth (about 5 minutes), adding flour as needed to prevent sticking. Place dough in a greased bowl; turn over to grease top. Cover and let rise in a warm place until doubled (about 1½ hours).

Punch dough down, knead briefly on floured board to release air, then divide into 24 equal pieces. Shape each into a smooth ball and place balls 2 inches apart on greased baking sheets. Cover and let rise in a warm place until puffy (about 25 minutes).

Brush buns with egg yolk mixture; then sprinkle tops with crushed sugar. Bake in a preheated 375° oven for about 15 minutes or until nicely browned. Transfer to racks to cool. Serve warm or reheated. Makes 2 dozen.

The celebrated health-spa town of Bath, England, was a fashionable destination for members of 18th century English society. Bath was thought to produce the best of everything, including the sweet buns that became popular to serve with tea.

Portuguese Sweet Bread

Many Americans know this tender, golden bread as "Hawaiian Sweet Bread"—not surprising, since residents of the Islands have adopted it as their own. But it was the Portuguese immigrants to Hawaii who first popularized the bread there in the late 19th century. The springy, slightly sweet bread is most often seen as a plain round loaf, sometimes with a hole in the center; our recipe shows you how to shape it more fancifully, too, into coils or braids for handsome loaves or buns.

¼ cup instant mashed potato granules or powder
⅔ cup boiling water
⅔ cup sugar
¼ cup instant nonfat dry milk
½ cup (¼ lb.) butter or margarine, cut into pieces
2 packages active dry yeast
⅓ cup warm water (about 110°)
5 to 5½ cups all-purpose flour
3 eggs
1 teaspoon salt
½ teaspoon vanilla
¼ teaspoon lemon extract
1 egg, beaten
Sugar (optional)

In a small pan, beat potato granules into the ⅔ cup boiling water. Stir in the ⅔ cup sugar, the milk, and butter. Let cool to 110° (butter need not melt completely).

Meanwhile, in a large bowl, dissolve yeast in warm water. Stir in cooled potato mixture. Add 2 cups of the flour and beat until blended. Stir in the 3 eggs, salt, vanilla, and lemon extract until smoothly blended. Then beat in 1½ cups more flour.

Mix in enough of the remaining flour (1 to 1½ cups) to make a stiff dough. Turn dough out onto a floured board and knead until smooth and satiny (5 to 20 minutes), adding flour as needed to prevent sticking. Place dough in a greased bowl; turn over to grease top. Cover and let rise in a warm place until doubled (about 1 hour).

Punch dough down and knead briefly on a lightly floured board to release air. Let dough rest for 10 minutes; then shape in one of the following ways.

For coiled loaves, divide dough in half. Roll each portion into a 30-inch-long rope. For each loaf, coil a rope into a greased 9-inch pie pan, starting at outside edge and ending in center; twist rope slightly as you lay it in pan.

For coiled buns, divide dough into 12 equal portions. Roll each into a 12-inch-long rope. On greased 12 by 15-inch baking sheets, coil each rope into a round bun, starting at outside edge and ending in center; twist rope slightly as you coil it. Make buns 2½ to 3 inches in diameter and space them at least 2 inches apart.

For braided loaves, divide dough into 6 equal portions. Roll each into a 14-inch-long rope. For each loaf, arrange 3 ropes side by side on a greased 12 by 15-inch baking sheet. Pinch together at top and loosely braid; pinch ends together and tuck underneath.

For round loaves, divide dough in half. Shape each half into a smooth ball; place each in a greased 9-inch pie pan. Gently flatten each into a round about 8 inches in diameter.

Cover and let rise in a warm place until almost doubled (35 to 45 minutes for loaves, 20 to 30 minutes for buns). Brush with beaten egg; sprinkle with sugar, if desired.

Bake in a preheated 350° oven (325° for glass pans) for 25 to 30 minutes for loaves, 20 to 25 minutes for buns, or until browned. Transfer to racks to cool. Serve warm or at room temperature. Makes 2 loaves or 1 dozen buns.

Banana Anadama Date Bread

New England's contribution to American cuisine includes such well-known items as Boston baked beans, clam chowder, and Vermont maple syrup. It also includes a hearty cornmeal-and-molasses bread known as "anadama."

There are many different recipes for anadama bread; our version is sweetened with banana and dates. It gets its rounded shape from a pie pan, and its pleasing crunch from the cornmeal. Serve it warm with butter.

1½ cups whole wheat flour
¾ cup yellow cornmeal
¾ teaspoon salt
½ teaspoon baking soda
1 package active dry yeast
2½ tablespoons salad oil
⅓ cup light molasses
1 cup plus 2 tablespoons very warm water (120° to 130°)
3 to 3½ cups all-purpose flour
½ cup mashed ripe banana
1 cup diced pitted dates
About 1 teaspoon yellow cornmeal

In large bowl of an electric mixer, combine whole wheat flour, the ¾ cup cornmeal, salt, baking soda, and yeast. Stir in oil, molasses, and water; beat at medium speed for 2 minutes. Add ¼ cup of the all-purpose flour and beat at high speed for 2 minutes. With a heavy-duty mixer or wooden spoon, stir in the banana and enough of the remaining all-purpose flour (about 2½ cups) to make a stiff dough.

Turn dough out onto a floured board and knead until smooth (about 5 minutes), adding flour as needed to prevent sticking. Knead dates into dough, a portion at a time. Place dough in a greased bowl; turn over to grease top. Cover and let rise in a warm place until doubled (about 1½ hours).

Grease a 9-inch pie pan and sprinkle with the 1 teaspoon cornmeal. Punch dough down, knead briefly on floured board to release air, and shape into a smooth ball. Place in pie pan, cover, and let rise in a warm place until almost doubled (about 45 minutes).

Bake in a preheated 375° oven (350° for a glass pan) for 35 to 40 minutes or until browned. Turn out onto a rack to cool. Slice or cut in wedges to serve. Makes 1 large loaf.

A popular tale about the origin of anadama bread concerns a disgruntled New England fisherman on one of the countless evenings when his unimaginative wife, Anna, presented him with his usual dinner of cornmeal mush and molasses. Disgusted, he mixed the ingredients together to form a bread dough, and while it baked, he's said to have muttered, "Anna, damn her."

Sourdough Breads

For generations, sourdough has mystified cooks and aroused their curiosity. Many stories have been told about Gold Rush pioneers and the measures they took to guard the ingredients of their sourdough starter—that mysterious, self-perpetuating leavening substance that gave them sure-fire hotcakes morning after morning.

In this chapter, we show you how to make your own sourdough starter (page 86) and how to use it to make breads with that characteristically tangy sourdough taste. The secret is in the fermentation, which is caused by harmless bacteria that are naturally present in such foods as raw milk, cultured buttermilk, and yogurt.

Sourdough starters become more active and sour as time passes, so if yours is a young starter (under 6 months), you'll be wise to start out with pancakes and waffles, or with breads that call for packaged yeast, baking powder, or baking soda as well as sourdough starter (most of ours do).

Interested in adding sourdough to your own favorite recipes? You can add as much as 1 cup starter to most yeast doughs if you reduce the total amount of liquid by ¼ to ½ cup. And you'll probably need to use every bit of the flour called for in the recipe—or a little more.

Bubbly Sourdough Starter (page 86) puts the magic flavor into (clockwise from lower left) Sourdough French Bread (two loaves; page 91), Sourdough Whole Wheat Pan Bread (page 85), braided Sourdough Potato Bread (page 84), Finnish Farmer Sourdough Rye (page 88), and round Sourdough Potato Bread (page 84).

Super Sourdough Refrigerator Bread

This recipe is proof that producing good sourdough flavor doesn't have to take up an entire day. Like Super-simple Refrigerator Bread (page 12), this bread meets you halfway—it goes together in two stages. You can even divide the task between two cooks: one to mix the no-knead dough today, another to bake it on the morrow.

1 package active dry yeast
1¾ cups warm water (about 110°)
1 teaspoon sugar
1 cup sourdough starter, at room temperature
⅓ cup *each* sugar and salad oil
1 tablespoon salt
2 eggs, well beaten
About 8 cups all-purpose flour

In a large bowl, combine yeast, ¼ cup of the warm water, and the 1 teaspoon sugar. Let stand until bubbly (about 15 minutes). Stir in remaining 1½ cups water, the starter, sugar, oil, salt, and eggs. Beat in 4 cups of the flour, 1 cup at a time, beating well after each addition. With a heavy-duty mixer or wooden spoon, gradually mix in as much of the remaining flour as dough will absorb. Place dough in a greased bowl; turn over to grease top. Cover and refrigerate for at least 4 hours or up to 24 hours.

To continue, punch dough down and divide in half. With greased hands, shape each half into a smooth loaf. Place each in a greased 9 by 5-inch loaf pan; cover and let rise in a warm place until loaves rise 1 inch above pan sides (about 2 hours). Bake in a preheated 350° oven (325° for glass pans) for 30 to 35 minutes or until well browned. Turn out onto a rack to cool. Makes 2 loaves.

The "sourdoughs"—prospectors— of the Gold Rush days used their starters for more than baking. Heated up, starter made a poultice for wounds. It was also applied like glue to chink log cabins. And, if kept long enough, it produced strong drink, or "hooch."

Sourdough Potato Bread

Pictured on page 82

Round or braided, these moist and tender loaves keep well for several days. The secret is mashed potatoes, which also add a delectably springy texture and a bit of extra nutrition.

1 package active dry yeast
5½ to 6 cups all-purpose flour
¼ cup sugar
2 teaspoons salt
Instant mashed potatoes (amount for 2 servings) plus milk, butter, and salt as specified on package
¾ cup milk
¼ cup butter or margarine, melted and cooled
2 eggs
1 cup sourdough starter, at room temperature
1 egg white beaten with 2 tablespoons water
Poppy seeds (optional)

In large bowl of an electric mixer, combine yeast, 2 cups of the flour, sugar, and salt.

In a pan, prepare instant mashed potatoes according to package directions. Then stir in the ¾ cup milk, the ¼ cup butter, the eggs, and starter; stir until blended.

Add potato mixture to dry ingredients and beat with mixer at medium speed for 2 minutes, scraping bowl occasionally. Add 1½ cups of the remaining flour and beat at medium speed for 2 minutes longer. With a heavy-duty mixer or wooden spoon, beat in enough of the remaining flour (about 1½ cups) to make a stiff dough.

Turn dough out onto a floured board; knead until smooth (5 to 20 minutes), adding flour as needed to prevent sticking. Place dough in a greased bowl; turn over to grease top. Cover and let rise in a warm place until doubled (1½ to 2 hours).

Punch dough down; knead briefly on a lightly floured board to release air, and divide in half.

For round loaves, shape each half into a smooth ball and place each on a lightly greased 12 by 15-inch baking sheet. With a razor blade or sharp floured knife, cut ½-inch-deep slashes in tops of loaves, in a ticktacktoe pattern.

For braided loaves, divide each half into thirds. Roll each piece to form a rope about 18 inches long. Place 3 ropes on a lightly greased 14 by 17-inch baking sheet; pinch tops together and braid loosely. Pinch ends together and tuck underneath. Repeat for second loaf.

Cover loaves and let rise in a warm place until almost doubled (about 45 minutes). Evenly brush loaves with egg white mixture. Sprinkle braided loaves with poppy seeds, if desired.

Bake in a preheated 350° oven for about 35 minutes or until loaves are richly browned. Let cool on racks. Makes 2 large loaves.

Oatmeal Sourdough Bread

For those who like to start their day the oatmeal way, here's a change of pace from porridge.

2½ cups rolled oats, regular or quick-cooking
⅓ cup instant nonfat dry milk
2¼ cups very hot tap water
1 package active dry yeast
¾ cup sourdough starter, at room temperature
About 7 cups all-purpose flour
¼ cup molasses or honey
¼ cup salad oil
2 teaspoons salt
1 teaspoon baking soda

In a large bowl, combine 1 cup of the rolled oats, the dry milk, and hot water. Stir well, then let cool to 110°. Meanwhile, whirl the remaining 1½ cups rolled oats in a blender until reduced to a flour.

Stir yeast into oat-milk mixture and let stand until dissolved. Add sourdough starter, oat flour, and 2½ cups of the all-purpose flour; beat to blend. Cover and let stand in a warm place until thick and bubbly (about 1½ hours).

Stir dough sponge down, then stir in molasses, oil, salt, and baking soda. Gradually beat in another 2 cups all-purpose flour. With a heavy-duty mixer or wooden spoon, gradually beat in enough of the remaining flour (about 2½ cups) to make a stiff dough.

Turn out onto a floured board and knead until smooth and no longer sticky (about 15 minutes), adding flour as needed to prevent sticking. Place dough in a greased bowl; turn over to grease top. Cover and let rise in a warm place until doubled (about 1½ hours).

Punch dough down and divide into thirds. Knead each piece briefly on a lightly floured board to release air; shape each into a smooth loaf and place in a greased 4½ by 8½-inch loaf pan. Cover and let rise in a warm place until loaves are about ½ inch above pan rims (45 to 60 minutes).

Bake in a preheated 375° oven (350° for glass pans) for 35 minutes or until well browned. Turn out onto racks to cool. Makes 3 loaves.

Sourdough Whole Wheat Pan Bread

Pictured on page 82

This recipe combines sourdough starter with whole wheat flour for a bread with a chewy crust, hearty flavor, and light texture.

1 cup *each* milk and boiling water
1 package active dry yeast
3 cups whole wheat flour
4½ to 5 cups all-purpose flour
¾ cup sourdough starter, at room temperature
¼ cup molasses
1 tablespoon salt
3 tablespoons butter or margarine, at room temperature
1 teaspoon baking soda

In a large bowl, combine milk and boiling water; let cool to about 110°. Stir in yeast and let stand until dissolved. Stir in whole wheat flour, 1 cup of the all-purpose flour, and sourdough starter; beat until smooth and elastic (about 5 minutes). Cover bowl with plastic wrap and let stand in a warm place until mixture is very bubbly and spongy-looking (about 1 hour).

Stir in molasses, salt, butter, and baking soda. Gradually mix in enough of the remaining flour (about 3 cups) to make a very stiff dough. Turn dough out onto a well-floured board and knead until smooth (10 to 20 minutes), adding flour as needed to prevent sticking. Place dough in a greased bowl; turn over to grease top. Cover and let rise in a warm place until doubled (1 to 1½ hours).

Punch dough down, knead briefly on a lightly floured board to release air, and divide in half. Shape each half into a loaf, and place each in a well-greased 4½ by 8½-inch loaf pan. Cover and let rise in a warm place until almost doubled (35 to 45 minutes).

Bake in a preheated 375° oven (350° for glass pans) for about 35 minutes or until browned. Turn out onto a rack to cool. Makes 2 loaves.

Old-fashioned Sourdough Starter

A good sourdough starter is a wonderful thing to have on hand for baking—but it's a bit tricky to make, since there are so many uncontrollable factors involved.

Temperature is the main variable; you'll need to find a warm place (80° to 90°) to put your starter while it ferments. Some good spots are on top of a water heater or refrigerator, or near (but not directly over) a gas range pilot light.

The light in an electric oven can provide enough heat, too. Adjust the racks so the top of the container will be 2 to 2½ inches below the oven light. Turn the oven on for a minute or so—just until the air inside feels a little warmer than room temperature; then turn the oven off. Place the starter inside, close the door, and turn on the light (or prop the door open just enough to keep the light on).

Once you have a starter, be patient: the older the starter, the better the results will be when you bake. Young starters (under 6 months) are best used in pancakes and waffles, or in breads that call for other leavening.

Sourdough Starter

Pictured on facing page and on page 82

Fill a 3 to 6-cup glass, ceramic, plastic, or stainless steel container with hot water and let stand. In a pan, heat 1 cup **skim milk or low-fat milk** to 90° to 100° on a thermometer. Remove from heat and stir in 3 tablespoons **plain (unflavored) yogurt.** Drain water from warmed container, wipe dry, and pour in milk mixture. Cover tightly; if using a screw-top jar with a metal lid, place a double layer of plastic wrap over mouth of jar before screwing on lid. Let stand in a warm place (see above).

After 18 to 24 hours, starter should be about the consistency of yogurt—a curd forms and mixture doesn't flow readily when container is slightly tilted. (It may also form smaller curds suspended in clear liquid.) If some clear liquid has risen to top of milk during this time, simply stir it back in. However, if liquid has turned light pink, milk is beginning to break down; discard and start again.

After curd has formed, gradually stir 1 cup **all-purpose flour** into starter until smooth. Cover tightly and let stand in a warm place (80° to 90°) until mixture is full of bubbles and has a good sour smell (2 to 5 days).

If clear liquid forms during this time, stir it back into starter. But if liquid is pink, spoon out and discard all but ¼ cup starter; then blend in a mixture of 1 cup *each* warm skim milk or low-fat milk (90° to 100°) and flour. Cover tightly and let stand again in a warm place until bubbly and sour smelling. To store, cover and refrigerate. Makes about 1½ cups.

To maintain an ample supply, replenish your starter every time you use it with equal amounts of warm skim or low-fat milk (90° to 100°) and flour. For example, if you used ½ cup of the starter in a recipe, blend in a mixture of ½ cup *each* warm skim or low-fat milk and flour. Cover tightly and let stand in a warm place for several hours or until bubbly; then cover and refrigerate.

For consistent flavor, continue using the same type of milk you used originally. Always bring your starter to room temperature before using it (this takes 4 to 6 hours).

If you bake regularly—once a week—the starter should stay lively and active. You can check your starter occasionally to see if it's active by spooning out ¼ cup of it and blending it with a mixture of ½ cup *each* warm skim or low-fat milk (90° to 100°) and flour. Cover and let stand in a warm place. Check often; it should bubble again in 4 to 8 hours. You can combine this mixture with the original starter after the test. But if it doesn't bubble, you'll have to make a new starter.

If you don't bake often, it's best to discard about half your starter and replenish it with warm milk and flour about every 2 months.

Sourdough Starter *(Recipe on facing page)*

1 *Heat skim milk to 90° to 100° on a thermometer. Remove from heat and stir in 3 tablespoons plain (unflavored) yogurt; low-fat yogurt will give the tangiest flavor.*

2 *Let mixture stand, tightly covered, in a warm place for 18 to 24 hours or until a curd forms. If any colorless liquid has formed on top, simply stir it back in.*

3 *Gradually stir 1 cup all-purpose flour into milk mixture; then cover and let stand in a warm place until bubbly—2 to 5 days.*

4 *Finished starter is bubbly and spongy looking, and has a good sour aroma. Keep it refrigerated, but always bring it to room temperature and let it get bubbly again before using it.*

Can't-Believe-It Sourdough Rye

Caraway, anise, whole wheat, and rye—what happens when you mix all these earthy flavors with sourdough? You bake up a taste that's almost too good to be true, which is how this bread got its name.

- **1½ cups warm water (about 110°)**
- **1 cup sourdough starter, at room temperature**
- **1 cup all-purpose flour**
- **About 4½ cups whole wheat flour**
- **1 cup rye flour**
- **1½ teaspoons *each* sugar and salt**
- **¼ cup caraway seeds**
- **1 teaspoon anise seeds**
- **Melted butter or margarine**

In a large bowl, mix warm water with sourdough starter, then stir in all-purpose flour, 2 cups of the whole wheat flour, and rye flour. Cover and let stand in a warm place for 24 hours.

In another bowl, mix 1½ cups whole wheat flour with sugar, salt, caraway seeds, and anise seeds; beat into sourdough mixture. Spread ½ cup whole wheat flour on a board and turn dough out onto it. Knead until silky and resilient (at least 20 minutes), adding whole wheat flour as needed to prevent sticking.

Shape dough into 2 loaves and place each in a lightly greased 4½ by 8½-inch loaf pan. Cover and let rise in a warm place until almost doubled (about 3 hours). Brush tops with melted butter.

Bake in a preheated 375° oven (350° for glass pans) for 35 to 40 minutes or until well browned. Turn out onto a rack to cool. Makes 2 loaves.

Finnish Farmer Sourdough Rye

Pictured on page 82

Rye—one of the few grains that ripen in a short northern growing season—has been the staple flour in Finland throughout that country's history. Like most Finnish breads today, this simple yeast bread is made with part wheat flour and part rye flour, making the dough easier to handle. But unlike most Finnish breads, it gets extra-robust flavor from sourdough starter.

Deep creases pressed into each loaf before baking make it easy to pull apart into narrow, fingerlike chunks for eating.

- **1 package active dry yeast**
- **1½ teaspoons sugar**
- **1 cup warm water (about 110°)**
- **1½ teaspoons salt**
- **2 teaspoons salad oil**
- **2 tablespoons caraway seeds**
- **¾ cup sourdough starter, at room temperature**
- **1½ cups rye flour**
- **2 to 2¼ cups all-purpose flour**
- **Melted butter or margarine**

In a large bowl, combine yeast, sugar, and warm water; let stand until bubbly (about 15 minutes). Stir in salt, oil, caraway seeds, and starter. With a heavy-duty mixer or wooden spoon, beat in ½ cup *each* of the rye and all-purpose flours. Add remaining 1 cup rye flour and beat well. Gradually beat in all but about 1 cup of remaining all-purpose flour.

When dough becomes too stiff to mix, turn out onto a floured board and knead until smooth and satiny (about 10 minutes), adding flour as needed to prevent sticking. Place dough in a greased bowl; turn over to grease top. Cover and let rise in a warm place until doubled (about 1 hour).

Punch dough down and divide in half. Knead each portion on a lightly floured board to release air, and shape into a smooth ball. Place each ball on a greased 12 by 15-inch baking sheet and pat into an 8 or 9-inch round. Cover loosely with plastic wrap and let rise in a warm place until almost doubled (about 45 minutes).

Using the handle of a long wooden spoon (see illustration below), press straight down through dough to pan in rows about 1 inch apart. Brush tops lightly with melted butter.

Make creases about 1 inch apart by pressing dough with handle of a long wooden spoon.

Bake in a preheated 375° oven for about 35 minutes or until well browned. Brush lightly with more melted butter and let cool on racks. Makes 2 loaves.

Sourdough Three Wheat Batter Bread

When three favorite morsels of wheat—the ground, the cracked, and the germ—are brought to buoyant life by sourdough starter, the resulting loaf makes wide-awake breakfast toast. And besides terrific flavor, you get the surprisingly moist and springy texture of batter bread, baked in a coffee can.

As with other batter breads, remember to beat this one vigorously; because the soft, sticky dough is never kneaded, the mixing stage is your only opportunity to develop the gluten for a light, well-risen texture.

This recipe's nonsourdough counterpart appears on page 24 and is pictured on page 3.

1 package active dry yeast
¼ cup warm water (about 110°)
⅛ teaspoon ground ginger
3 tablespoons honey
1 large can (13 oz.) evaporated milk or 1½ cups fresh milk
1 cup sourdough starter, at room temperature
1 teaspoon salt
2 tablespoons salad oil
2½ cups all-purpose flour
1½ cups whole wheat flour
½ cup *each* wheat germ and cracked wheat

In a large bowl, combine yeast, water, ginger, and 1 tablespoon of the honey; let stand until bubbly (about 20 minutes). Stir in remaining honey, the milk, starter, salt, and oil. In another bowl, stir together all-purpose flour, whole wheat flour, wheat germ, and cracked wheat; add to liquid ingredients, 1 cup at a time, beating well after each addition.

Spoon batter into 2 well-greased 1-pound coffee cans or into 1 well-greased 2-pound coffee can; cover with well-greased plastic lids. Let rise in a warm place just until dough pushes lids off (60 to 75 minutes—watch carefully).

Immediately bake, uncovered, on lowest rack of a preheated 350° oven for 45 minutes for 1-pound cans or about 1 hour for a 2-pound can, or until well browned. Let cool in cans on a rack for 5 minutes; then loosen crust around edges of cans with a thin knife, slide bread from cans, and let cool in an upright position on rack. Makes 2 small loaves or 1 large loaf.

Orange Sourdough Batter Bread

Festive with orange juice, nuts, and raisins, this batter bread also boasts the zest of sourdough. A great choice for busy bakers, it requires no kneading, and it rises quickly. It's baked in a soufflé dish or other straight-sided casserole; thinly sliced, it makes delicious cinnamon toast.

⅓ cup orange juice
2 packages active dry yeast
3 tablespoons sugar
1 tablespoon grated orange peel
1 large can (13 oz.) evaporated milk or 1½ cups fresh milk
1 cup sourdough starter, at room temperature
1 teaspoon salt
2 tablespoons butter or margarine, melted
4 to 4½ cups all-purpose flour
1 cup golden raisins
½ cup chopped walnuts or almonds

In a 2-quart pan, heat orange juice to about 110°, then stir in yeast and 1 tablespoon of the sugar; let stand until bubbly. Stir in remaining sugar, orange peel, milk, sourdough starter, salt, and butter. Transfer to a large bowl and, with a heavy-duty mixer or wooden spoon, beat in flour, 1 cup at a time, to make a dough that is heavy and stiff but too sticky to knead; with last cup of flour, add raisins and nuts.

Spoon dough into a well-greased 2½-quart soufflé dish or other straight-sided casserole. Cover and let rise in a warm place until dough is ¾ to 1 inch above rim of dish (about 1 hour). Bake in a preheated 350° oven for 65 to 75 minutes or until loaf is well browned. Let cool in baking dish on a rack for about 10 minutes; then turn bread out onto rack to cool completely. Makes 1 large loaf.

The first sandwich is commonly credited to John Montagu, Earl of Sandwich, who lived in 18th century England. Often hurried at mealtime, he found it convenient to tuck a piece of meat between slices of bread and eat it with his hands—considered very vulgar at the time.

Sourdough French Bread *(Recipe on facing page)*

1 *Just before bread is ready to bake, place a rimmed baking sheet on the lowest oven rack and pour in boiling water about ¼ inch deep; this creates steam for crustiness.*

2 *Cut ½-inch-deep slashes in top of risen loaf; besides adding a decorative touch, this allows steam to escape and prevents cracks from forming as bread bakes.*

3 *Brush loaf with cornstarch mixture, then slide from cardboard onto top baking sheet in oven. Cornmeal allows the loaf to slide easily.*

4 *After loaf has baked for 10 minutes, quickly brush again with cornstarch mixture to help develop a chewy, glossy crust.*

5 *For a San Francisco-style feast, serve fresh sourdough French bread with a fisherman's stew and chilled white wine. The bread makes great dunking in any kind of sauce.*

Sourdough French Bread

Pictured on facing page and on page 82

Rivaling the best of San Francisco sourdough, this tangy, crusty loaf can turn a simple wine-and-cheese picnic into a feast. On a cold day, it can work the same magic with a hearty soup or stew. You can use this recipe to make brown-and-serve miniature loaves, too. Or try the flavor variations that follow.

- **1 package active dry yeast**
- **1½ cups warm water (about 110°)**
- **1 cup sourdough starter, at room temperature**
- **About 6 cups all-purpose flour**
- **2 teaspoons *each* salt and sugar**
- **Cornmeal**
- **1 teaspoon cornstarch**
- **½ cup water**

In a large bowl, dissolve yeast in warm water. Add starter, 4 cups of the flour, the salt, and sugar; stir until smooth. Cover and let rise in a warm place until doubled (about 1½ hours).

Stir in enough of the remaining flour (about 1½ cups) to make a very stiff dough. Turn dough out onto a lightly floured board and knead until smooth and satiny (about 10 minutes), adding flour as needed to prevent sticking. Divide dough in half. (If you have only one oven, place one half in a greased bowl, cover, and let stand at room temperature until the first loaf is placed in the oven.)

For an oblong loaf, roll dough back and forth, elongating it into a 14-inch log. For a round loaf, shape dough into a smooth ball, pinching a seam underneath. Or shape each half into 3 small oblong or round loaves. Set each loaf (or 3 small ones) on a piece of stiff cardboard sprinkled with ¼ cup cornmeal. Cover lightly with plastic wrap; let rise in a warm place until puffy and almost doubled (1 hour for large loaves, 45 minutes for small).

Adjust oven racks so they are at the two lowest positions. Place a 12 by 15-inch baking sheet on top rack as oven preheats to 400°. Just before bread is ready to bake, place a rimmed baking sheet on the lower rack and pour in boiling water to a depth of about ¼ inch.

Meanwhile, heat cornstarch and water to boiling, stirring; let cool slightly. With a razor blade or sharp knife, cut ½-inch-deep slashes on top of loaf (make diagonal slashes on oblong loaves, tick-tacktoe pattern on round loaves). Evenly brush cornstarch mixture over entire surface of loaf. Slip loaf off cardboard onto top baking sheet in oven. (At this point, if using only one oven, punch down remaining dough and knead briefly to release air; shape and let rise; then bake as directed.)

Bake at 400°; after 10 minutes (7 for small loaves), brush again with cornstarch mixture. Bake for about 25 minutes longer (20 for small loaves) or until loaves are golden and sound hollow when tapped. Let cool on racks. Makes 2 large or 6 small loaves.

Brown-and-Serve French Bread

Prepare **Sourdough French Bread** and bake at 400° for 10 minutes (7 for small loaves). Brush again with cornstarch mixture. After 8 more minutes (5 for small loaves) or when surface of loaves is no longer wet, remove from oven; let cool on racks. Wrap each loaf separately in foil and freeze.

To finish baking, unwrap desired number of loaves and set them (frozen or thawed) on a lightly greased baking sheet. Bake in a preheated 400° oven for 35 minutes for large frozen loaves (30 if thawed), or 30 minutes for small frozen loaves (25 if thawed), or until loaves are golden brown and sound hollow when tapped.

Sourdough Cheese Bread

Follow directions for **Sourdough French Bread,** stirring in 2 cups shredded **sharp Cheddar cheese** when you add the flour to make a very stiff dough.

Sourdough Onion Bread

Follow directions for **Sourdough French Bread,** but omit salt. Stir in 1 package **dry onion soup mix** (amount for 3 or 4 servings) when you add the flour to make a very stiff dough.

Sourdough Tortilla Bread

Follow directions for **Sourdough French Bread,** but stir in ¼ cup *each* **salad oil, light molasses,** and **dark corn syrup** with the starter. Omit sugar. When stirring in enough flour to make a very stiff dough, reduce amount of all-purpose flour in this step to about 1 cup, and add 1½ cups **masa harina** (dehydrated masa flour).

Buttery Sourdough Pan Rolls

Feathery light in texture, buttery rich in flavor, these sourdough pan rolls are also relatively carefree to make. As for Buttery Pan Rolls on page 20, you just drop the dough by spoonfuls into the pan, let rolls rise briefly, then bake.

- **2 packages active dry yeast**
- **½ cup warm water (about 110°)**
- **4 cups all-purpose flour**
- **¼ cup sugar**
- **1 teaspoon salt**
- **10 tablespoons butter or margarine, melted and cooled**
- **1 egg**
- **1 cup sourdough starter, at room temperature**
- **½ cup warm milk (about 110°)**

In a small bowl, dissolve yeast in warm water. In a large bowl, stir together 2 cups of the flour, the sugar, and salt. Then add yeast mixture, 6 tablespoons of the melted butter, the egg, starter, and milk.

Beat with a heavy-duty mixer or wooden spoon for about 5 minutes or until well blended and smooth. Gradually beat in the remaining 2 cups flour. Cover and let rise in a warm place until doubled (about 45 minutes).

Pour 2 tablespoons of the remaining melted butter into a 9 by 13-inch baking pan, tilting pan to coat bottom. Stir dough down and drop into pan by large spoonfuls, making about 15 rolls. Cover and let rise in a warm place until light and puffy (about 30 minutes).

Drizzle the remaining 2 tablespoons melted butter over rolls. Bake in a preheated 425° oven (400° for a glass pan) for 15 to 20 minutes or until browned. Turn out onto a plate and serve hot. Pull rolls apart to separate. Makes about 15 rolls.

In medieval times, bakers faced severe fines if they violated laws regulating the weight and price of bread. To guard against accusations of shortchanging customers, many bakers gave an extra, free roll with each dozen sold. From this practice came the term "baker's dozen."

Cottage Cheese Sourdough Pan Rolls

Cottage cheese makes these rolls moist and light, sourdough makes them tangy. Served instead of regular pan rolls, they make an interesting change of pace with any meal. And compared with other yeast breads, they're quite speedy.

If you fancy the combination of sourdough and dill, add 2 teaspoons dill weed with the cottage cheese.

- **1 package active dry yeast**
- **¼ cup warm water (about 110°)**
- **1 cup cottage cheese**
- **1 cup sourdough starter, at room temperature**
- **1 egg**
- **2 teaspoons baking powder**
- **¼ teaspoon baking soda**
- **1 teaspoon salt**
- **1 tablespoon sugar**
- **About 4½ cups all-purpose flour**
- **2 tablespoons firm butter or margarine**

In a small bowl, dissolve yeast in warm water. In a blender or food processor, whirl cottage cheese, sourdough starter, and egg until smooth.

In a large bowl, combine baking powder, baking soda, salt, sugar, and 4 cups of the flour. With your fingers, work in butter until no large particles remain. Stir in cheese mixture and yeast mixture.

Turn dough out onto a floured board and knead until smooth (about 10 minutes), adding flour as needed to prevent sticking. Place dough in a greased bowl; turn over to grease top. Cover and let rise in a warm place until doubled (about 45 minutes).

Punch dough down. Divide into 18 pieces and shape each into a smooth ball. Arrange balls in two greased 8-inch round baking pans. Cover and let rise until puffy (25 to 30 minutes). Bake in a preheated 350° oven (325° for glass pans) for 30 to 35 minutes or until golden. Turn out onto racks to cool. Makes 1½ dozen rolls.

Sourdough Bagels

Crossing New York's famous boiled bun with San Francisco's famous leavening produces a cosmopolitan sensation—a bagel that's both chewy and sour. You may have tasted the onion kind and the poppy seed kind, but until you try sourdough, too, you can scarcely consider yourself a true bagel connoisseur.

Though this recipe is slightly different from our regular bagel recipe (page 46), the technique is basically the same, so you can refer to the photo sequence on page 47.

1 package active dry yeast
1 cup warm water (about 110°)
3 tablespoons sugar
1 teaspoon salt
½ cup sourdough starter, at room temperature
About 4 cups all-purpose flour
About 3 quarts boiling water
1 egg, lightly beaten

In large bowl of an electric mixer, dissolve yeast in warm water. Add sugar, salt, starter, and 2½ cups of the flour. Beat on medium speed until dough pulls away from sides of bowl in stretchy strands (about 5 minutes).

With a heavy-duty mixer or wooden spoon, gradually beat in 1 more cup flour. Turn dough out onto a floured board and knead until smooth and satiny (about 10 minutes), adding flour as needed to prevent sticking. Place dough in a greased bowl; turn over to grease top. Cover and let rise in a warm place until doubled (about 1 hour).

Punch dough down; knead briefly on a lightly floured board to release air, then divide into 12 equal pieces. Form each into a smooth ball, cover, and let rest for 15 minutes.

To shape, hold each ball with both hands and poke your thumbs through center. With one thumb in the hole, work around perimeter, shaping bagel like a doughnut, 2½ to 3 inches across. Place shaped bagels, 2 inches apart, on two greased 12 by 15-inch baking sheets. Cover lightly and let stand until puffy (about 20 minutes).

In a 5 to 6-quart kettle, bring 3 quarts water to boiling; adjust heat to keep it boiling gently. Carefully lift bagels off baking sheet with wide metal spatula and drop, 3 at a time, into water. Boil until puffy (about 1 minute per side). Lift out with a slotted spoon or spatula and drain briefly on a towel.

Arrange bagels, slightly apart, on the same baking sheets (no need to wash them) and brush tops with beaten egg. Bake in a preheated 375° oven for about 20 minutes or until golden. Let cool on a rack. Makes 1 dozen.

Sourdough Cheese Griddle Muffins

Sharp Cheddar cheese pairs up with sourdough starter to give these griddle muffins tangy flavor. Split them to serve plain or toasted, or fill with sandwich ingredients. The muffins are basically square, but with a homey, irregular shape.

1 package active dry yeast
1 cup warm water (about 110°)
¼ cup *each* instant nonfat dry milk and salad oil
½ cup sourdough starter, at room temperature
1½ teaspoons sugar
About 4 cups all-purpose flour
1 cup (about ¼ lb.) shredded very sharp Cheddar cheese
About ½ cup yellow cornmeal

In large bowl of an electric mixer, dissolve yeast in warm water. Beat in dry milk, oil, starter, and sugar. Gradually add about 1½ cups of the flour and beat on medium speed until dough pulls away from sides of bowl in stretchy strands (about 5 minutes). Beat in cheese.

With a heavy-duty mixer or wooden spoon, gradually add 2 to 2½ cups more flour, beating to make a stiff, moist dough. Turn out onto a floured board and knead until smooth (about 10 minutes), adding flour as needed to prevent sticking (dough will be very soft). Place dough in a greased bowl; turn over to grease top. Cover and let rise in a warm place until doubled (about 1½ hours).

Punch dough down and knead briefly to release air; cover and let stand for 10 minutes. Roll out on a lightly floured board to form a rectangle about 9 by 15 inches and ½ inch thick. Cut into fifteen 3-inch squares.

Grease 2 baking sheets (at least 12 by 15 inches) and sprinkle lightly with cornmeal. Arrange squares about 2 inches apart on pans and sprinkle lightly with more cornmeal. Cover loosely with plastic wrap and let rise in a warm place until puffy (about 20 minutes).

To bake, carefully transfer muffins to a moderately hot ungreased griddle, using a metal spatula and placing muffins about 1 inch apart. Cook for 10 minutes per side or until dark golden brown. Serve warm as they bake, or set on racks to cool. Wrapped airtight, muffins can be refrigerated for up to 3 days; freeze for longer storage. Makes 15 muffins.

Sourdough Blueberry Bread

Pictured on facing page

Sourdough starter is a versatile sort of thing. Not only does it create savory breads with piquant personality; it also marries well with the sweet flavors of many quick loaf breads and coffee cakes.

A quick bread to remember when planning your next special brunch, this one delivers rich, blueberry glory with every sourdough crumb. It bakes in an ovenproof frying pan or Dutch oven; you cut it into wedges to serve.

1½ cups all-purpose flour
½ cup whole wheat flour
½ teaspoon salt
¾ teaspoon baking soda
½ cup sugar
1 egg
½ cup *each* salad oil and milk
¾ cup sourdough starter, at room temperature
1 cup fresh, well-drained canned, or frozen blueberries (thaw and pat dry, if frozen)
Sugar (optional)

In a medium-size bowl, stir together all-purpose flour, whole wheat flour, salt, baking soda, and the ½ cup sugar. In another bowl, beat egg lightly, then stir in oil and milk. Add to dry ingredients with starter and stir until well combined. Gently fold in berries.

Turn batter into a well-greased heavy 10-inch frying pan (with ovenproof handle) or 5 to 6-quart Dutch oven. Sprinkle top with additional sugar, if desired.

Bake, uncovered, in a preheated 375° oven for 35 to 40 minutes or until a wooden pick inserted in center comes out clean. Serve warm or cool, cut into wedges. Makes 8 to 12 servings.

Sourdough Applesauce-Bran Bread

Quick breads have extra moistness as well as a pleasing sour flavor when you begin with sourdough starter. This one can be sliced to eat as soon as it's cool; or, for a mellow, slightly more sour flavor, wrap it airtight, then store it in the refrigerator for up to a week.

1½ cups whole wheat flour
⅓ cup *each* unprocessed bran and wheat germ
1 teaspoon *each* baking powder and salt
½ teaspoon baking soda
1 egg
¾ cup sugar
⅓ cup salad oil
1 cup sourdough starter, at room temperature
1 cup applesauce

In a bowl, combine flour, bran, wheat germ, baking powder, salt, and baking soda; mix until well blended, and set aside.

In a medium-size bowl, beat egg lightly, then beat in sugar and oil until well blended; add starter and applesauce, beating until smooth. Stir in flour mixture, mixing just until blended.

Turn batter into a well-greased 9 by 5-inch loaf pan and bake in a preheated 350° oven (325° for a glass pan) for about 1 hour and 10 minutes or until a wooden pick inserted in center comes out clean.

Let cool in pan on a rack for about 10 minutes, then turn out onto rack to cool completely. Makes 1 loaf.

Sourdough Banana-Nut Bread

Like Sourdough Applesauce-Bran Bread (above), this bread can be "aged" in the refrigerator to allow the flavor to develop. Also like Sourdough Applesauce-Bran Bread, it is fruity and delicious.

2¼ cups all-purpose flour
1 teaspoon *each* baking powder and salt
½ teaspoon baking soda
¾ teaspoon *each* ground cinnamon and nutmeg
1 egg
¼ cup granulated sugar
½ cup firmly packed brown sugar
⅓ cup salad oil
1 cup sourdough starter, at room temperature
1 cup mashed ripe bananas (about 3 small bananas)
1 teaspoon vanilla
½ teaspoon grated lemon peel
1 cup chopped nuts
1 cup raisins (optional)

In a small bowl, combine flour, baking powder, salt, baking soda, cinnamon, and nutmeg, mixing well; set aside.

(Continued on page 96)

Sourdough Blueberry Bread *(Recipe on facing page)*

1 *Fold blueberries in gently so that they don't get crushed and stain the batter.*

2 *Turn batter into a well-greased, heavy 10-inch frying pan with an ovenproof handle, or a Dutch oven; spread out evenly. To form a sweet, slightly crisp crust, sprinkle with sugar.*

3 *Bake bread until top is golden and a wooden pick inserted in center comes out clean—this means it's done. If pick has batter clinging to it, bake the bread a few minutes longer.*

4 *Fat wedges of Sourdough Blueberry Bread are a cheery addition to the breakfast table. Sweet and fruity, the bread gets added character from whole wheat flour and sourdough starter.*

In a medium-size bowl, beat egg lightly; add granulated sugar, brown sugar, and oil and beat until well blended. Beat in sourdough starter, bananas, vanilla, and lemon peel; stir in nuts. Add raisins, if desired; then add flour mixture, mixing just until blended.

Turn batter into a well-greased 9 by 5-inch loaf pan. Bake in a preheated 350° oven (325° for a glass pan) for about 1 hour and 10 minutes or until a wooden pick inserted in center comes out clean. Let cool in pan on a rack for about 10 minutes, then turn out onto rack to cool completely. Makes 1 loaf.

Sourdough Streusel Coffee Cake

Sourdough fans don't stop with plain loaves of bread, but soon venture afield to fancier items, such as this streusel-crunchy coffee cake. A rich nutmeat filling combines with sourdough starter and orange peel to create scintillating flavor.

Nut streusel (recipe follows)
½ cup (¼ lb.) butter or margarine
½ cup *each* granulated sugar and firmly packed brown sugar
1 tablespoon grated orange peel
3 eggs
½ cup sourdough starter, at room temperature
2 cups all-purpose flour
1½ teaspoons *each* baking powder and baking soda
½ teaspoon salt
1 cup sour cream
¾ cup raisins

Prepare nut streusel and set aside. In large bowl of an electric mixer, beat butter, granulated sugar, and brown sugar until fluffy. Beat in orange peel, eggs, and starter. In another bowl, combine flour, baking powder, baking soda, and salt.

With mixer on low speed, add flour mixture to butter mixture alternately with sour cream, beating well after each addition; add raisins with last addition of flour. Spoon ⅓ of the batter into a well-greased and floured 9-inch plain or fluted tube cake pan (2 to 2½-quart size). Sprinkle with ⅓ of the nut streusel; repeat layers two more times.

Bake in a preheated 350° oven for 60 to 65 minutes or until a wooden pick inserted in center comes out clean. Let cake cool in pan on a rack for 10 minutes, then turn out onto rack to cool completely. Makes 8 to 10 servings.

Nut streusel. In a small bowl, stir together ½ cup firmly packed **brown sugar,** 1½ teaspoons **ground cinnamon**, and ½ cup finely chopped **almonds** until well combined.

Surprise Rolls

Within each of these sourdough–whole wheat rolls waits a wonderful sweet or savory surprise. Sometimes it's a nip of fruit, sometimes a morsel of cheese. The rolls make a tidy little snack or a quick and nutritious breakfast—at home or on the road.

½ cup stone-ground whole wheat flour
2 tablespoons sugar
1 teaspoon baking soda
½ teaspoon salt
1 egg
1 cup sourdough starter, at room temperature
3 tablespoons melted butter or margarine
Fillings: Chopped dried apricots or dates, or Swiss cheese (cut into ½-inch cubes)

In a bowl, stir together flour, sugar, baking soda, and salt. In another bowl, beat egg and blend in starter and butter. Add egg mixture to dry ingredients and stir until well combined. Quickly fill 12 greased 2 to 2½-inch muffin cups ⅓ full; add 1 teaspoon fruit or 1 cube cheese to each cup and top evenly with remaining batter. Bake in a preheated 400° oven for 15 to 20 minutes or until a wooden pick inserted in center comes out clean. Turn out onto a rack to cool. Makes 12 rolls.

In the mid-19th century, the first high-speed steel rollers were used to grind grain, until then crushed by millstones. But because it clogged the rollers, the wheat germ had to be removed from the grain before grinding, which meant about a 90 percent nutritional loss from the grain. This explains why, in recent nutrition-conscious times, there has been a revival of interest in "stone-ground" flour.

Sourdough Pancakes & Waffles

During the California Gold Rush of 1849, sourdough starter was a necessity of life. The rugged "forty-niners" carried their starters with them wherever they went, for without starter, they would have no baked goods. Cooking in pits in the ground or over campfires, they made breads, biscuits, and flapjacks such as the ones below.

History is history, however—and you don't have to be a pioneer to enjoy these old-time pancakes and waffles!

- **1 cup whole wheat flour**
- **1 cup all-purpose flour**
- **½ cup sourdough starter, at room temperature**
- **2 cups warm buttermilk (about 110°)**
- **2 eggs**
- **¼ cup *each* milk and salad oil**
- **2 tablespoons sugar**
- **1 teaspoon baking soda**
- **½ teaspoon salt**

In a large bowl, combine whole wheat flour, all-purpose flour, starter, and buttermilk; beat until blended. Cover and let stand at room temperature for about 45 minutes (or cover and refrigerate overnight).

Beat together eggs, milk, and oil. Add to flour mixture and stir until blended. Combine sugar, baking soda, and salt. Stir into batter, then let stand for 5 minutes.

For pancakes, drop batter by spoonfuls onto a moderately hot greased griddle. Cook until tops are bubbly and appear dry; turn and cook until other sides are browned. Makes about 2 dozen 4-inch pancakes.

For waffles, bake in a preheated electric waffle iron, following manufacturer's directions; waffles should be richly browned. Serve immediately. Or let cool on racks, package airtight, and freeze; reheat frozen waffles in a toaster. Makes twelve 4-inch-square waffles.

Sourdough Blueberry Pancakes

Follow recipe for **Sourdough Pancakes & Waffles,** stirring in ¾ cup fresh, canned (well-drained), or frozen (thawed and patted dry) **blueberries** just before baking.

Sourdough Oatmeal Pancakes

Follow recipe for **Sourdough Pancakes & Waffles,** substituting 1 cup **rolled oats** for 1 cup of either the whole wheat or the all-purpose flour.

Sourdough Crêpes

You can serve these tangy sourdough crêpes in all the ways you serve regular French crêpes. For breakfast, butter them and spread with preserves or sprinkle with sugar. For a lunch or dinner entrée, wrap them around any kind of savory filling, then heat in the oven before serving.

Make the crêpes ahead of time, if you like. They keep well in the refrigerator for up to a week, or you can freeze them for longer storage.

- **¾ cup sourdough starter, at room temperature**
- **1 cup warm water (about 110°)**
- **1¼ cups all-purpose flour**
- **2 eggs**
- **3 tablespoons salad oil**
- **½ teaspoon *each* salt and baking soda**
- **1 tablespoon sugar**
- **Butter or margarine**

In a bowl, stir together starter, water, and flour until smoothly blended. Cover and let stand in a warm place until very bubbly (about 8 hours).

Beat together eggs and oil, then stir into batter. Also combine salt, baking soda, and sugar; sprinkle over batter and stir well to blend. Cover lightly and let stand at room temperature for about 15 minutes.

Place a 6 or 7-inch crêpe pan or other flat-bottomed frying pan over medium heat. When pan is hot, add ¼ teaspoon butter or margarine and swirl to coat surface. At once, pour in 1½ to 2 tablespoons batter, quickly tilting pan so batter flows over entire flat surface (don't worry if there are a few little holes). Cook until surface appears dry and edge is lightly browned. With a spatula, turn and brown other side. Turn crêpe out of pan onto a plate. Repeat, stacking crêpes, until all batter is used. If you don't plan to use the baked crêpes within a few hours, cool, package airtight, and refrigerate for as long as a week. Let crêpes warm to room temperature before separating them; they tear if cold. Makes 12 to 16 crêpes.

Griddle & Fried Breads

Just because it's bread doesn't mean that it has to be baked in the oven! Many of the world's favorite breads are cooked in another way: they're fried, either on a hot griddle or in oil. Included among the fried breads are ethnic specialties such as Mexican tortillas, English crumpets, and Hungarian langos, as well as such all-American treats as doughnuts, pancakes, and waffles.

Country of origin is by no means the only way in which these breads vary: some are leavened with yeast and some with baking powder or baking soda; some are unleavened flatbreads. There are breads that would make sweet surprises at breakfast or dessert, and those that are traditionally served with the spiciest of dinners. You can also choose between breads of airy lightness and those with an earthier texture.

Bread bakers who seek variety and a little adventure as well as good, homemade flavor and nutrition are certain to find them all in the following collection of recipes.

Hot from the griddle or freshly deep-fried, these tempting breads are (clockwise from bottom) Pumpkin Waffles with walnut-orange butter (page 105), Norwegian Lefse (page 101), Cinnamon Doughnut Twists (page 108), Langos with garlic cloves (page 108), and Old-fashioned Cake Doughnuts (page 107).

Corn Tortillas

As taco "shells" or tostada "platters," or simply stacked, warm and tempting, on the dinner table, corn tortillas lend their golden goodness to almost every Mexican meal. With a tortilla press, shaping the dough is much easier. But we also explain how to do the job with a rolling pin.

- **2 cups masa harina (dehydrated masa flour)**
- **1¼ to 1⅓ cups warm water**

Mix masa flour with enough warm water to make dough hold together well. Using your hands, shape dough into a smooth ball. Divide into 12 equal pieces, then roll each into a ball. (For small tortillas, divide dough into 24 equal pieces.)

To shape with a tortilla press: Place a square of wax paper on bottom half of tortilla press, and place 1 ball of dough on paper, slightly off center toward edge farthest from handle. Flatten it slightly with the palm of your hand. Cover with a second square of wax paper. Lower top half of press (being careful not to wrinkle paper), and press down firmly on lever until tortilla measures about 6 inches in diameter (4 inches for small tortillas). Stack paper-covered tortillas.

To shape with a rolling pin: Use two cloths that have been dipped in water and wrung dry. Flatten a ball of dough slightly and place between the cloths. Roll with light, even strokes until cake is about 6 inches in diameter (4 inches for small tortillas). Carefully pull back cloths, trim tortilla to a round shape if necessary, and sandwich it between two squares of wax paper. Repeat, stacking paper-covered tortillas.

To cook: Carefully peel off top piece of wax paper. Turn over tortilla, paper side up, onto an ungreased griddle preheated to medium-hot, or into a heavy frying pan over medium-high heat. As tortilla becomes warm, you'll be able to peel off remaining paper.

Cook for about 1½ to 2 minutes, turning frequently, until tortilla looks dry (it should be soft) and is lightly flecked with brown specks; it will puff up briefly.

Serve tortillas immediately. Or let cool, wrap airtight, and store in refrigerator or freezer. To reheat, stack tortillas (thawed, if frozen), wrap in foil, and place in a preheated 350° oven for about 15 minutes or until hot and steamy. Makes 1 dozen 6-inch or 2 dozen 4-inch corn tortillas.

Sesame Seed Tortillas

Pebbly-surfaced with sesame seeds, our fresh and chewy flour tortillas offer delicious, if untraditional, flavor. The little griddle breads are easy to shape with a rolling pin, and they make pleasing companions to soups and stews. For variety, try rye and whole wheat tortillas, too.

- **½ cup sesame seeds**
- **About 3 cups all-purpose flour**
- **2 teaspoons baking powder**
- **¾ teaspoon salt**
- **¼ cup solid vegetable shortening**
- **1 cup warm water (about 110°)**

In a wide frying pan over medium heat, toast sesame seeds, shaking pan frequently, until seeds are golden (about 2 minutes); set aside and let cool.

In a large bowl, combine toasted sesame seeds, 3 cups flour, baking powder, and salt; cut in shortening, using a pastry blender or two knives, until mixture is in fine crumbs. Add water and stir to mix well, then turn out onto a floured board. Knead, adding flour as needed to prevent sticking, just until dough is well blended and smooth (4 to 5 minutes). Cover with plastic wrap and let stand for about 30 minutes.

Divide dough into 12 equal pieces. Shape each into a ball and press flat on a floured board to form a circle; then roll out to form a thin 8 to 9-inch tortilla.

To cook, place tortillas, one or two at a time, on a hot ungreased griddle or heavy frying pan; bubbles should form underneath the surface almost immediately. Cook, turning over several times, for 2 to 3 minutes or until surface begins to brown.

Stack tortillas as they're cooked, and cover with foil to keep warm. If making ahead, let cool on a rack, then wrap and refrigerate for 2 to 3 days; freeze for longer storage. To reheat, stack tortillas (thawed, if frozen), wrap in foil, and place in a preheated 350° oven for about 15 minutes or until hot and steamy. Makes 12.

Rye Tortillas with Caraway

Follow directions for **Sesame Seed Tortillas,** but omit sesame seeds. Reduce all-purpose flour to 1½ cups and add 1½ cups **rye flour** along with 2 teaspoons **caraway seeds.**

Whole Wheat Tortillas with Wheat Germ

Follow directions for **Sesame Seed Tortillas,** but omit sesame seeds and all-purpose flour. Add 3 cups **whole wheat flour** along with ¼ cup **toasted wheat germ.**

Chapaties

The tortilla, the crêpe, the blini, and the pancake—all these griddle breads from diverse nations have gained universal popularity. But what about *chapaties*? Stacked on dinner tables throughout India, at meals both humble and grand, these chewy rounds of wheat bread help temper the fiery seasonings in other dishes. Chapaties, one of the world's simplest breads, taste just as delicious with mild Western foods as with hot and spicy Indian curries.

About 2 cups whole wheat flour
1 teaspoon salt
About ⅔ cup warm water

In a bowl, stir together 2 cups flour and salt. Stirring gently with a fork, add water slowly until a crumbly dough forms. With your hands, mix dough until it holds together; add a few more drops of water, if needed. On a floured board, knead until smooth but still sticky (about 3 minutes). Wrap airtight in plastic wrap and let stand at room temperature for 30 minutes.

Divide dough into 16 equal pieces, shape into smooth balls, and flatten each with your hand. On a floured board, roll each flattened ball into a circle about 5 inches in diameter, using light, even strokes. Stack circles, separating them with sheets of wax paper. If made ahead, seal in a plastic bag and refrigerate until next day.

Place a circle of dough on an ungreased griddle preheated to medium-low, or in a heavy frying pan over medium-low heat. After about 1 minute, top will darken slightly; at this point, press top of dough with a wide spatula. Blisters will gradually form and push up spatula; press them down. When bottom is lightly browned (about 1 more minute), turn bread over and cook until other side is lightly browned (about 2 minutes). Place breads on a baking sheet, cover with a damp towel, and keep hot in a preheated 225° oven while cooking remaining dough. Serve hot. Makes 16 chapaties.

Norwegian Lefse

Pictured on page 98

Pliant, soft, and delicately sour, potato *lefse* has always been something of a Scandinavian secret. But this treat from the far north is too delicious not to share. Roll it around sausage or cheese for a Norwegian "taco," or daub it with butter and sugar for a Norwegian "crêpe."

About 2½ pounds russet potatoes
Boiling water
2 tablespoons butter or margarine
¼ cup milk
1 teaspoon salt
3 to 3½ cups all-purpose flour
Salad oil

Peel potatoes and cut into quarters; cover with boiling water and cook until tender (about 30 minutes). Drain and mash until very smooth. Measure potatoes; you should have 4 cups. Stir in butter, milk, and salt, mixing well. Let cool to room temperature.

Gradually mix in enough of the flour (about 2 cups) to make a nonsticky dough. On a floured board, knead gently to shape into a smooth log. Divide into 24 equal pieces; do not cover.

If possible, cover rolling pin with stockinet. Shape each piece of dough into a smooth ball. On a pastry cloth or floured board, roll each ball into a thin 8 to 10-inch round. Turn rounds and keep coated with flour (using as little as possible) to prevent sticking.

Shake excess flour off each round and place on a medium-hot, lightly oiled griddle or frying pan. It will start to bubble; bake until bubbles are lightly browned (about 1½ minutes). With a spatula, turn and bake other side. Serve warm. Or let cool on racks, wrap airtight, refrigerate for up to 4 days, or freeze. To reheat (thaw first, if frozen), stack and wrap in foil; place in a preheated 325° oven for 10 to 15 minutes. Makes 24 lefse.

"Bread" as a synonym for money was in common use during the 17th century and earlier. "Breadwinner," for family provider, followed later.

Crumpets

Pictured on facing page

Crumpets have holes for a reason: How else, ask the British, can a generous amount of butter properly permeate each moist and springy bite?

Crumpets are probably best described as a cross between an English muffin and a pancake. They're served warm, either freshly baked or toasted, with butter and jam or honey.

You'll need some kind of metal rings to contain the simple yeast batter while it bakes. You can use 3-inch flan rings or open-topped cooky cutters. Or you can do as we did—use tuna cans with the tops and bottoms removed.

1 package active dry yeast
1 teaspoon sugar
¼ cup warm water (about 110°)
⅓ cup milk, at room temperature
1 egg
About 4 tablespoons butter or margarine, melted
1 cup all-purpose flour
½ teaspoon salt

In a large bowl, combine yeast, sugar, and water; let stand until bubbly (about 15 minutes). Blend in milk, egg, and 1 tablespoon of the butter. Add flour and salt and beat until smooth. Cover and let stand in a warm place until almost doubled (about 45 minutes).

Brush a griddle or heavy frying pan and the inside of each 3-inch ring with butter. Heat rings on griddle over low heat; pour about 3 tablespoons batter into each ring. Bake for about 7 minutes or until holes appear and tops are dry. Remove rings and turn crumpets to brown other side lightly (about 2 minutes). Repeat with remaining batter.

Serve warm or let cool on a rack and toast just before serving. Makes 7 or 8 crumpets.

Blini—little round buckwheat pancakes—were invented by the early Slavs to represent the sun they worshipped at the spring equinox. Centuries later, in Russia, blini were topped with sour cream and beluga caviar to provide high-fashion nibbling for the Czarist aristocrats.

Blini

On Shrove Tuesday (just before the 40 days of Lent), during festivities in many European countries, pancakes are eaten. The flour in the pancakes represents the staff of life; the eggs symbolize creation, and the milk, purity. During *Maslenitsa*, Russia's pre-Lenten "Butter Festival," the little buckwheat pancakes called blini are consumed by the dozen.

Our version of blini is topped with butter, sour cream, onions, hard-cooked eggs, and dill—humbler fare than the Russian aristocrats' caviar. Of course, you can try caviar, too, if you wish; there are several inexpensive varieties available.

⅔ cup milk
1 package active dry yeast
¼ cup warm water (about 110°)
1 teaspoon sugar
⅔ cup all-purpose flour
¼ cup buckwheat pancake mix
¼ teaspoon salt
2 eggs, separated
3 tablespoons sour cream
Butter or margarine
Toppings (suggestions follow)

Bring milk to scalding in a small pan over medium heat; let cool. In a large bowl, combine yeast, water, and sugar; let stand until bubbly (5 to 15 minutes). In another bowl, combine flour, pancake mix, and salt; then add to yeast mixture along with milk, egg yolks, and sour cream. Beat until smooth and well blended (about 3 minutes). Cover and let stand at room temperature until mixture is spongy and has a slightly sour smell (about 4 hours).

In a bowl, beat egg whites until soft, moist peaks form. Gently fold into batter; let stand for 30 minutes.

Heat a griddle or wide frying pan over medium-high heat; brush lightly with butter. Ladle 3 tablespoons batter onto griddle for each pancake; cook until tops are dry and bubbles break (about 3 minutes). Turn and brown other side. Stack pancakes and keep them warm while preparing remaining pancakes. Pass toppings at the table. Makes 4 servings (16 pancakes).

Toppings. Offer ½ cup (¼ lb.) **butter** or margarine, melted; ½ pint (1 cup) **sour cream; 1 mild red onion,** thinly sliced; 4 hard-cooked **eggs,** chopped; and fresh or dry **dill weed.**

Crumpets *(Recipe on facing page)*

1 *For the rings in which crumpets cook, we've used tuna cans with their tops and bottoms removed. Brush griddle and inside of rings with melted butter; place rings on griddle.*

2 *When the yeast batter has risen, it will be thick and full of bubbles; use a quarter-cup measure or a small ladle to scoop it up.*

3 *Pour about 3 tablespoons batter into each ring on griddle. Bake for about 7 minutes, or until holes appear and tops are dry.*

4 *Using tongs, lift rings off of griddle. If crumpets stick to rings, use a knife to loosen them until the rings can be removed easily.*

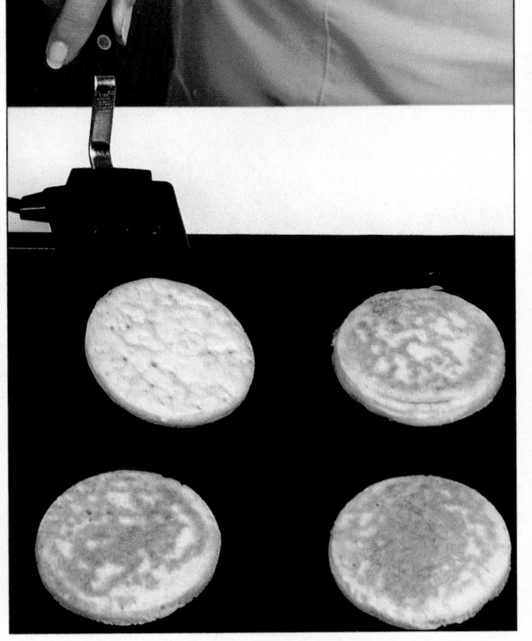

5 *Turn crumpets and cook for about 2 minutes, until other side is lightly browned. Serve at once; or let cool on a rack and toast before serving.*

6 *Afternoon tea and crumpets—a delightful custom of British origin. Try crumpets for breakfast, too, or top them with melted cheese for lunch.*

Bainbridge Buttermilk & Bourbon Hotcakes

Their tongue-twisting mouthful of a name says a lot about these golden hotcakes, invented on Bainbridge Island in Washington state. With each truly tongue-tempting melt-in-your-mouthful, they make better eating than speaking. Try them for Sunday breakfast, with powdered sugar, melted butter, and jam, or with the more conventional maple syrup.

1 egg, separated
¾ cup buttermilk
1 tablespoon salad oil
2 tablespoons bourbon
⅔ cup all-purpose flour
2 tablespoons cornmeal
½ teaspoon *each* baking powder and baking soda
¼ teaspoon salt
Butter or margarine

In a medium-size bowl, beat egg white just until stiff, moist peaks form. In a large bowl, beat egg yolk, buttermilk, oil, and bourbon together until frothy; then blend in flour, cornmeal, baking powder, baking soda, and salt. Fold beaten white into mixture.

Preheat a griddle or wide frying pan over medium heat; when hot, melt enough butter to coat cooking surface. Spoon batter (about 3 tablespoons for each cake) onto griddle; spread to make 3-inch circles. Cook until tops are bubbly and appear dry; turn and cook until other sides are browned. Add butter as needed. Makes about 1 dozen pancakes.

Old-fashioned Oatmeal Pancakes

No modern-day speedy breakfast, these cakelike pancakes demand a little extra preparation time in return for their rich, oaten goodness. You start them the night before, to let the oats and buttermilk blend to creamy tenderness. (Besides, many sleepy cooks appreciate having a ready-made batter at hand in the morning.) With your first syrup-doused mouthful, you'll agree that these special pancakes are well worth the effort.

2 cups regular rolled oats
About 2 cups buttermilk
2 eggs
4 tablespoons butter or margarine, melted and cooled
½ cup raisins (optional)
½ cup all-purpose flour
2 tablespoons sugar
1 teaspoon *each* baking powder and baking soda
½ teaspoon ground cinnamon
¼ teaspoon salt

In a bowl, combine oats and 2 cups of the buttermilk; stir until well blended. Cover and refrigerate until next day.

In a bowl, beat eggs lightly and add to oat mixture, along with butter and raisins, if desired; stir just until blended. In another bowl, stir together flour, sugar, baking powder, baking soda, cinnamon, and salt; add to oat mixture and stir just until moistened. If batter seems too thick, add more buttermilk (up to 3 tablespoons).

Preheat a griddle or wide frying pan over medium heat; grease lightly. Spoon batter, about ⅓ cup for each cake, onto griddle, and spread out to make circles 4 inches in diameter. Cook until tops are bubbly and appear dry; turn and cook until other sides are browned. Makes about 1½ dozen pancakes.

Crêpes

France's contribution to the world's pancake stack may surprise you with its versatility. How can anything so papery-thin and fragile also prove so practical? Yet crêpes enclose everything from leftover turkey to berries with cream, brightening any occasion from family breakfast to midnight buffet. They freeze nicely, too, even for months; before unwrapping to use, let them thaw, so they won't stick together and tear as you separate them.

3 eggs
⅔ cup all-purpose flour
1 cup milk
About 4 teaspoons butter or margarine

In a blender or food processor, whirl eggs and flour until smooth; then add milk and blend until thoroughly combined. Or combine eggs and flour in a medium-size bowl and blend with a wire whisk; add milk and mix until smooth.

Place a 6 or 7-inch crêpe pan or other flat-bottomed frying pan over medium heat. When pan is hot, add ¼ teaspoon of the butter and swirl to coat surface. Stir batter and pour in about 2 tablespoons, quickly tilting pan so batter flows over entire surface. If heat is correct and pan is hot enough, crêpe sets at once, forming tiny bubbles—don't worry if there are a few small holes. (If batter makes a smooth layer, pan isn't hot enough.) Cook until surface is dry and edge is lightly browned.

Turn with a spatula and cook until other side is lightly browned. Turn out onto a plate. Repeat to make each crêpe, stirring batter occasionally; stack crêpes. If made ahead, let cool; then place wax paper between crêpes, package airtight (in quantities you expect to use), and refrigerate for up to a week; freeze for longer storage. Bring crêpes to room temperature before separating. Makes about 18 crêpes.

Bacon-Sesame Waffles

You start with a crunchy cornmeal batter, and add a sprinkling of sesame seeds and a crisp strip of bacon just before baking.

8 slices bacon
2 cups all-purpose flour
½ cup cornmeal
5 teaspoons baking powder
½ teaspoon salt
2 eggs, separated
2 cups milk
½ cup salad oil
2 teaspoons vanilla
8 teaspoons sesame seeds

In a wide frying pan over medium heat, fry bacon until crisp; lift out, drain, and cut each slice in half.

In a large bowl, combine flour, cornmeal, baking powder, and salt. Add egg yolks, milk, oil, and vanilla; stir just until blended. In small bowl of an electric mixer, beat egg whites until stiff, moist peaks form; then gently fold into batter.

Preheat waffle iron according to manufacturer's directions. Sprinkle about 2 teaspoons sesame seeds evenly over grid, and place ½ slice bacon on each of the iron's waffle sections. Pour batter over top, close waffle iron, and cook for about 5 minutes or until waffles are golden. Makes sixteen 4½-inch-square waffles.

Pumpkin Waffles

Pictured on page 98

Heady with all the spice sensations usually associated with pumpkin pie, these hearty waffles make a good choice for a holiday breakfast. Serve them with walnut-orange butter (recipe below) and maple syrup.

Walnut-orange butter (recipe follows)
2¼ cups all-purpose flour
4 teaspoons baking powder
2 teaspoons ground cinnamon
1 teaspoon *each* ground allspice and ginger
½ teaspoon salt
¼ cup firmly packed brown sugar
1 cup canned pumpkin
2 cups milk
4 eggs, separated
¼ cup butter or margarine, melted

Prepare walnut-orange butter and set aside. In a small bowl, stir together flour, baking powder, cinnamon, allspice, ginger, salt, and sugar. In a larger bowl, combine pumpkin, milk, and egg yolks; add flour mixture and butter; stir to blend.

In small bowl of an electric mixer, beat egg whites until soft peaks form; fold into batter.

Following manufacturer's directions, preheat a waffle iron and pour batter onto grid; cook for about 5 minutes or until waffles are richly browned and crisp. Top with walnut-orange butter. Makes about twenty-four 4½-inch-square waffles.

Walnut-orange butter. Blend ½ cup (¼ lb.) **butter** or margarine (softened), ½ cup chopped **walnuts,** and ½ teaspoon grated **orange peel.**

According to legend, the first waffles were invented quite by accident in medieval Scotland. A weary crusader, waiting for his wife to finish baking his supper of oatcakes, sat down to rest—right on top of some cakes she had left to cool on the bench. His coat of mail imprinted them with a pretty woven pattern, so the couple named the cakes "waffres," which is the Scottish word for woven.

French Crullers *(Recipe on facing page)*

1 *Stir vigorously with a wooden spoon for 1 minute; dough will form a heavy ball and clean sides of pan.*

2 *As you beat in each egg, mixture separates and becomes slippery, but smooths out again after each egg is completely incorporated into mixture.*

3 *Spoon dough into a large pastry bag fitted with a #6 star tip; form rings, using greased 3-inch circles of foil as guides.*

4 *Slide both cruller and foil into hot oil, turning them over so that foil floats free. Remove foil with tongs and discard.*

5 *When crullers are browned, remove from pan and drain on paper towels. While still warm, dip in sugar glaze.*

6 *Pretty to look at and ethereally light, melt-in-your-mouth French crullers can make a party out of a coffee break.*

French Crullers

Pictured on facing page

Their name taken from *krullen*, the Dutch word for "curl," our airy crullers get their curlicue surface from being pressed through a pastry bag. But baking tradition credits this version not to the Dutch, but to the French. Light and crisp as éclairs, French crullers are the daintiest of doughnuts.

3 tablespoons sugar
½ teaspoon salt
¼ cup butter or margarine
1 cup water
1¼ cups all-purpose flour
4 eggs
1 teaspoon *each* grated lemon peel and vanilla
¼ teaspoon ground mace
Sugar glaze (recipe follows)
Salad oil

Cut 14 circles of heavy-duty foil, each 3 inches in diameter. Grease one side of each and set 1 inch apart on baking sheets, greased side up.

In a heavy 2½ to 3-quart pan, combine sugar, salt, butter, and water. Bring to a full boil over medium heat, stirring until butter has melted. Remove from heat, add flour all at once, and beat vigorously with a wooden spoon until smooth. Return to heat and stir vigorously for 1 minute; dough should form a heavy ball and clean sides of pan.

Remove from heat and add eggs, one at a time, beating vigorously after each. With the last egg, also beat in lemon peel, vanilla, and mace.

Spoon dough into a large pastry bag fitted with a #6 star tip. Using outer edges of foil circles as guides, make 3-inch rings with dough, overlapping ends slightly. Let stand, uncovered, for 20 to 30 minutes. Meanwhile, prepare sugar glaze.

Into a deep 3 or 4-quart pan, pour salad oil to a depth of 2 inches; heat to 365° to 375° on a deep-frying thermometer. With a slotted spatula, lift a cruller and foil; slide both into the oil, turning them over so foil floats free; use tongs to remove foil. Fry 2 or 3 crullers at a time, turning often, until golden brown (about 7 minutes). Lift from oil with slotted spatula; drain on paper towels. While warm, dip in glaze. Makes 14 crullers.

Sugar glaze. In a bowl, blend 1½ cups **powdered sugar,** 3 tablespoons **hot water,** and ½ teaspoon **vanilla** until smooth.

Old-fashioned Cake Doughnuts

Pictured on page 98

Here's as tempting an after-school treat as any that Grandmother ever served.

About 3½ cups all-purpose flour
3 teaspoons baking powder
1 teaspoon *each* salt and ground nutmeg
¼ teaspoon *each* ground cloves and mace
4 eggs
⅔ cup sugar
⅓ cup milk
⅓ cup butter or margarine, melted and cooled
1 teaspoon *each* vanilla and grated lemon peel
Salad oil
Powdered sugar frosting (recipe follows)
Flaked coconut or chopped nuts (optional)

In a bowl, stir 3 cups of the flour together with baking powder, salt, nutmeg, cloves, and mace. In large bowl of an electric mixer, beat eggs on high speed until very light and fluffy. Gradually add sugar, beating until mixture is very thick and lemon-colored. Reduce speed to low, then blend in milk, butter, vanilla, and lemon peel.

Gradually beat flour mixture into egg mixture to make a stiff dough (if dough seems soft, beat in about ¼ cup of the remaining flour). Cover and refrigerate for 2 hours or until next day.

When ready to shape doughnuts, divide dough in half; cover and refrigerate one half. Turn other half out onto a floured board and dust lightly with some of the remaining ¼ cup flour. Roll dough out to ½-inch thickness. Using a well-floured 3-inch doughnut cutter (dip it in flour after each cut), cut out doughnuts and holes and place slightly apart on a lightly floured baking sheet. Reroll and cut scraps. Repeat with remaining half of dough. Let doughnuts and holes stand, uncovered, at room temperature for 15 to 20 minutes.

Into a deep 3 to 4-quart pan, pour oil to a depth of 2 inches and heat to 375° to 400° on a deep-frying thermometer. Gently add 2 or 3 doughnuts or holes at a time and fry, turning often, until golden brown (1½ to 2 minutes). Lift from oil with a slotted spoon or spatula; drain on paper towels.

Serve plain, or let cool completely and spread with powdered sugar frosting and sprinkle with flaked coconut or chopped nuts, if desired. Makes about 2 dozen doughnuts and holes.

(Continued on next page)

Powdered sugar frosting. Blend 3 cups **powdered sugar,** 2 tablespoons soft **butter** or margarine, ¼ teaspoon **vanilla,** and 2 or 3 tablespoons hot **water.**

Cinnamon Doughnut Twists

Pictured on page 98

Cinnamon-spicy through and through, these twisted doughnuts say a warm and fragrant "welcome home" to tired goblins after Halloween adventuring. They're good at other times, too—serve them for a lazy weekend breakfast, or on a chill night with hot cider by the fire.

2 packages active dry yeast
¼ cup warm water (about 110°)
1½ cups milk
½ cup sugar
1 teaspoon salt
½ teaspoon ground cinnamon
⅓ cup butter or margarine, cut into pieces
2 eggs
About 5¼ cups all-purpose flour
Salad oil
1 cup sugar
4 teaspoons ground cinnamon

In a large bowl, dissolve yeast in water. Meanwhile, in a medium-size pan, combine milk, the ½ cup sugar, salt, the ½ teaspoon cinnamon, and butter. Heat over medium heat to about 110° (butter need not melt completely). Add milk mixture, eggs, and 2 cups of the flour to yeast mixture. Beat until smooth. With a heavy-duty mixer or wooden spoon, mix in 3 more cups of the flour until smooth (dough will be soft and sticky). Cover and let rise in a warm place until almost doubled (about 1 hour).

Beat dough with a wooden spoon to release air. Turn out onto a well-floured board (dough will be very sticky). Roll dough around to coat all over with flour so it won't stick to board. With a floured rolling pin, roll dough into a rectangle ½ inch thick, 8 inches wide, and 18 inches long. With a floured knife, cut dough crosswise into 1-inch strips.

To form each twist, fold one strip in half crosswise and, from the center, loosely twist the strands together; press two loose ends together to seal (see illustration below). Leave uncovered on floured board to rise (if room is warm), or transfer to floured pans and let rise in a warm place, uncovered, until almost doubled (20 to 30 minutes).

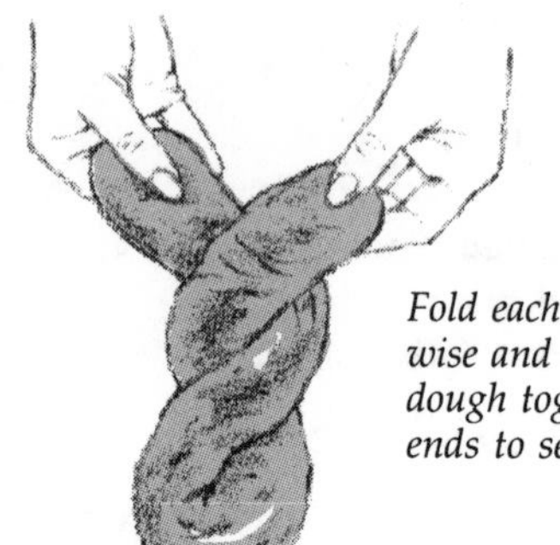

Fold each strip in half crosswise and twist strands of dough together; then pinch ends to seal.

Into a deep frying pan or 5-quart pan, pour salad oil to a depth of 1½ to 2 inches and heat to 365° to 375° on a deep-frying thermometer. Gently add doughnuts, a few at a time, and fry, turning often, until golden brown (about 3 minutes). Lift from oil with a slotted spoon or spatula; drain on paper towels.

Mix the 1 cup sugar and the 4 teaspoons cinnamon together in a bag. Add warm doughnuts, 1 or 2 at a time, and shake to coat. Makes about 18 doughnuts.

Among the many wonderful baked goods brought by immigrants to the United States, the Dutch **olykoek** *("oily cake") gave us our delicious discovery of doughnuts.*

Langos

Pictured on page 98

Puffy and chewy, these little rounds of garlic-rubbed fried bread owe their creation to Hungarian frugality. On baking day in Hungary, dough scraps are traditionally saved, rolled into circles, and slashed in several places for an extra-chewy interior; then they're deep-fried to a tempting golden brown. Served warm, the aromatic morsels make delicious companions to spicy soups and stews. Our *langos*—just one of numerous versions—start with potato bread dough.

1 large russet potato (about ½ lb.)
2 cups water
1 package active dry yeast
1 teaspoon salt
½ teaspoon *each* ground ginger and baking soda
About 3 cups all-purpose flour
3 tablespoons cornstarch
Salad oil
Salt
Garlic cloves, peeled

Scrub and slice potato (do not peel). In a 1 to 1½-quart pan, boil potato in the 2 cups water (covered) until very tender (about 20 minutes). Drain, reserving liquid; then smoothly mash potato and set aside.

Measure ¾ cup of the reserved potato liquid; pour into a large bowl and let cool to 110°. Dissolve yeast in liquid, then mix in potato, the 1 teaspoon salt, ginger, and baking soda.

Stir together 2½ cups of the flour and the cornstarch, then gradually beat into yeast mixture with a wooden spoon (dough will be crumbly). Turn out onto a floured board and knead until smooth, adding flour as needed to prevent sticking.

Place dough in a greased bowl; turn over to grease top. Cover and let rise in a warm place until doubled (about 1½ hours).

Punch dough down; knead briefly on floured board to release air. Divide dough into 16 pieces, shaping each into a smooth ball. Place balls about 2 inches apart on 2 greased baking sheets; cover and let rise at room temperature until almost doubled (about 45 minutes).

Flatten balls into 4-inch rounds. Cut 4 or 5 slits in each with a knife; pull slits to open (see illustration below). Place rounds well apart on greased baking sheets. Dust with flour, cover, and let rise until puffy (about 30 minutes).

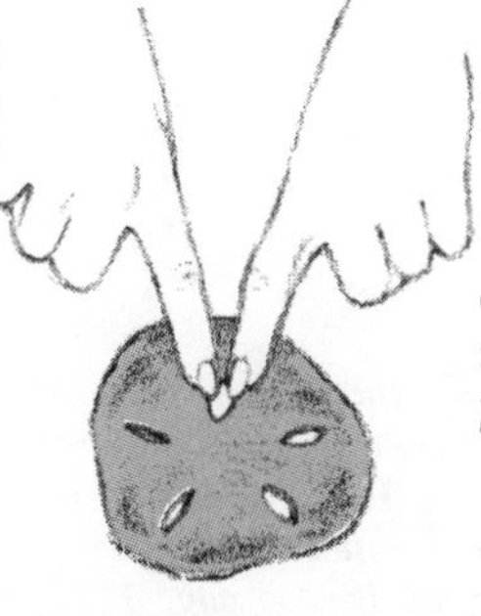

Cut 4 or 5 slits in each round; use your fingers to pull slits open.

Into a deep 10 to 12-inch frying pan, pour oil to a depth of 1½ inches and heat to 365° to 375° on a deep-frying thermometer. Fry one round of bread at a time, turning until golden brown on both sides (1½ to 2 minutes total). Lift from oil with a slotted spoon or spatula, let drain briefly, then set on folded paper towels. Sprinkle lightly with salt.

Serve warm or cool, with cloves of garlic to rub onto langos just before eating. Makes 16.

Nepalese Bread

At dinnertime, high in the Himalayas, the Nepalese spread butter and chutney on hot, spiced wedges of their traditional fried bread. The whole wheat dough puffs as it cooks, forming a miniature "pillow" with a hollow interior. Serve it with chutney as the Nepalese do; it's also wonderful for breakfast with just butter, or butter and honey.

About 2 cups whole wheat flour
2 tablespoons sugar
½ teaspoon *each* baking powder and salt
¼ teaspoon *each* ground cinnamon, cloves, and nutmeg
1 egg
½ cup milk
Salad oil

In a medium-size bowl, stir together 2 cups whole wheat flour, sugar, baking powder, salt, cinnamon, cloves, and nutmeg.

In a small bowl, lightly beat egg, then stir in milk. Add egg mixture to dry ingredients and mix well. Work with your hands until dough forms a ball; dough should be soft but not sticky.

Divide dough into 4 equal parts; shape each into a ball, cover lightly with plastic wrap, and let rest about ½ hour. On a lightly floured board, roll out each ball into an 8 to 8½-inch circle. With a sharp knife, cut each into quarters.

Into a deep 10 to 12-inch frying pan, pour salad oil to a depth of about 1½ inches and heat to 375° to 400° on a deep-frying thermometer. Using a slotted spoon or spatula, lower 1 portion of dough at a time into hot oil; when it returns to the surface, immediately turn it over, using 2 spoons. Continue to cook, turning frequently, for about 2 minutes, or until puffed and browned. Lift out and drain well on paper towels. Repeat until all are cooked. Serve warm or at room temperature. To reheat, wrap loosely in foil and place in a preheated 350° oven for 5 minutes or until heated through. Makes 16.

Quick Breads

The term "quick breads" generally refers to breads leavened without yeast—which means that their preparation time is attractively brief. This category includes such popular items as sweet loaf breads, muffins, biscuits, and easy coffee cakes.

Many are quietly nourishing, packed with good things—fruits, nuts, seeds, even zucchini and rhubarb. Some of them make tempting fare for breakfast or teatime snacks; others are savory accompaniments to dinner.

The loaf breads keep well when tightly wrapped and stored in the refrigerator for as long as a week; you can freeze them for longer storage. Usually they become easier to slice and more flavorful if you wait a day before serving. Muffins, scones, and biscuits are best served freshly baked and still warm from the oven. Coffee cakes, too, are best that way, but if you keep them covered they'll stay fresh for a time, and will taste great at room temperature or reheated.

In this chapter, you'll also learn how to make your own butter (see page 119).

Spicy fragrances fill the kitchen when you bake these wholesome treats. Clockwise from lower left are Whole Wheat Dinner Muffins (page 125), Currant Soda Bread (page 121), Wheat Germ Zucchini Bread (page 114), and Apricot Nut Loaves (page 112).

Curra
Tap

Apricot Nut Loaf

Pictured on page 111

Tangy apricots and plump raisins mingle with walnuts in this moist and richly flavored bread.

- **¾ cup dried apricots**
- **Lukewarm water**
- **1 medium-size orange (juice and rind)**
- **½ cup raisins**
- **Boiling water**
- **⅔ cup sugar**
- **2 tablespoons butter or margarine, melted**
- **1 egg**
- **2 cups all-purpose flour**
- **2 teaspoons baking powder**
- **1 teaspoon *each* salt and baking soda**
- **½ cup chopped walnuts**
- **1 teaspoon vanilla**

Cover apricots with lukewarm water and let stand for 30 minutes; drain. Use a vegetable peeler to remove thin outer peel from half the orange; then squeeze all juice from both halves. Force apricots, raisins, and the thin orange peel through medium blade of a food grinder (or finely chop with a knife).

Add enough boiling water to orange juice to make 1 cup, and pour into bowl with ground fruit. Mix in sugar and butter; beat in egg. In a separate bowl, stir together flour, baking powder, salt, and baking soda until thoroughly blended. Stir dry ingredients into apricot mixture until blended. Add nuts and vanilla. Spoon into a well-greased 9 by 5-inch loaf pan.

Bake in a preheated 350° oven (325° for a glass pan) for 50 minutes or until bread begins to pull away from sides of pan and a wooden pick inserted in center comes out clean. Let cool in pan for 10 minutes; then turn out onto a rack to cool completely. Makes 1 loaf.

"To know the color of one's bread," an expression in Julius Caesar's time, meant to know one's social rank. Lower-class Romans ate dark bread; the upper crust ate white.

Applesauce Raisin Bread

If the whole loaf of this spicy bread doesn't disappear the first time you serve it, slice the leftovers for a delicious version of buttered toast.

- **1 egg**
- **1 cup applesauce**
- **4 tablespoons butter or margarine, melted**
- **½ cup granulated sugar**
- **¼ cup firmly packed brown sugar**
- **2 cups all-purpose flour**
- **2 teaspoons baking powder**
- **¾ teaspoon salt**
- **½ teaspoon baking soda**
- **½ teaspoon ground cinnamon**
- **1 teaspoon ground nutmeg**
- **½ cup raisins**
- **1 cup coarsely chopped pecans or walnuts**

In a large bowl, beat egg lightly; stir in applesauce, butter, granulated sugar, and brown sugar, mixing until well combined. Blend in flour, baking powder, salt, baking soda, cinnamon, and nutmeg. Stir in raisins and nuts.

Turn batter into a well-greased 9 by 5-inch loaf pan, or a plain or fluted 1-quart ring mold. Bake in a preheated 350° oven (325° for a glass pan) for 1 hour or until a wooden pick inserted in center comes out clean. Let cool in pan for 10 minutes, then turn out onto a rack to cool completely. Makes 1 loaf.

Old-fashioned Lemon Bread

While it's hot from the oven, you poke this loaf with a skewer until it's full of holes, then drizzle it with a sweet, lemony glaze. When finished, the bread is easy to slice and has a fine, even texture, much like a poundcake.

- **1½ cups all-purpose flour**
- **1 cup sugar**
- **1 teaspoon baking powder**
- **½ teaspoon salt**
- **2 eggs**
- **½ cup *each* milk and salad oil**
- **1½ teaspoons grated lemon peel**
- **Lemon glaze (recipe follows)**

In a large bowl, stir together flour, sugar, baking powder, and salt. In a small bowl, lightly beat eggs, then beat in milk, oil, and lemon peel. Add liquid mixture to flour mixture and stir just until blended.

Pour batter into a greased and flour-dusted 9 by 5-inch loaf pan. Bake in a preheated 350° oven (325° for a glass pan) for 40 to 45 minutes or until a wooden pick inserted in center comes out clean.

Prepare lemon glaze. When bread finishes baking, use a long wooden skewer to poke numerous holes all the way to bottom of loaf. Drizzle hot glaze over top so that it slowly soaks into bread. Let bread cool in pan for about 15 minutes; then turn out onto a rack to cool completely. Makes 1 loaf.

Lemon glaze. In a small pan, combine 4½ tablespoons **lemon juice** and ⅓ cup **sugar.** Place over medium heat and cook, stirring, until sugar dissolves.

Tangerine Oatmeal-Date Loaf

Tangerine peel and juice combine with rolled oats to flavor this moist fruit bread that's laden with sweet chopped dates. (You can use oranges when tangerines aren't in season.) Wrap the loaf tightly to keep it fresh at room temperature for about a week, or freeze it for longer storage.

- **1 cup boiling water**
- **1 package (about 8 oz.) pitted dates, chopped**
- **¼ cup butter or margarine**
- **1½ tablespoons grated tangerine or orange peel**
- **1 cup fresh tangerine juice or orange juice**
- **2 eggs, lightly beaten**
- **2 cups *each* all-purpose flour and regular or quick-cooking rolled oats**
- **⅔ cup sugar**
- **2 teaspoons *each* baking soda and baking powder**
- **1 teaspoon salt**
- **1 cup chopped walnuts**

Pour boiling water over dates and butter. Stir until butter has melted; set aside. When mixture has cooled to room temperature, stir in tangerine peel, juice, and eggs. In a large bowl, stir together flour, oats, sugar, baking soda, baking powder, salt, and nuts until thoroughly blended. Add date mixture to dry ingredients and stir just until moistened.

Pour batter into a greased and flour-dusted 9 by 5-inch loaf pan (or into two 3⅜ by 7⅜-inch pans).

Bake in a preheated 350° oven (325° for a glass pan) for about 1 hour and 20 minutes (about 1 hour for the smaller pans) or until bread begins to pull away from sides of pan and a wooden pick inserted in center comes out clean. Let cool in pan for 10 minutes; then turn out onto a rack to cool completely. Makes 1 large loaf or 2 small loaves.

Spicy Pineapple-Zucchini Bread

Versatile zucchini combines happily with pineapple in this moist, tender bread that's flecked with green. The zucchini should be shredded coarsely and handled as little as possible, to avoid making it watery.

- **3 eggs**
- **1 cup salad oil**
- **2 cups sugar**
- **2 teaspoons vanilla**
- **2 cups coarsely shredded unpeeled zucchini (about 4 medium-size)**
- **1 can (8¼ oz.) crushed pineapple, well drained**
- **3 cups all-purpose flour**
- **2 teaspoons baking soda**
- **1 teaspoon salt**
- **½ teaspoon baking powder**
- **1½ teaspoons ground cinnamon**
- **¾ teaspoon ground nutmeg**
- **1 cup *each* finely chopped walnuts and currants**

In a large bowl, beat eggs until frothy; add oil, sugar, and vanilla; continue beating until mixture is thick and foamy. Stir in zucchini and pineapple. In a separate bowl, stir together flour, baking soda, salt, baking powder, cinnamon, nutmeg, walnuts, and currants until thoroughly blended. Stir gently into zucchini mixture just until blended. Spoon batter equally into two greased and flour-dusted 9 by 5-inch loaf pans.

Bake in a preheated 350° oven (325° for glass pans) for 1 hour or until bread begins to pull away from sides of pans and a wooden pick inserted in center comes out clean. Let cool in pans for 10 minutes; then turn out onto racks to cool completely. Makes 2 loaves.

Wheat Germ Zucchini Bread

Pictured on page 111

When your zucchini patch provides you with an abundant harvest, celebrate with this appetizing and nutritious bread.

Use a food processor or the coarsest surface of your grater to shred the zucchini. Also, be sure to blend the mixture gently when you add the zucchini, to avoid crushing it and making the mixture too wet.

- **3 eggs**
- **1 cup salad oil**
- **1 cup *each* granulated sugar and firmly packed brown sugar**
- **3 teaspoons maple flavoring**
- **2 cups coarsely shredded unpeeled zucchini (about 4 medium-size)**
- **2½ cups all-purpose flour**
- **½ cup toasted wheat germ**
- **2 teaspoons *each* baking soda and salt**
- **½ teaspoon baking powder**
- **1 cup finely chopped walnuts**
- **⅓ cup sesame seeds**

Beat eggs until frothy; add oil, sugars, and maple flavoring, and continue beating until mixture is thick and foamy. Stir in zucchini. In a separate bowl, stir together flour, wheat germ, baking soda, salt, baking powder, and walnuts until thoroughly blended; stir gently into zucchini mixture just until blended. Spoon batter equally into two greased and flour-dusted 9 by 5-inch loaf pans, and sprinkle evenly with sesame seeds.

Bake in a preheated 350° oven (325° for glass pans) for 1 hour or until bread begins to pull away from sides of pans and a wooden pick inserted in center comes out clean. Let cool in pans for 10 minutes; then turn out onto racks to cool completely. Makes 2 loaves.

Banana-Apricot Nut Bread

Piquant nuggets of dried apricots, liberally laced through this fruit-and-nut bread, blend with the more delicate flavor of ripe banana to make a rich-tasting, moist, and tender treat. Like other banana breads, it's a great way to use up bananas that have ripened past their peak.

- **2 cups all-purpose flour**
- **1 teaspoon baking powder**
- **½ teaspoon *each* baking soda and salt**
- **1 cup sugar**
- **½ cup *each* chopped dried apricots and chopped walnuts**
- **¾ cup mashed ripe banana (about 2 bananas)**
- **½ cup milk**
- **1 egg**
- **¼ cup butter or margarine, melted**

In a bowl, stir together flour, baking powder, baking soda, salt, sugar, apricots, and nuts until thoroughly blended. In a separate bowl, combine banana, milk, egg, and butter; stir into dry ingredients just until well blended. Pour batter into a greased 4½ by 8½-inch loaf pan.

Bake in a preheated 350° oven (325° for a glass pan) for 1¼ hours or until bread begins to pull away from sides of pan and a wooden pick inserted in center comes out clean. (Or bake for 1 hour in a 9 by 5-inch pan, or 45 minutes in two 3⅜ by 7⅜-inch pans.) Let cool in pan for 10 minutes; then turn out onto a rack to cool completely. Makes 1 large loaf or 2 small loaves.

Whole Wheat Banana Bread

Whole wheat flour lends full-bodied flavor to this moist banana bread, which has a light, cakelike texture.

- **½ cup (¼ lb.) butter or margarine, melted**
- **1 cup sugar**
- **2 eggs, lightly beaten**
- **1 cup *each* mashed ripe banana (about 3 bananas) and all-purpose flour**
- **½ teaspoon salt**
- **1 teaspoon baking soda**
- **1 cup whole wheat flour**
- **⅓ cup hot water**
- **½ cup chopped walnuts**

In a large bowl, combine butter and sugar, then mix in beaten eggs and banana, blending until smooth. In a separate bowl, stir together all-purpose flour, salt, baking soda, and whole wheat flour until thoroughly blended. Add dry ingredients to banana mixture alternately with hot water. Stir in chopped nuts. Spoon batter into a greased 9 by 5-inch loaf pan.

Bake in a preheated 325° oven (300° for a glass pan) for about 1 hour and 10 minutes or until bread begins to pull away from sides of pan and a wooden pick inserted in center comes out clean. Let cool in pan for 10 minutes; then turn out onto a rack to cool completely. Makes 1 loaf.

Poppy Seed Loaf

Crunchy poppy seeds give an exciting burst of flavor to this mellow, moist tea bread. Paired with a tangy apricot spread, it's a good choice to serve with midmorning coffee or with a fruit salad for lunch.

¼ cup butter or margarine, softened
1 cup sugar
2 eggs
1 teaspoon grated orange peel
2 cups all-purpose flour
2½ teaspoons baking powder
½ teaspoon salt
¼ teaspoon ground nutmeg
1 cup milk
⅓ cup poppy seeds
½ cup chopped nuts
½ cup golden raisins (optional)
Tangy apricot spread (recipe follows)

Beat together butter and sugar until creamy; add eggs, one at a time, beating well after each addition. Mix in orange peel. In a separate bowl, stir together flour, baking powder, salt, and nutmeg until thoroughly blended. To creamed mixture, add flour mixture alternately with milk, stirring until well blended; then stir in poppy seeds, nuts, and raisins, if used. Turn batter into a well-greased and flour-dusted 9 by 5-inch loaf pan.

Bake in a preheated 350° oven (325° for a glass pan) for 1 hour and 10 minutes or until bread begins to pull away from sides of pan and a wooden pick inserted in center comes out clean. Let cool in pan for 10 minutes, then turn out onto a rack to cool completely. Meanwhile, prepare tangy apricot spread; pass at the table to spread on slices of bread. Makes 1 loaf.

Tangy apricot spread. Beat together ½ cup (¼ lb.) **butter** or margarine (softened), ¼ cup **apricot jam,** 1 teaspoon grated **lemon peel,** and 1 tablespoon **lemon juice.**

Brown Bread

Try thick slices of this dark, rich-tasting bread with baked beans and your favorite sausages for supper. If you like, you can make small cylindrical loaves by baking the bread in 1-pound vegetable or fruit cans instead of in a regular loaf pan.

3 tablespoons butter or margarine, softened
¾ cup firmly packed brown sugar
2 cups buttermilk
3 tablespoons light molasses
2 cups whole wheat or graham flour
1 cup all-purpose flour
½ cup wheat germ
2 teaspoons baking soda
1 teaspoon salt
1 cup *each* raisins and chopped walnuts

In a large bowl, beat butter and sugar together until creamy. Then mix in buttermilk and molasses. In a separate bowl, stir together whole wheat flour, all-purpose flour, wheat germ, baking soda, and salt until thoroughly blended; add to buttermilk mixture and beat until well combined. Stir in raisins and chopped nuts. Spoon batter into a well-greased 9 by 5-inch loaf pan, or divide evenly among 4 well-greased and flour-dusted 1-pound cans, filling them no more than ⅔ full.

Bake in a preheated 350° oven (325° for a glass pan) for 1 hour and 20 minutes (45 minutes for 1-pound cans) or until bread begins to pull away from sides of pan and a wooden pick inserted in center comes out clean. Let cool in pan (or cans) for 10 minutes; then turn out onto a rack to cool completely. (If baked in cans, loosen crust around edges of cans with a thin knife, then slide bread out of cans onto rack to cool completely.) Makes 1 large loaf or 4 small loaves.

Superstition has long surrounded the art of bread baking. Showing respect for their staff of life, German bakers took care never to turn their backs to the oven. A Spanish custom, if a piece of bread drops to the floor, is to pick it up, kiss it, and place it on the table again; this ritual is said to help a soul escape from purgatory.

Date-Nut Loaf

Dates are nature's answer to a sweet tooth. Because these sugary fruits contain relatively large amounts of potassium, iron, and niacin, as well as some protein and fiber, you can enjoy them with a clear conscience. In fact, dates were such an important food source in their native Middle East that they were known as "bread of the desert."

Laden with nuts and raisins as well as dates, this dark, satisfying bread is a nutritional powerhouse. It's especially good spread with cream cheese.

1¼ cups all-purpose flour
1 teaspoon *each* baking powder and baking soda
½ cup sugar
¼ teaspoon salt
½ teaspoon ground cinnamon
1 package (8 oz.) pitted dates, chopped
½ cup *each* golden raisins and chopped walnuts
2 tablespoons butter or margarine
½ teaspoon vanilla
1 cup hot water
1 egg

In a large bowl, stir together flour, baking powder, baking soda, sugar, salt, cinnamon, dates, raisins, and walnuts until thoroughly blended. In a separate bowl, stir together butter, vanilla, and hot water until butter has melted; then stir in egg. Pour butter mixture into dry ingredients and stir just until well blended. Pour batter into a greased 4½ by 8½-inch loaf pan.

Bake in a preheated 325° oven (300° for a glass pan) for 1 hour and 25 minutes or until bread begins to pull away from sides of pan and a wooden pick inserted in center comes out clean. (Or bake for 1 hour in a 9 by 5-inch pan, or 45 minutes in two 3⅜ by 7⅜-inch pans.) Let cool in pan for 10 minutes; then turn out onto a rack to cool completely. Makes 1 large loaf or 2 small loaves.

Not until the 1850s was baking powder commercially available in America. Before that, bakers relied on pearlash, a purified form of potash, to leaven breads made without yeast.

Honey Peanut Loaf

Tucked into lunch boxes or served for snacks, this honey-sweetened bread will win applause from peanut butter fans.

½ cup (¼ lb.) butter or margarine, softened
½ cup chunk-style peanut butter
¼ cup firmly packed brown sugar
2 eggs
½ cup *each* honey and buttermilk
1 teaspoon vanilla
2 cups all-purpose flour
1 teaspoon *each* baking powder and baking soda
⅛ teaspoon salt

In a large bowl, beat together butter, peanut butter, and brown sugar until well blended. Add eggs, one at a time, and beat until fluffy. Stir in honey, buttermilk, and vanilla. In a separate bowl, stir together flour, baking powder, baking soda, and salt until thoroughly blended. Stir into creamed mixture. Spoon batter into a greased 9 by 5-inch loaf pan.

Bake in a preheated 325° oven (300° for a glass pan) for 55 minutes or until bread begins to pull away from sides of pan and a wooden pick inserted in center comes out clean. Let cool in pan for 10 minutes; then turn out onto a rack to cool completely. Makes 1 loaf.

Persimmon Bread

Bright orange persimmons are a colorful signal that autumn is here. These November fruits, with their jellylike texture, also add brightness to the home baker's kitchen—try them in this quick bread.

1 teaspoon baking soda
1 cup persimmon purée (recipe follows)
2½ cups all-purpose flour
½ cup *each* sugar and lightly packed brown sugar
2½ teaspoons baking powder
1 teaspoon *each* salt, ground cinnamon, and ground nutmeg
1 egg
⅓ cup milk
3 tablespoons salad oil
1 cup chopped walnuts

Stir baking soda into persimmon purée; let stand for 5 minutes. In a small bowl, combine flour, sugars, baking powder, salt, cinnamon, and nutmeg; set aside.

In a large bowl, beat egg lightly, then beat in milk, oil, and persimmon mixture. Add flour mixture and stir just until blended. Stir in nuts.

Spoon mixture evenly into a greased 9 by 5-inch loaf pan. Bake in a preheated 350° oven (325° for a glass pan) for about 1¼ hours or until a wooden pick inserted in center comes out clean. Let cool in pan for 10 minutes, then turn out onto a rack to cool completely. Makes 1 loaf.

Persimmon purée. Let **persimmons** ('Hachiya' variety) ripen until soft and jellylike. Cut in half and scoop out pulp with a spoon. Discard skin, seeds, and stem. In a blender or food processor, whirl pulp, a little at a time, until smooth (2 or 3 persimmons will yield 1 cup purée). For each 1 cup purée, thoroughly stir in 1½ teaspoons **lemon juice.** To store, freeze 1-cup batches in rigid containers; thaw, covered, at room temperature.

Pumpkin-Pecan Tea Loaf

Fragrances of pumpkin and blended spices characterize this bread that's made in part from whole wheat flour. For a special breakfast treat, cut it into thick slices and toast lightly.

- **⅔ cup solid vegetable shortening**
- **2⅔ cups sugar**
- **4 eggs**
- **1 can (1 lb.) pumpkin**
- **⅔ cup water**
- **2½ cups all-purpose flour**
- **1 cup whole wheat flour**
- **2 teaspoons baking soda**
- **1½ teaspoons salt**
- **½ teaspoon baking powder**
- **½ teaspoon ground cardamom (optional)**
- **1 teaspoon *each* ground cloves and ground cinnamon**
- **1 cup *each* raisins and chopped pecans**

Beat together shortening and sugar until creamy. Beat in eggs. Add pumpkin and water; stir until blended. In another bowl, stir together all-purpose flour, whole wheat flour, baking soda, salt, baking powder, cardamom (if used), cloves, and cinnamon until thoroughly combined. Gradually add these dry ingredients to pumpkin mixture and stir until well blended. Stir in raisins and chopped pecans. Pour batter into two greased and flour-dusted 9 by 5-inch loaf pans (or three 3⅜ by 7⅜-inch pans).

Bake in a preheated 350° oven (325° for glass pans) for about 1¼ hours (about 1 hour for smaller pans) or until bread begins to pull away from sides of pans and a wooden pick inserted in center comes out clean. Let cool in pans for 10 minutes; then turn out onto racks to cool completely. Makes 2 medium-size or 3 small loaves.

Eggnog Almond Tea Loaf

When the Christmas spirit moves you, try this rich holiday quick bread made with eggnog. Enjoy it at home, or give it as a gift—either way, it spreads holiday cheer. For gift-giving, you might like to bake the bread in the small, inexpensive foil loaf pans available in supermarkets and housewares stores; you can wrap and give the little loaves still in their pans.

- **1 cup chopped blanched almonds**
- **2½ cups all-purpose flour**
- **¾ cup sugar**
- **3½ teaspoons baking powder**
- **1 teaspoon salt**
- **½ teaspoon *each* ground nutmeg and grated lemon peel**
- **1 egg**
- **3 tablespoons salad oil**
- **1¼ cups commercial eggnog**

Spread almonds on a rimmed baking sheet and toast in a 350° oven for 5 to 7 minutes or until golden, stirring frequently. In a large bowl, stir together flour, sugar, baking powder, salt, nutmeg, lemon peel, and toasted almonds. In a small bowl, beat egg lightly, then beat in oil and eggnog. Add liquid mixture to flour mixture and stir just until well blended. Pour batter into a greased and flour-dusted 9 by 5-inch loaf pan (or three 3½ by 5½-inch pans).

Bake in a preheated 350° oven (325° for a glass pan) for about 1 hour (about 40 minutes for small loaves) or until a wooden pick inserted in center comes out clean. Let cool in pan for 10 minutes, then turn out onto a rack to cool completely. Makes 1 large loaf or 3 small loaves.

Panettone

Baked in a paper bag, this quick-bread version of a traditional Milanese yeast bread is moderately sweet and has a cakelike texture.

1 egg
2 egg yolks
¾ cup sugar
½ cup (¼ lb.) butter or margarine, melted and cooled
1 teaspoon grated lemon peel
1 teaspoon *each* anise seeds and anise extract
¼ cup *each* pine nuts, raisins, and coarsely chopped, mixed candied fruit
2⅔ cups all-purpose flour
2 teaspoons baking powder
½ teaspoon salt
1 cup milk

In a large bowl, beat egg, egg yolks, and sugar together until thick and pale yellow. Beat in butter; then add lemon peel, anise seeds, anise extract, nuts, raisins, and candied fruit. In another bowl, stir together flour, baking powder, and salt. Blend half the dry ingredients into egg mixture. Stir in half the milk, add remaining dry ingredients, and mix well. Add remaining milk and blend.

Fold down top of a paper bag (one that measures 3½ by 6 inches on the bottom) to form a cuff so bag stands about 4 inches high. Butter inside of bag generously, set on a baking sheet, and pour in batter (or use a greased and flour-dusted panettone mold approximately 6 inches in diameter and 4 inches deep).

Bake in a preheated 325° oven for about 1¾ hours or until well browned and a wooden skewer inserted in center comes out clean. To serve hot, tear off paper bag and cut bread into wedges. To serve cold, wrap bread (still in bag) in a cloth, then in foil, and let cool completely to mellow the flavors. Makes 1 loaf.

A young Milanese baker's apprentice is credited with the invention of **panettone.** *To impress his boss, he created the sweet, fruited bread—or* **pane**—*and christened it with his own name—Tonio.*

All-summer Fruit Coffee Cake

As fresh summer fruits make their debut, you can change the ingredients of this versatile recipe to make a different fruit-streusel coffee cake each month. Use blueberries, cherries, apricots, nectarines, peaches, plums, or apples—each one offers its own special color, flavor, and texture. Serve the coffee cake warm for breakfast, or top servings with ice cream or whipped cream for dessert.

2 cups all-purpose flour
1 cup sugar
2 teaspoons baking powder
1 teaspoon salt
1½ teaspoons grated orange peel
½ cup (¼ lb.) firm butter or margarine
2 eggs
1 cup milk
1 teaspoon vanilla
3½ cups prepared fresh fruit: blueberries; pitted sweet cherries; pitted apricots, nectarines, or plums, sliced ½ inch thick; peeled and pitted peaches, sliced ½ inch thick; *or* peeled and cored apples, sliced ¼ inch thick
Streusel topping (recipe follows)

In a large bowl, stir together flour, sugar, baking powder, salt, and orange peel. Using a pastry blender or 2 knives, cut butter into flour mixture until it resembles cornmeal.

In another bowl, beat eggs lightly, then stir in milk and vanilla. Make a well in center of flour mixture and pour in egg mixture; stir just until moistened.

Spoon batter into a well-greased 7 by 11-inch baking pan; arrange prepared fruit evenly on top, pressing in lightly. Prepare streusel topping and scatter over fruit.

Bake in a preheated 350° oven (325° for a glass pan) for 1 hour or until a wooden pick inserted in center comes out clean. Let cool on a rack for 20 minutes; then cut into squares and serve warm. Or let cool completely, cover, and store at room temperature. To reheat, place cake, uncovered, in a 300° oven for about 10 minutes. Makes 8 servings.

Streusel topping. In a small bowl, combine ⅓ cup firmly packed **brown sugar,** ¼ cup **all-purpose flour,** and 1 teaspoon **ground cinnamon.** With your fingers, work in 2 tablespoons firm **butter** or margarine until well distributed. Stir in ½ cup chopped **almonds or walnuts.**

Butters for Your Bread

What better way to enhance fresh homemade bread than with fresh homemade butter? Making your own butter isn't the arduous task it once was—today, an electric mixer takes the place of the old wooden churn, so the delicate flavor of fresh butter is easy to achieve.

We also offer several fluffy butter spreads to top off your breads, rolls, toast, or hot griddle cakes. Each one starts with ½ cup of butter—either purchased or homemade. (If you wish, you can use margarine, but we think you'll prefer the flavor of real butter.) Naturally, the flavored butters spread more easily and melt faster when they're not ice-cold, so serve them at room temperature.

Fresh Butter

1 quart whipping cream, chilled
Cold water
Salt (optional)

In large bowl of an electric mixer, beat cream at medium speed until small lumps of butter form and thin buttermilk is floating among butter particles. (This takes 25 to 30 minutes; mixture spatters during the last stage, so you may want to cover mixer and bowl loosely with foil.) Scrape sides of bowl occasionally with a rubber spatula. Or whirl cream in a food processor fitted with a plastic blade; butter will form much faster.

Strain butter in a wire strainer, reserving buttermilk. Measure buttermilk and save for other uses; add its equal measure of cold water to butter in a bowl. Stir well; strain again and discard water. Repeat this washing process until water is clear.

With a heavy wooden spoon, work as much water as possible out of butter, draining off liquid as it accumulates. Add salt if desired (1 to 2 teaspoons or to taste), and blend evenly into butter. Pack butter into a bowl and serve immediately, or cover and refrigerate. Makes about 1 pound.

Cinnamon Butter

In a small bowl, beat ½ cup **butter** or margarine (softened) with 1 teaspoon **ground cinnamon** and 3 tablespoons **powdered sugar** until fluffy.

Date-Nut Butter

In a small bowl, beat together until fluffy ½ cup **butter** or margarine (softened), 3 tablespoons *each* **powdered sugar** and finely chopped **pitted dates,** and ¼ cup finely chopped **pecans or walnuts.**

Honey Butter

In a small bowl, beat ½ cup **butter** or margarine (softened) with ¼ cup **honey** until fluffy.

Orange Butter

In a small bowl, beat ½ cup **butter** or margarine (softened) with 1½ teaspoons grated **orange peel** and 3 tablespoons **powdered sugar** until fluffy.

Spice Butter

In a small bowl, beat until fluffy ½ cup **butter** or margarine (softened), 3 tablespoons firmly packed **brown sugar,** ¼ teaspoon *each* **ground cinnamon** and **allspice,** and ⅛ teaspoon **ground nutmeg.**

Peach Butter

Peel, pit, and chop 1 medium-size peach or nectarine; you should have ½ cup. Place fruit in a blender container or food processor. Add 1 teaspoon **lemon juice,** ½ cup **butter** or margarine (cut into chunks), 2 tablespoons firmly packed **brown sugar** or honey, and ¼ teaspoon **ground nutmeg;** blend until fluffy.

Buttermilk Coffee Cake

This sweet, moist, tender cake with a crunchy nut topping can be served from its own baking pan right out of the oven.

2¼ cups all-purpose flour
½ teaspoon *each* salt and ground cinnamon
1 cup firmly packed brown sugar
¾ cup *each* granulated sugar and salad oil
½ cup coarsely chopped walnuts
1¼ teaspoons ground cinnamon
1 teaspoon *each* baking soda and baking powder
1 egg
1 cup buttermilk

In a medium-size bowl, mix together flour, salt, the ½ teaspoon cinnamon, brown sugar, granulated sugar, and salad oil. Beat with an electric mixer on medium speed until well blended.

To prepare topping, transfer ¾ cup of this mixture to a small bowl and blend into it the nuts and the 1¼ teaspoons cinnamon; set aside.

To the remaining mixture, add baking soda, baking powder, egg, and buttermilk; blend until smooth. Pour mixture into a greased 13 by 9-inch baking pan, and smooth the top. Evenly spoon reserved topping over batter and lightly press it in. Bake in a preheated 350° oven (325° for a glass pan) for 25 to 30 minutes or until a wooden pick inserted in center comes out clean. Cut into squares. Makes about 12 servings.

Cheese-glazed Coffee Cake

This almond-flavored coffee cake appears complicated, but goes together quickly. It has a tender cream puff interior and a cream cheese glaze.

1 cup (½ lb.) firm butter or margarine
2 cups all-purpose flour
1 cup plus 2 tablespoons water
4 eggs
¾ teaspoon almond extract
Cheese glaze (recipe follows)
½ cup sliced almonds

In a small bowl, combine ½ cup of the butter with 1 cup of the flour, crumbling with your fingers to make fine crumbs; sprinkle with the 2 tablespoons water. Stir with a fork until pastry holds together. On a 12 by 15-inch baking sheet, pat pastry out into a 10-inch circle.

In a 2 to 3-quart pan over medium-high heat, place the 1 cup water and remaining ½ cup butter (cut into pieces); bring to a boil. Remove pan from heat, add remaining 1 cup flour all at once, and beat with a wooden spoon until blended. Reduce heat to medium. Return pan to heat and stir vigorously until dough forms a heavy ball and cleans sides of pan. Remove from heat and beat in eggs, one at a time, beating well after each addition. Add almond extract. Spread mixture evenly over pastry.

Bake in a preheated 400° oven for about 45 minutes or until cake is brown and looks crisp. Meanwhile, prepare cheese glaze. Let cake cool for 10 minutes, then drizzle with glaze and top with sliced almonds. Cut into wedges to serve. Makes 10 servings.

Cheese glaze. In a small bowl, blend 1 small package (3 oz.) **cream cheese** (softened), ¾ cup **powdered sugar,** 1 teaspoon **grated orange peel,** and 1 tablespoon **orange juice** until smooth.

Popovers

These fragile shells are nothing but crisp golden crusts and tasty air. The egg batter puffs as it bakes, forming hollows that you can fill with butter or preserves, or something creamy and savory.

For all their smashing good looks, popovers are easy to make. Measure the few ingredients accurately and avoid overbeating the batter, or the popovers won't rise as high. Once they're in the oven, resist the temptation to peek—popovers will collapse if a draft of air reaches them just as they're swelling above the cup.

You can bake popovers in your choice of containers: shiny, lightweight metal muffin pans; dark, heavy cast-iron popover pans; or ovenproof glass custard cups.

1 cup all-purpose flour
¼ teaspoon salt
1 teaspoon sugar (optional)
1 tablespoon butter or margarine, melted and cooled, or salad oil
1 cup milk
2 eggs

Grease containers (see choices below left). In large bowl of an electric mixer, stir together flour, salt, and sugar (if used) until thoroughly blended. Add butter, milk, and eggs; beat until very smooth (about 2½ minutes), scraping bowl frequently with a rubber spatula. Pour into greased containers, filling each about half full. In ovenproof cups of ⅓-cup size, batter will yield 12 popovers; ½-cup size will give you 10 popovers; 6-ounce size, 6 or 7 popovers.

For a richly browned shell with a fairly moist interior, bake on center rack in a preheated 400° oven for about 40 minutes or until well browned and firm to touch. For a lighter-colored popover, drier inside, bake in a preheated 375° oven for 50 to 55 minutes. Remove from pans and serve hot. (If you like your popovers especially dry inside, loosen them from pan but leave them sitting at an angle in cups; prick sides of each popover several times with a wooden pick and let stand in turned-off oven, door slightly ajar, for 8 to 10 minutes.) Makes 6 to 12 popovers.

Cheese Popovers

Follow directions for **Popovers,** but omit sugar and stir ½ cup finely shredded sharp Cheddar or Parmesan **cheese** into batter.

Orange Spice Popovers

Follow directions for **Popovers,** but add the 1 teaspoon **sugar** to batter along with ½ teaspoon grated **orange peel** and ¼ teaspoon **ground nutmeg.**

Savory Herb Popovers

Follow directions for **Popovers,** but omit sugar and add 1 small clove **garlic** (finely minced or pressed) and ¼ teaspoon **dry rosemary or oregano leaves** to batter.

In Ireland, soda bread is traditionally cooked over a smoldering peat fire. Irish cooks claim that this method gives the bread a special, authentically Irish flavor.

Irish Soda Bread

In Dublin, rounds of soda bread accompany every meal, from breakfast to high tea. Each warm, thick slice makes a delectable platter for butter and honey or marmalade.

4 to 4¼ cups all-purpose flour
1 teaspoon salt
3 teaspoons baking powder
1 teaspoon baking soda
¼ cup sugar (optional)
⅛ teaspoon ground cardamom or coriander (optional)
¼ cup firm butter or margarine
1 egg
1¾ cups buttermilk

In a large bowl, stir together 4 cups of the flour, the salt, baking powder, and baking soda (and sugar and cardamom, if used) until thoroughly blended. Cut in butter with a pastry blender or 2 knives until crumbly. In a separate bowl, beat egg lightly and mix with buttermilk; stir into dry ingredients until blended. Turn out onto a floured board and knead until smooth (2 to 3 minutes).

Divide dough in half and shape each half into a smooth, round loaf; place each loaf in a greased 8-inch cake or pie pan and press to make dough fill pans. With a razor blade or sharp floured knife, cut a ½-inch-deep cross in top of each loaf.

Bake in a preheated 375° oven (350° for glass pans) for 35 to 40 minutes or until nicely browned. Makes 2 loaves.

Currant Soda Bread

Pictured on page 111

Follow directions for **Irish Soda Bread,** using sugar but omitting cardamom or coriander. After cutting in butter, add 2 cups **currants or raisins** and, if desired, 1¼ teaspoons **caraway seeds.** Add egg and buttermilk and proceed as directed in recipe.

Whole Wheat Soda Bread

Follow directions for **Irish Soda Bread,** but substitute 2 cups **whole wheat flour** for 2 cups of the all-purpose flour. After cutting in butter, add 1 to 2 cups **raisins or** chopped **dates,** if you wish.

Buttermilk Biscuits

Make sure the honey pot is close at hand when you serve these old-fashioned biscuits. Offer the tender, flaky little breads with bacon and eggs for a satisfying breakfast, or with a country-style dinner of ham or fried chicken.

2 cups all-purpose flour
2½ teaspoons baking powder
¼ teaspoon salt
½ teaspoon baking soda
1 tablespoon sugar
⅓ cup firm butter, margarine, or solid vegetable shortening
¾ cup buttermilk

In a large bowl, stir together flour, baking powder, salt, baking soda, and sugar until thoroughly blended. Cut butter into chunks, add to bowl, and rub mixture together with your fingers until the largest pieces are no more than about ¼ inch in diameter. Pour in buttermilk and stir with a fork until dough sticks together and clings to the fork in a large lump. Turn dough onto a flour-dusted board, turning gently to coat all surfaces lightly with flour. Then knead, making about 10 turns.

Place dough in a lightly greased 9 or 10-inch round or square pan (you can use a cake pan, or a frying pan that can go into the oven). Pat dough out evenly to fill pan. With a flour-dusted 2 to 3-inch round cutter, cut straight down through dough, then lift cutter straight up to make each biscuit; cut close together to make as many as possible. Leave scraps in place.

Bake in a preheated 400° oven for 15 to 20 minutes or until golden brown on top. Serve hot directly from the pan. Makes 9 to 16 biscuits.

Buttermilk Scones

These fruit-laced, buttery scones are sure to please. And they go together so quickly, you can slip out of bed a little early and present them for breakfast any day of the week. They're fragrant with orange peel, and sweet with a sprinkling of cinnamon sugar that's baked to a delectable crispness. Serve them hot, with lots of butter and steaming cups of strong tea.

3 cups all-purpose flour
⅓ cup sugar
2½ teaspoons baking powder
½ teaspoon baking soda
¾ teaspoon salt
¾ cup firm butter or margarine, cut into small pieces
¾ cup chopped pitted dates or currants
1 teaspoon grated orange peel
1 cup buttermilk
About 1 tablespoon cream or milk
¼ teaspoon ground cinnamon mixed with 2 tablespoons sugar

In a large bowl, stir together flour, sugar, baking powder, baking soda, and salt until thoroughly blended. Using a pastry blender or 2 knives, cut butter into flour mixture until it resembles coarse cornmeal; stir in dates and orange peel. Make a well in center of butter-flour mixture; add buttermilk all at once. Stir mixture with a fork until dough cleans sides of bowl.

With your hands, gather dough into a ball; turn out onto a lightly floured board. Roll or pat into a ½-inch-thick circle. Using a 2 to 3-inch round cutter, cut into individual scones. Place 1½ inches apart on lightly greased baking sheets. Brush tops of scones with cream; sprinkle lightly with cinnamon mixture.

Bake in a preheated 425° oven for 12 minutes or until tops are light brown. Serve warm. Makes about 18 scones.

Whole Wheat Scones

Made with stone-ground whole wheat flour, these scones have a wholesome quality and a crumbly texture similar to cornbread. Try them with a hot and hearty breakfast on a cold winter's morning.

The raisin-studded millet variation following this recipe has a sweeter, lighter flavor than the whole wheat scones. Look for millet meal at health food stores.

2¼ cups stone-ground whole wheat flour
2 teaspoons baking powder
½ teaspoon *each* salt and baking soda
3 tablespoons sugar
½ cup (¼ lb.) firm butter or margarine
2 eggs, lightly beaten
⅓ cup milk

In a large bowl, stir together whole wheat flour, baking powder, salt, baking soda, and 2 tablespoons of the sugar until thoroughly blended. Cut butter into chunks, add to bowl, and rub mixture together with your fingers until it resembles cornmeal. Measure 1 tablespoon of the beaten egg and set aside. Stir milk into remaining egg until blended. With a fork, combine milk and egg mixture with flour mixture until evenly moistened.

With your hands, pat dough (it is sticky) into a ball and place on a floured board. Knead dough lightly 2 or 3 turns, then place on a lightly greased baking sheet and pat into a smooth circle about 8 inches in diameter. Use a floured sharp knife to cut circle into 8 wedges; leave wedges in place. Brush with reserved egg and sprinkle with remaining 1 tablespoon sugar.

Bake in a preheated 400° oven for 30 minutes or until golden brown. Let cool for about 5 minutes before serving. Makes 8 scones.

Millet Raisin Scones

Follow directions for **Whole Wheat Scones,** but omit whole wheat flour and add instead 1¼ cups **all-purpose flour** and 1 cup **millet meal.** Add ¾ cup **raisins** to dry ingredients. Substitute ¼ cup **sour cream** for milk.

Sesame-Wheat Germ Cornbread

Toasted sesame seeds lend a hearty, nutlike flavor and crunchiness to this cornbread. The wheat germ adds extra nutrition.

- **½ cup sesame seeds**
- **1½ cups all-purpose flour**
- **½ cup sugar**
- **1½ teaspoons salt**
- **1¼ teaspoons baking soda**
- **2 cups yellow cornmeal**
- **1 cup wheat germ**
- **2 cups buttermilk**
- **¾ cup salad oil or melted butter or margarine**
- **2 eggs, lightly beaten**

In a wide frying pan over medium heat, toast sesame seeds, shaking pan frequently, until seeds are golden (about 2 minutes); set aside. In a large bowl, stir together flour, sugar, salt, and baking soda until thoroughly blended. Mix in cornmeal, wheat germ, and sesame seeds. In a separate bowl, mix together buttermilk, salad oil, and eggs. Stir liquid mixture into dry ingredients just until blended. Pour into a greased 9 by 5-inch loaf pan.

Bake in a preheated 375° oven (350° for a glass pan) for about 55 minutes or until a wooden pick inserted in center comes out clean. Let cool in pan for 5 minutes; then turn out onto a rack to cool completely. Makes 1 large loaf.

Mexican Cornbread

Borrowing flavors from Mexico, this savory cornbread combines Cheddar cheese with green chiles. Sour cream adds rich moistness, and the creamed corn contributes texture. You can control the spiciness of the bread by the number of chiles you add.

- **2 eggs**
- **¼ cup salad oil**
- **1 to 4 canned green chiles**
- **1 small can (about 9 oz.) creamed-style corn**
- **½ cup sour cream**
- **1 cup yellow cornmeal**
- **½ teaspoon salt**
- **2 teaspoons baking powder**
- **2 cups (about 8 oz.) shredded sharp Cheddar cheese**

In a large bowl, beat eggs and oil until well blended. Rinse seeds out of chiles, finely chop chiles, and add to egg mixture. Then add corn, sour cream, cornmeal, salt, baking powder, and 1½ cups of the cheese; stir until thoroughly blended. Pour into a greased 8 or 9-inch round or square pan. Sprinkle remaining ½ cup cheese over top.

Bake in a preheated 350° oven (325° for a glass pan) for 1 hour or until a wooden pick inserted in center comes out clean. Makes 1 loaf.

We owe our traditional American cornbread to Indians, who introduced many delicacies made from corn to the early settlers. The Algonquins' version, called "appone," gradually became known as "corn pone."

Sweet Breakfast Muffins

The secret of making good, pebbly-topped muffins is to treat the batter tenderly. When you blend the liquid ingredients with the dry ingredients, stir just enough to moisten them, with about 12 to 15 circular strokes that scrape the bottom of the bowl. The batter should look lumpy. Over-mixing can cause tough, coarse-textured muffins.

½ cup all-purpose flour
¾ cup whole wheat flour
2 teaspoons baking powder
½ teaspoon salt
1 egg
¼ cup melted butter or margarine, or salad oil
½ cup granulated sugar or firmly packed brown sugar, or 3 tablespoons honey
½ cup milk

In a large bowl, stir together all-purpose flour, whole wheat flour, baking powder, and salt until thoroughly blended; make a well in center. In a separate bowl, lightly beat egg; stir in melted butter, sugar or honey, and milk. Pour all at once into flour well. Stir just enough to moisten all the dry ingredients. Spoon batter into greased or paper-lined 2½-inch muffin cups, filling each about ⅔ full.

Bake in a preheated 375° oven for about 25 minutes or until well browned and tops spring back when lightly touched. Makes about 9 muffins.

Cinnamon Nut-topped Muffins

Follow directions for **Sweet Breakfast Muffins** and fill muffin cups. In a bowl, combine 2 tablespoons packed **brown sugar,** 2 tablespoons chopped **walnuts or pecans,** and ½ teaspoon **ground cinnamon.** Just before baking, sprinkle tops of muffins evenly with sugar-nut mixture. Makes about 9 muffins.

Fresh Apple Muffins

Follow directions for **Sweet Breakfast Muffins,** but add ½ teaspoon **ground cinnamon** to dry ingredients. Stir in 1 cup shredded (unpeeled) **tart apple** with the butter. Reduce milk to ⅓ cup. Makes about 10 muffins.

Rhubarb Muffins

Hot muffins for breakfast can inspire the stubbornest sleepyhead to rise and shine. They're also a good choice for a leisurely weekend brunch. And they're versatile—depending on ingredients, they may have a wide range of flavors and textures.

Moist, tender, and slightly tart, these cinnamon-topped muffins prove that rhubarb grows for more purposes than pie.

1¼ cups firmly packed brown sugar
½ cup salad oil
1 egg
2 teaspoons vanilla
1 cup buttermilk
1½ cups diced rhubarb
½ cup chopped walnuts
2½ cups all-purpose flour
1 teaspoon *each* baking soda and baking powder
½ teaspoon salt
Cinnamon topping (recipe follows)

In a large bowl, combine sugar, oil, egg, vanilla, and buttermilk; beat well. Stir in rhubarb and walnuts.

In a separate bowl, stir together flour, baking soda, baking powder, and salt until thoroughly blended. Stir dry ingredients into rhubarb mixture just until blended. Spoon batter into greased or paper-lined 2½-inch muffin cups, filling them about ⅔ full. Prepare cinnamon topping; scatter over filled cups and press lightly into batter.

Bake in a preheated 400° oven for 20 to 25 minutes or until muffins are delicately browned and tops spring back when lightly touched. Makes about 20 muffins.

Cinnamon topping. Combine 1 tablespoon melted **butter** or margarine with ⅓ cup **sugar** and 1 teaspoon **ground cinnamon.**

In England, the term "muffin" refers to the bread that Americans know as "English muffins." Until the 1930s, they were sold on London streetcorners by bell-ringing "muffin men."

Oatmeal Muffins

Oatmeal gives a distinctive texture to these rather sweet muffins. They're delicious plain or with butter and honey for breakfast or a midmorning snack.

1 cup regular or quick-cooking rolled oats
1 cup buttermilk
1 cup all-purpose flour
½ teaspoon *each* salt and baking soda
1½ teaspoons baking powder
½ cup (¼ lb.) butter or margarine, melted and cooled
½ cup firmly packed brown sugar
1 egg, beaten

Combine oats and buttermilk; let stand for 30 minutes. Stir together flour, salt, baking soda, and baking powder until thoroughly blended. Add melted butter, sugar, and egg to oatmeal mixture and mix well. Stir in dry ingredients just until blended. Spoon batter into greased or paper-lined 2½-inch muffin cups, filling each about ⅔ full.

Bake in a preheated 350° oven for about 25 minutes or until muffins are browned and tops spring back when lightly touched. Makes 1 dozen muffins.

Ready-bake Bran Muffins

Freshly baked bran muffins for busy-morning breakfasts are a luxury easily achieved. These wholesome, almost cakelike muffins are made from a fruit-laced batter that keeps, ready to bake, in the refrigerator for about two weeks. You make the number of muffins you want, and they bake light and tender while the coffee brews.

3 cups whole-bran cereal
1 cup boiling water
2 eggs, lightly beaten
2 cups buttermilk
½ cup salad oil
1 cup raisins, currants, chopped pitted dates, or chopped pitted prunes
2½ teaspoons baking soda
½ teaspoon salt
1 cup sugar
2½ cups all-purpose flour

In a large bowl, mix bran cereal with boiling water, stirring to moisten evenly. Set aside until cool, then add eggs, buttermilk, oil, and fruit and blend well. In a separate bowl, stir together baking soda, salt, sugar, and flour until thoroughly blended; then stir into bran mixture.

To store for later use, refrigerate batter in a tightly covered container for as long as two weeks, and bake muffins at your convenience, stirring batter to distribute fruit evenly before each use.

Spoon batter into greased or paper-lined 2½-inch muffin cups, filling each about ⅔ full. Bake in a preheated 425° oven for about 20 minutes or until tops spring back when lightly touched. Makes 2 to 2½ dozen muffins.

Whole Wheat Dinner Muffins

Pictured on page 111

These robust, whole grain muffins can substitute nicely for bread at dinner. Serve them with fried chicken, roast pork or lamb, baked ham, or salads. For a change of pace, you can omit the wheat germ and substitute ¾ cup whole-bran cereal; you can also vary the muffins' flavor by using brown sugar or honey instead of granulated sugar.

1 cup all-purpose flour
1 cup whole wheat flour
¼ cup wheat germ
3 teaspoons baking powder
½ teaspoon salt
1 egg
¼ cup melted butter or margarine, or salad oil
¼ cup granulated sugar or firmly packed brown sugar, or 2 tablespoons honey
1 cup milk

In a large bowl, stir together all-purpose flour, whole wheat flour, wheat germ, baking powder, and salt until thoroughly blended; make a well in the center. In a separate bowl, lightly beat egg; stir in melted butter, sugar or honey, and milk. Pour all at once into flour well. Stir just enough to moisten all the dry ingredients. Spoon batter into greased or paper-lined 2½-inch muffin cups, filling each about ⅔ full.

Bake in a preheated 375° oven for about 25 minutes or until muffins are well browned and tops spring back when lightly touched. Makes about 1 dozen muffins.

Index

All about bread, 4–9
All-summer fruit coffee cake, 118
Almond
bear claws, buttery, 69
Christmas wreath, cherry-, 70
croissants, 54
loaves, fish-shaped, 64
tea loaf, eggnog, 117
Alsatian kugelhof, 65
Anadama date bread, banana, 81
Anise bread, 61
Apple filling, for streuselkuchen, 64
Apple muffins, fresh, 124
Applesauce-bran bread, sourdough, 94
Applesauce raisin bread, 112
Apricot
nut bread, banana-, 114
-nut filling, for Danish coffee cake, 60
nut loaf, 112
spread, tangy, 115
Arab pocket bread, 40
Armenian peda bread, 40
Armenian thin bread, 44

Bacon & potato casserole bread, 38
Bacon-sesame waffles, 105
Bagels, 46
pumpernickel, 46
sourdough, 92
whole wheat, 46
Bainbridge buttermilk & bourbon hotcakes, 104
Baking bread, 9
Baking in quantity, 53
Baking powder, 5
Baking soda, 5
Banana
anadama date bread, 81
-apricot nut bread, 114
bread, whole wheat, 114
-nut bread, sourdough, 94
Basic loaf (with short-cut bread mix), 36
Basic white bread, 15
Basket bread, golden, 74
Basque sheepherder's bread, 38
Bath buns, 80
Batter bread
Cheddar-caraway, 25
corn-herb, 18
light wheat, 18
mushroom, 25
orange-rye, 18
orange sourdough, 89
Parmesan-dill, 26
raisin-nut, 18
rich white, 18
sourdough three wheat, 89
three wheat, 24
whole grain cereal, 24
Bear claws, buttery almond, 69
Beet bread, 31
Belgian cramique, 72
Biscuit buns, whole wheat, 49
Biscuits, buttermilk, 122
Blini, 102
Blueberry bread, sourdough, 94
Blueberry pancakes, sourdough, 97
Bourbon hotcakes, Bainbridge buttermilk &, 104
Braid, Greek Easter egg, 76
Braid, tricolor, 43
Bran, 21
Bran bread, sourdough applesauce-, 94
Bran muffins, ready-bake, 125
Bread flour, 21
Bread mix, short-cut, 36
Bread sculpture, fanciful, 79
Bread sticks, chewy, 52
Bread sticks, party, 52
Breakfast muffins, sweet, 124
Brioches, 57
Brown-and-serve French bread, 91
Brown bread, 115
Bubble loaf, poppy seed, 16
Bubble loaf, pumpkin spice, 78
Buns
Bath, 80
Swedish letter (Lussekätter), 73
whole wheat biscuit, 49
whole wheat onion, 20
Butter croissants, quick, 56
Butterhorn dinner rolls, 48
Buttermilk
biscuits, 122
& bourbon hotcakes, Bainbridge, 104
coffee cake, 120
scones, 122
Butters, 105, 119
Buttery almond bear claws, 69
Buttery pan rolls, 20
Buttery sourdough pan rolls, 92

Cake doughnuts, old-fashioned, 107
Can't-believe-it sourdough rye, 88
Caraway, rye tortillas with, 100
Caraway batter bread, Cheddar-, 25
Cardamom raisin loaf, 37
Carrot bread, 31
Casserole bread, bacon & potato, 38
Cereal batter bread, whole grain, 24
Challah, 44
Chapaties, 101
Cheddar-caraway batter bread, 25
Cheese
bread, sourdough, 91
croissants, chile &, 54
croissants, ham &, 54
filling, for streuselkuchen, 64
-glazed coffee cake, 120
griddle muffins, sourdough, 93
loaves, golden Swiss, 34
popovers, 121
ring, herb-, 37
Cherry-almond Christmas wreath, 70
Chewy bread sticks, 52
Chile & cheese croissants, 54
Chocolate
-almond croissants, 54
croissants, 54
egg streusel, for pan dulce, 67
Christmas wreath, cherry-almond, 70
Christopsomo, 76
Cinnamon
butter, 119
doughnut twists, 108
-nut filling, for Danish coffee cake, 60
nut loaf, 37
nut-topped muffins, 124
Cinnamon *(cont'd.)*
pretzels, sweet, 68
rolls, giant, 68
swirl loaf, 16
Cloverleaf dinner rolls, 48
Coffee cake
all-summer fruit, 118
buttermilk, 120
cheese-glazed, 120
Danish, 60
poppy seed, 62
sourdough streusel, 96
Colomba di Pasqua, 77
Cornbread, Mexican, 123
Cornbread, sesame-wheat germ, 123
Corn-herb batter bread, 18
Cornmeal, 21
Corn tortillas, 100
Cottage cheese sourdough pan rolls, 92
Cracked wheat, 21
Cracked wheat twin-top bread, 35
Cramique, Belgian, 72
Crêpes, 104
Crêpes, sourdough, 97
Croissants, 54
almond, 54
chile & cheese, 54
chocolate, 54
chocolate-almond, 54
fruit, 54
ham & cheese, 54
quick butter, 56
whole wheat, 56
Croutons, rosemary, 34
Crullers, French, 107
Crumpets, 102
Crusts, custom-made, 33
Crusty water rolls, 49
Currant soda bread, 121
Custom-made crusts, 33

Danish coffee cake, 60
Dark mixed grain bread, 16
Dark rye bread, 26
Date
bread, banana anadama, 81
loaf, tangerine oatmeal-, 113
-nut butter, 119
-nut loaf, 116
Dill batter bread, Parmesan-, 26
Dinner muffins, whole wheat, 125
Dinner rolls, 48
Doughnuts, French crullers, 107
Doughnuts, old-fashioned cake, 107
Doughnut twists, cinnamon, 108
Dresden-style stollen, 72

Easter dove (colomba di Pasqua), 77
Easter egg braid, Greek, 76
Eggnog almond tea loaf, 117
Egg streusel, for pan dulce, 67
Elevations, high, baking at, 9
Equipment, baking, 9
European sour bread, 28

Fanciful bread sculpture, 79
Fan-tan dinner rolls, 48
Fats, 5
Finnish farmer sourdough rye, 88
Fish-shaped almond loaves, 64
Flavorings, 5

Flour, 5, 21
Flours & grains, 21
Freeform loaves, 8
Freezer rye bread, 17
Freezer whole wheat bread, 16
Freezing bread, for storing, 9
French bread
  brown-and-serve, 91
  light & crusty, 39
  sourdough, 91
French crullers, 107
Fresh apple muffins, 124
Fresh butter, 119
Fried breads, griddle &, 98–109
Fruit coffee cake, all-summer, 118
Fruit croissants, 54

German soft pretzels, 51
Giant cinnamon rolls, 68
Giant upside-down pecan rolls, 67
Gluten flour, 21
Golden basket bread, 74
Golden sculpture dough, 79
Golden Swiss cheese loaves, 34
Graham flour, 21
Grains, flours &, 21
Greek Easter egg braid, 76
Griddle & fried breads, 98–109
Griddle muffins, sourdough cheese, 93

Ham & cheese croissants, 54
Herb batter bread, corn-, 18
Herb bread, 16
Herb-cheese ring, 37
Holiday breads, 70–78, 117
Honey bread, triticale, 35
Honey butter, 119
Honey peanut loaf, 116
Hotcakes, Bainbridge buttermilk & bourbon, 104
Hot cross bread, 75

Irish soda bread, 121

Kneading dough, 7
Kugelhof, Alsatian, 65
Kulich, 75

Langos, 108
Leavenings, 5
Lefse, Norwegian, 101
Lemon bread, old-fashioned, 112
Letter buns, Swedish (Lussekätter), 73
Light & crusty French bread, 39
Light wheat batter bread, 18
Limpa, 29
Liquids, 5
Los Angeles peda bread, 41
Lussekätter (Swedish letter buns), 73

Maple wheat swirls, 65
Masa harina, 91, 100
Mexican cornbread, 123
Millet, 21
Millet bread, 32
Millet raisin scones, 123
Mini-loaves of peda, 43
Mix, short-cut bread, 36
Mixed grain bread, dark, 16
Mixing dough, 7
Molasses pumpernickel bread, 28
Muffins
  cinnamon nut-topped, 124
  fresh apple, 124
  oatmeal, 125
  ready-bake bran, 125
  rhubarb, 124
  sourdough cheese griddle, 93
  sweet breakfast, 124
  whole wheat dinner, 125
Mushroom batter bread, 25

Nepalese bread, 109
Norwegian lefse, 101
Nut
  batter bread, raisin-, 18
  bread, banana-apricot, 114
  bread, sourdough banana-, 94
  loaf, apricot, 112
  loaf, cinnamon, 37
  loaf, date-, 116
  -topped muffins, cinnamon, 124

Oatmeal, 21
  bread, pebble-top, 32
  -date loaf, tangerine, 113
  muffins, 125
  pancakes, old-fashioned, 104
  pancakes, sourdough, 97
  sourdough bread, 85
Old-fashioned cake doughnuts, 107
Old-fashioned lemon bread, 112
Old-fashioned oatmeal pancakes, 104
Old-fashioned sourdough starter, 86
One-rise whole wheat bread, 12
Onion
  boards, 45
  bread, sourdough, 91
  buns, whole wheat, 20
  pan rolls, 37
Orange
  butter, 119
  butter, walnut-, 105
  -rye batter bread, 18
  sourdough batter bread, 89
  spice popovers, 121

Pan bread, sourdough whole wheat, 85
Pancakes
  Bainbridge buttermilk & bourbon hotcakes, 104
  old-fashioned oatmeal, 104
  sourdough blueberry, 97
  sourdough oatmeal, 97
  & waffles, sourdough, 97
Pan dulce, 67
Panettone, 118
Pan rolls
  buttery, 20
  buttery sourdough, 92
  cottage cheese sourdough, 92
  dinner, 48
  onion, 37
Pans, 8
Parker House dinner rolls, 49
Parmesan-dill batter bread, 26
Party bread sticks, 52
Peach butter, 119
Peanut loaf, honey, 116
Peasant rye bread, sponge-method, 17
Pebble-top oatmeal bread, 32
Pecan rolls, giant upside-down, 67
Pecan tea loaf, pumpkin-, 117
Peda, mini-loaves of, 43
Peda, whole wheat, 43
Peda bread, Armenian, 40
Peda bread, Los Angeles, 41
Persimmon bread, 116
Pineapple-zucchini bread, spicy, 113
Pizza crust, 36
Pocket bread, Arab, 40
Popovers, 120
  cheese, 121
  orange spice, 121
  savory herb, 121
Poppy seed
  bubble loaf, 16
  coffee cake, 62
  filling, for streuselkuchen, 64
  loaf, 115
Portuguese sweet bread, 80
Potato
  bread, 31
  bread, sourdough, 84
  casserole bread, bacon &, 38
Potica, 61
Pretzels
  soft, German, 51
  sweet cinnamon, 68
  whole wheat, 51
Pumpernickel bagels, 46
Pumpernickel bread, molasses, 28
Pumpkin
  -pecan tea loaf, 117
  spice bubble loaf, 78
  waffles, 105

Quantity refrigerator bread, 53
Quick breads, 110–125
Quick butter croissants, 56

Raisin
  bread, applesauce, 112
  loaf, cardamom, 37
  -nut batter bread, 18
  scones, millet, 123
Ready-bake bran muffins, 125
Refrigerator bread
  quantity, 53
  super-simple, 12
  super sourdough, 84
Reheating bread, after storing, 9
Rhubarb muffins, 124
Rich white batter bread, 18
Ring, herb-cheese, 37
Rising, 8
Rolls
  buttery pan, 20
  buttery sourdough pan, 92
  cottage cheese sourdough pan, 92
  crusty water, 49
  dinner, 48
  giant cinnamon, 68
  giant upside-down pecan, 67
  onion pan, 37
  surprise, 96
  See also Buns
Rosemary bread, 34
Rosemary croutons, 34

Rye, 21
batter bread, orange-, 18
bread, 15
bread, dark, 26
bread, freezer, 17
bread, sponge-method peasant, 17
can't-believe-it sourdough, 88
Finnish farmer sourdough, 88
limpa, 29
molasses pumpernickel bread, 28
tortillas with caraway, 100

Sally Lunn, 78
Savory herb popovers, 121
Savory yeast breads, 22–57
Scones
buttermilk, 122
millet raisin, 123
whole wheat, 122
Sculpture, fanciful bread, 79
Sesame seed tortillas, 100
Sesame waffles, bacon-, 105
Sesame-wheat germ cornbread, 123
Shaping dough, 8
Sheepherder's bread, Basque, 38
Short-cut bread mix, 36
Soda bread
currant, 121
Irish, 121
whole wheat, 121
Soft pretzels, German, 51
Sour bread, European, 28
Sourdough
applesauce-bran bread, 94
bagels, 92
banana-nut bread, 94
batter bread, orange, 89
blueberry bread, 94
blueberry pancakes, 97
bread, oatmeal, 85
brown-and-serve French bread, 91
cheese bread, 91
cheese griddle muffins, 93
crêpes, 97
French bread, 91
oatmeal pancakes, 97
onion bread, 91
pancakes & waffles, 97
pan rolls, buttery, 92
pan rolls, cottage cheese, 92
potato bread, 84
refrigerator bread, super, 84
rye, can't-believe-it, 88
rye, Finnish farmer, 88
starter, 86
streusel coffee cake, 96
surprise rolls, 96
three wheat batter bread, 89
tortilla bread, 91
whole wheat pan bread, 85
Spice bubble loaf, pumpkin, 78
Spice butter, 119
Spice popovers, orange, 121
Spicy pineapple-zucchini bread, 113
Spinach bread, 31
Sponge-method peasant rye bread, 17
Spread, tangy apricot, 115
Starter, sourdough, 86
Sticks, bread, chewy, 52
Sticks, bread, party, 52
Stollen, Dresden-style, 72
Storing bread, 9
Streusel, for pan dulce, 67
Streusel, nut, for sourdough streusel coffee cake, 96
Streusel coffee cake, sourdough, 96
Streuselkuchen, 62
Streusel topping, for all-summer fruit coffee cake, 118
Streusel topping, for streuselkuchen, 64
Sugar and salt, 5
Super-simple refrigerator bread, 12
Super sourdough refrigerator bread, 84
Surprise rolls, 96
Swedish letter buns (Lussekätter), 73
Sweet & festive yeast breads, 58–81
Sweet bread, Portuguese, 80
Sweet breakfast muffins, 124
Sweet cinnamon pretzels, 68
Swirl loaf, cinnamon, 16
Swirls, maple wheat, 65
Swiss cheese loaves, golden, 34

Tangerine oatmeal-date loaf, 113
Tangy apricot spread, 115
Tea loaf, eggnog almond, 117
Tea loaf, pumpkin-pecan, 117
Techniques, yeast bread, 10–21
Thin bread, Armenian, 44
Thin bread, white flour, 45
Three wheat batter bread, 24
Three wheat batter bread, sourdough, 89
Tomato bread, 31
Tools, the baker's, 9
Tortilla bread, sourdough, 91
Tortillas
corn, 100
rye, with caraway, 100
sesame seed, 100
whole wheat, with wheat germ, 101
Tricolor braid, 43
Tricolor pan loaves, 43
Triticale, 21
Triticale honey bread, 35
Troubleshooting guide, 13
Twin-top bread, cracked wheat, 35
Twists, cinnamon doughnut, 108

Understanding yeast baking, 7
Upside-down pecan rolls, giant, 67

Vanocka, 70
Vegetable breads, 31

Waffles
bacon-sesame, 105
pumpkin, 105
sourdough pancakes &, 97
Walnut filling, for potica, 61
Walnut-orange butter, 105
Water rolls, crusty, 49
What's in a loaf—and why, 5
Wheat batter bread, light, 18
Wheat germ, 21
cornbread, sesame-, 123
whole wheat tortillas with, 101
zucchini bread, 114
Wheat swirls, maple, 65
White batter bread, rich, 18
White bread, basic, 15
White flour thin bread, 45
Whole grain cereal batter bread, 24
Whole wheat
Arab pocket bread, 40
bagels, 46
banana bread, 114
biscuit buns, 49
bread, freezer, 16
bread, one-rise, 12
croissants, 56
dinner muffins, 125
flour, 21
onion buns, 20
pan bread, sourdough, 85
peda, 43
pretzels, 51
scones, 122
soda bread, 121
tortillas with wheat germ, 101
Wreath, cherry-almond Christmas, 70

Yeast, 5
baking with, 7
bread techniques, 10–21
breads, savory, 22–57
breads, sweet & festive, 58–81

Zucchini bread, spicy pineapple-, 113
Zucchini bread, wheat germ, 114
Zuñi bread, 29

Metric Conversion Table

To change	To	Multiply by
ounces (oz.)	grams (g)	28
pounds (lbs.)	kilograms (kg)	0.45
teaspoons	milliliters (ml)	5
tablespoons	milliliters (ml)	15
fluid ounces (fl. oz.)	milliliters (ml)	30
cups	liters (l)	0.24
pints (pt.)	liters (l)	0.47
quarts (qt.)	liters (l)	0.95
gallons (gal.)	liters (l)	3.8
Fahrenheit temperature (°F)	Celsius temperature (°C)	5/9 after subtracting 32